Communications
in Computer and Information Science   607

Commenced Publication in 2007
Founding and Former Series Editors:
Alfredo Cuzzocrea, Dominik Ślęzak, and Xiaokang Yang

More information about this series at http://www.springer.com/series/7899

Tatsiana Okrut · Yuras Hetsevich
Max Silberztein · Hanna Stanislavenka (Eds.)

Automatic Processing of Natural-Language Electronic Texts with NooJ

9th International Conference, NooJ 2015
Minsk, Belarus, June 11–13, 2015
Revised Selected Papers

 Springer

Editors
Tatsiana Okrut
United Institute of Informatics Problems
Minsk
Belarus

Yuras Hetsevich
United Institute of Informatics Problems
Minsk
Belarus

Max Silberztein
Université de Franche-Comté
Paris
France

Hanna Stanislavenka
United Institute of Informatics Problems
Minsk
Belarus

ISSN 1865-0929   ISSN 1865-0937 (electronic)
Communications in Computer and Information Science
ISBN 978-3-319-42470-5   ISBN 978-3-319-42471-2 (eBook)
DOI 10.1007/978-3-319-42471-2

Library of Congress Control Number: 2016944166

Printed on acid-free paper

This Springer imprint is published by Springer Nature
The registered company is Springer International Publishing AG Switzerland

Preface

NooJ is a linguistic development environment that provides tools for linguists to construct and accumulate linguistic resources that formalize a large gamut of linguistic phenomena: typography, orthography, lexicons for simple words, multiword units and discontinuous expressions, inflectional and derivational morphology, local, structural, and transformational syntax, and semantics. In 2011, the European Metanet initiative endorsed NooJ, and it is now distributed as an open source software on the European Metashare platform. More than 3,000 copies of NooJ are downloaded each year.

Currently, there are NooJ modules available for over 50 languages. Linguists, researchers in social sciences, and more generally all professionals who analyze large corpora of texts have contributed to its development, year after year, and participated in the annual international NooJ conference.

NooJ 2015 received 51 submissions. The present volume contains 20 articles selected from the 35 papers that were presented at the International NooJ 2015 Conference, which was held during June 11–13 at the United Institute of Informatics Problems of the National Academy of Sciences in Minsk, Belarus. These articles are organized in three parts: "Corpora, Vocabulary and Morphology" contains four articles; "Syntax and Semantics" contains seven articles; "Applications" contains nine articles.

The articles in the first part involve the construction of large texts and dictionaries:

– Ivan Reentovich, Yuras Hetsevich, Valery Varanovich, Evgenia Kachan, and Hanna Kazlouskaya's article "First One Million Corpora for Belarusian NooJ Module" describes the construction of a large corpus and its organization in sections (fiction, medical, scientific texts, etc.) that has been parsed with NooJ in order to perform several experiments.
– Dhekra Najar and Slim Mesfar's article "A Large Terminological Dictionary of Arabic Compound Words" presents a new dictionary for Arabic that formalizes the morphology of multiword expressions in Arabic and classifies them into 20 semantic domains.
– Maximiliano Duran's article "The Annotation of Compound Suffixation Structure of Quechua Verbs" presents a morphological set of rules that expand a dictionary of 1,500 verbs in Quechua by adding sequences of suffixes to each verb. The resulting dictionary has been applied to a corpus of texts to evaluate the precision and recall of the morphological rules.
– Serena Pelosi's article "Morphological Relations for the Automatic Expansion of Italian Sentiment Lexicons" proposes a method to help construct a lexicon of sentiment terms rapidly, using a basic dictionary of 5,000 adjectives of sentiments, suffixation rules, as well as syntactic clues in order to detect new terms automatically in texts.

The articles in the second part involve the construction of syntactic and semantic grammars:

- Max Silberztein's article "Transformational Analysis of Transitive Sentences" discusses the feasibility of implementing a large-coverage set of transformational rules in order to take into account all the possible syntactic operations that might be applied to an elementary sentence.
- Xavier Blanco Escoda's article "A Hierarchy of Semantic Labels for Spanish Dictionaries" presents a comprehensive system of semantic hierarchy used to describe dictionary entries in Spanish. Currently, this system contains 700 semantic labels that are actual words rather than abstractions.
- Yuras Hetsevich, Tatsiana Okrut, and Boris Lobanov's article "Grammars for Sentence into Phrase Segmentation: Punctuation Level" describes a prosodic system that can annotate phrases according to four types of intonation: finality, non-finality, interrogation, and exclamation.
- Mario Monteleone's article "Local Grammars and Formal Semantics: Past Participles vs. Adjectives in Italian" presents a set of local grammars that can solve ambiguities between adjectives and past participles in Italian.
- Kristina Kocijan and Sara Librenjak's article "Recognizing Verb-Based Croatian Idiomatic MWUs" presents a set of grammars that can detect idioms in Croatian and evaluates it by applying it to a Web corpus sample.
- Paula Carvalho, Cristina Mota, and Anabela Barreiro's article "Paraphrasing Human Intransitive Adjective Constructions in Port4NooJ" presents the new linguistic resources of the Port4NooJ system, which aims at generating paraphrases in Portuguese automatically. These new resources include 15 lexicon-grammar tables that provide extremely rich information.
- Nadia Ghezaiel and Kais Haddar's article "Study and Resolution of Arabic Lexical Ambiguity Through the Transduction on Text Automaton" presents a set of local grammars that are applied to Arabic texts in cascade in order to solve various types of ambiguities.

The articles in the third part describe various NLP software applications built with NooJ:

- Vadim Zahariev, Stanislau Lysy, Alena Hiuntar, and Yury Hetsevich's article "Grapheme-to-Phoneme and Phoneme-to-Grapheme Conversion in Belarusian with NooJ for TTS and STT Systems" proposes a grammar-based system to automatically transcribe oral texts (transcribed in a phonetic representation) into an orthographical transcription, using syntactic grammars whose linguistic units are phonemes rather than words.
- Maria Pia di Buono's article "Semi-Automatic Indexing and Parsing Information on the Web with NooJ" presents a search engine capable of parsing users' queries in natural language, using a representation model both for the users' queries and for the documents. The system is tested on the Italian Wikipedia database.

- Lesia Kaigorodova, Yuras Hetsevich, Kiryl Nikalaenka, U.A. Sychou, R.A. Prakapovich, and S. Gerasuto's article "Language Modelling for Robots–Human Interaction" presents a system that manages robot–human interactions, based on a simplified language whose syntax and semantics are formalized using NooJ grammars.
- Alessandro Maisto and Raffaele Guarasci's article "Morpheme-Based Recognition and Translation of Medical Terms" proposes a system capable of analyzing complex medical terms in English (e.g., "otolaryngology") and in Italian, using morpho-semantic rules.
- Yuras Hetsevich and Julia Borodina's article "Using NooJ for Processing of Satellite Data" presents a system that can parse satellite telemetry data and translate it into Belarusian.
- Mohamed Aly Fall Seideh, Héla Fehri, Kais Haddar, and Abdelmajid Ben Hamadou's article "Named Entity Recognition from Arabic–French Herbalism Parallel Corpora" presents a system that uses parallel texts in Arabic and French and uses bilingual dictionaries as well as syntactic grammars to find the corresponding translation of terms in Botanical medicine.
- Alena Veka and Yauheniya Yakubovich's article "Automatic Translation from Belarusian into Spanish Based on Using NooJ's Linguistic Resources" describes a Belarusian–Spanish dictionary that can be used to automatically translate words, idiomatic expressions, and phrases, from Belarusian to Spanish.
- Farida Yamouni's article "A French–Tamazight MT System for Computer Science" describes the construction of an MT system that can process multiword terms in the vocabulary of computer science, using a French–Tamazight electronic dictionary as well as translation grammars.
- Valérie Collec Clerc's article "Mixed Prolog and NooJ Approach in Japanese Benefactive Constructions" presents a system that recognizes Japaneses sentences that contain benefactive auxiliaries, using a set of NooJ linguistic resources (dictionaries and grammars for named entities), associated with a set of Prolog pragmatic rules that take the relationship between the speaker and the listener into account in order to produce the resulting correct sentences.

This volume should be of interest to all users of the NooJ platform because it presents the latest development of the software, its latest linguistic resources, as well as new software applications.

In particular, linguists and computational linguists who work on Arabic, Belarusian, Croatian, English, French, Italian, Japanese, Portuguese, Spanish, Quechua, or Tamazight will find in this volume state-of-the-art linguistic studies for these languages.

We think that the reader will appreciate the importance of this volume, both for the intrinsic value of each linguistic formalization and the underlying methodology, as well as for the potential for developing NLP applications.

June 2016 The Editors

Organization

The International NooJ 2015 Conference was organized by the United Institute of Informatics Problems of the National Academy of Sciences of Belarus in cooperation with Université de Franche-Comté and the NooJ International Association.

General Conference Chair

Max Silberztein   Université de Franche-Comté, France

Organizing Committee

Yuras Hetsevich	United Institute of Informatics Problems, Belarus
Max Silberztein	Université de Franche-Comté, France
Barys Lobanov	United Institute of Informatics Problems, Belarus
Tatsiana Okrut	United Institute of Informatics Problems, Belarus
Julia Baradzina	United Institute of Informatics Problems, Belarus
Dzmitry Dzenisiuk	United Institute of Informatics Problems, Belarus
Alena Hiuntar	United Institute of Informatics Problems, Belarus
Stanislau Lysy	United Institute of Informatics Problems, Belarus
Lesia Kaigorodova	United Institute of Informatics Problems, Belarus

Scientific Committee

Xavier Blanco	Autonomous University of Barcelona, Spain
Krzysztof Bogacki	University of Warsaw, Poland
Héla Fehri	University of Gabès, Tunisia
Yuras Hetsevich	United Institute of Informatics Problems, Belarus
Svetla Koeva	University of Sofia, Bulgaria
Peter Machonis	Florida International University, USA
Slim Mesfar	University of Manouba, Tunisia
Johanna Monti	University of Sassari, Italy
Max Silberztein	Université de Franche-Comté, France
Marko Tadic	University of Zagreb, Croatia
François Trouilleux	Université Blaise-Pascal, France
Simonetta Vietri	University of Salerno, Italy
Igor Sovpel	Belarusian State University, Belarus
Alexander Zubov	Minsk State Linguistic University, Belarus
Vladimir Golenkov	Belarusian State University of Informatics and Radioelectronics, Belarus
Alena Hiuntar	United Institute of Informatics Problems, Belarus
Stanislau Lysy	United Institute of Informatics Problems, Belarus
Lesia Kaigorodova	United Institute of Informatics Problems, Belarus

Contents

Application

Corpora, Vocabulary and Morphology

The First One-Million Corpus for the Belarusian NooJ Module

Ivan Reentovich[1(✉)], Yuras Hetsevich[1], Valery Voronovich[2], Evgenia Kachan[2], Hanna Kozlovskaya[2], Angelina Tretyak[2], and Uladzimir Koshchanka[3]

[1] United Institute of Informatics Problems, Minsk, Belarus
mwshrewd@gmail.com, Yury.Hetsevich@gmail.com
[2] Belarusian State University, Minsk, Belarus
gamrat.vvv@gmail.com, evgeniakacan@gmail.com,
malavita3000@gmail.com, angelina_tret@mail.ru
[3] The Centre for the Belarusian Culture, Language and Literature Research,
National Academy of Sciences of Belarus, Minsk, Belarus
koshul@gmail.com

Abstract. In this article the first one-million corpus for the Belarusian NooJ module is represented. The given corpus has been built up of texts, patched up into sections by different subject categories. From the broad list of possible subject categories in the sections the corpus focuses on fiction, historic, medical, scientific, sociological literature, etc. Given a great number of similar subject categories, the first one-million corpus can be considered as a first subject collection of texts for the Belarusian NooJ module.

The text corpus is expected to be suitable for research in the following aspects: word polysemy processing of various texts, polysemic punctuation marks processing, and a new lexical items search.

The first one-million corpus for the Belarusian NooJ module can be fully applicable in many fields of linguistic research.

Keywords: Corpora · Belarusian NooJ-module · Statistical analysis · Part-of-Speech tagging · Machine-learning algorithms · Levenshtein algorithm · The machine-learning model · Counter-check · Spelling errors · Concatenation-in-paradigm · Unknown words search · Known words search · Clustering · Belarusian N-Corpus · Text processing

1 Introduction

The chosen subject "First One-million Corpus for the Belarusian NooJ module" is among the most important, integral parts of future research in the field of speech recognition and synthesis. It is really a great step on the way to new investigations of the Belarusian language in the world of NooJ and linguistics.

The purpose of this paper is to introduce the elaboration, creation stages as well as stages of "deep" analysis and practical application of the first one-million corpus for the Belarusian NooJ module in the context of different aspects and approaches.

© Springer International Publishing Switzerland 2016
T. Okrut et al. (Eds.): NooJ 2015, CCIS 607, pp. 3–15, 2016.
DOI: 10.1007/978-3-319-42471-2_1

Besides, the first one-million Belarusian corpus for the Belarusian NooJ module will be applicable for solving the following fundamental tasks: optimizing and expanding the development of high-quality linguistic algorithms for the electronic text pre-processing in the TTS (Text-to-Speech) system.

Two Belarusian corpora were developed for NooJ [1] – the 1-VERSION corpus (1 million corpus.noc) and the MAIN corpus (First 1MLN Corpus for the Belarusian NooJ Module.noc). To make the process of corpus creation more productive, a special (descriptive) algorithm has been worked out.

2   Descriptive Algorithm for the First One-Million Corpus for the Belarusian NooJ Module

The main work on corpus compilation and analysis with the help of this algorithm was fulfilled on the basis of 1-VERSION corpus (Table 1).

According to this algorithm, the 1-VERSION corpus has been built-up of 338 unar-ranged text units, the MAIN –of 1 570 text units, patched up into sections of different subject categories (As is seen from A Appendix (Fig. 15)). From the broad list of possible subject categories in the sections, the MAIN corpus focuses on fiction, historical, medical, scientific, sociological literature.

3   The Dictionary of Naturalized Lexical- and Grammatical Information for the Whole List of Unknown Unique Words (File *UNKNOWNS.dic*)

3.1   "Purity" Check of the Corpus '1 million corpus.noc'

To get better results on the task of the Dictionary of Naturalized Lexical- and Gram-matical Information creation, it is necessary to realize the more extended "purity" check of the corpus '1 million corpus.noc'. From this corpus, with the help of Levenshtein algorithm [2], the search of wordforms with the high (0.8) level of similarity of one wordform to another was realized. As a result, comparing the created dictionaries of known (about 150 000) and unknown (about 50 000) wordforms, the authors have found almost 30 % of similar wordforms, which, as a matter of fact, must belong to known wordforms, despite the fact that the NooJ program has recognized them as unknown.

Below, the general problem points are given in terms of "purity" check of the whole text corpus, which may rather effectively be solved using the abovementioned Levensh-tein algorithm:

1. the occurence of Latin letters in many words in the texts of the Belarusian corpus;
2. dialectal words of the Belarusian language;
3. Russian words;
4. orthographic mistakes;
5. different letter case processing.

Table 1. Descriptive algorithm of the first one-million corpus for the Belarusian NooJ module

№	Action	Result
1	Text material collecting and **subject specification** for prospective corpora	The draft corpus for the Belarusian NooJ module is made. (The name is **1 million corpus – Very big[.noc]**). Chosen subjects: **without the subject specification.** **(TEXT TOTAL: 338)**
2	The **"purity" check** of the developed corpus: *1. Unknown or unidentified symbols;* *2. [In addition]: words with apostrophe (');* *3. [In addition]: words with hyphen/ (–) symbol.* 2, 3 [All possible word occurrences with *apostrophe (')* and *hyphen (-)* **must be** searched in texts of the corpus because the NooJ program is unable (in the process of Linguistic Analysis) to parse them correctly (in a context such words are **incorrectly** lexically divided): **e.g. *1) над' ехаць (incorrect);* ***2) цёмна- сіні (incorrect).*** *(In both cases the words are divided by the **space** and NooJ can't identify them as one unit).* **E.g. 1) над'ехаць (correct);** 2) цёмна-сіні (correct)]	1. There are NO ANY **unknown or unidentified symbols** in the given corpus (all texts must be encoded to UTF-8). 2. **5818** wordforms with apostrophe (') are found in the given corpus. (The special NooJ-grammar **SearchWordFormsWithApostrophe(FIRST VERSION).nog** has been applied in this case) 3. In the given corpus we detected: — **25 615 occurrences** of all wordforms with hyphen/ (–) symbol (The special NooJ-grammar **SearchWordFormsWithHyphen.fst** has been applied in this case); — **19 728 occurrences** of all unique (1 occurrence per match) wordforms with hyphen/ (–) symbol (The special NooJ-grammar **SearchWordFormsWithHyphen.fst** has been applied in this case); — **23 663 occurrences** of all wordforms with hyphen/ (–) symbol using special **<WORDFORMWITHHYPHEN> query**. (After the realization of Linguistic Analysis throughout the corpus, applying necessary NooJ resources **general_be.nod [4, 5]** and **SearchWordFormsWithHyphen.nog**); — **18 351 occurrences** of all unique (1 occurrence per match) wordforms with hyphen/ '–' symbol, using special **<WORDFORMWITHHYPHEN> query**. (Such results were got after the realization of Linguistic Analysis throughout the corpus, applying necessary NooJ resources **general_be.nod** and **SearchWordFormsWithHyphen.nog**).
3	The **wordforms** total is counted in the developed corpus	Wordforms (ALL) (**<WF>** = *1 884 971*) Wordforms (ALL, unique [1 occurrence per match]) (**<WF>** = *197 712*)
4	The **unknown words search** is realized from the developed corpus	Unknown words (ALL) (**<UNK>** = *140 235*) Unknown words (ALL, unique [1 occurrence per match]) (**<UNK>** = *50 186*)
5	Creation of the dictionary of unknown (**<UNK>**) unique word usage [*.dic]	File *UNKNOWNS.dic* (*49 749* unknown words (after the necessary correction of the unique **<UNK>** = *50 186* result))
6	Creation of the dictionary of naturalized lexical- and grammatical information for the whole list of unknown unique words (on the basis of the file *UNKNOWNS.dic*)	[The **more extended "purity"** check of the developed corpus. (The **"disposal"** of Roman alphabet letters and other problematic cases in texts of the corpus)]

7	The **known words search** is realized from the developed corpus	Known words (ALL) (**<DIC>** = *1 750 447*) Known words (ALL, unique [1 occurrence per match]) (**<DIC>** = *148682*)
8	Realization of the developed corpus **time consuming operation of lexical information selection**	The **whole dictionary** is created on the basis of the given corpus: *1 mil c_BE.dic (197 712 **unique occurrences**)*
9	The **punctuation marks search** is realized from the developed corpus	Punctuation marks (ALL) (**<P>** = *605 512*) Punctuation marks (ALL, unique [1 occurrence per match]) (**<P>** = *61*)
10	The **digrams search check** is realized from the developed corpus	Digrams *Concordance* (**Digrams** = *1 787 305* [occurrences]) *Dictionary* (*1 mil cor VB_(digrams).dic*)
11	The **Part of Speech tagging of words** is realized within the developed corpus	Parts of Speech (**<NOUN>** = *523 193*) –>ALL (**<NOUN>** = *58 376*) –> unique [1 occurrence per match] (**<VERB>** = *326 739*) –> ALL (**<VERB>** = *45 682*) –> unique [1 occurrence per match] (**<ADJECTIVE>** = *194 682*) –> ALL (**<ADJECTIVE>** = *38 218*) –> unique [1 occurrence per match] (**<ADVERB>** = *172935*) –> ALL (**<ADVERB>** = *3 869*) –> unique [1 occurrence per match]

These issues are also solved in the NooJ program, though it takes far more time and effort, because the program has to process a large scope of information.

3.2   Statistical Analysis of the Text Corpus '*1 million corpus.noc*'

The following steps have been taken at this stage:

1. The corpus '*1 million corpus.noc*' Linguistic Analysis (As is seen from A Appendix (Fig. 16)).
2. The search of wordforms (all wordforms, which are present in the corpus) using special queries (<WF>, <UNK>, <DIC>, <NOUN>, <VERB>, <ADJEC-TIVE>, <ADVERB>).
3. Export of the matches into text files (*.txt).
4. Text files with exported data are stored in a special database, where the unique wordform clustering was realized and the number of wordforms was counted.

3.3   Machine-Learning Algorithms Application for the Part-of-Speech Tagging [3] of Unknown Wordforms

1. The **main attribute of a wordform** for the Part-of-speech tagging process with the machine-learning algorithms, specified for the purpose, was *three ending letters* of each wordform in the dictionary of unknown wordforms. (As is seen from Fig. 1.)

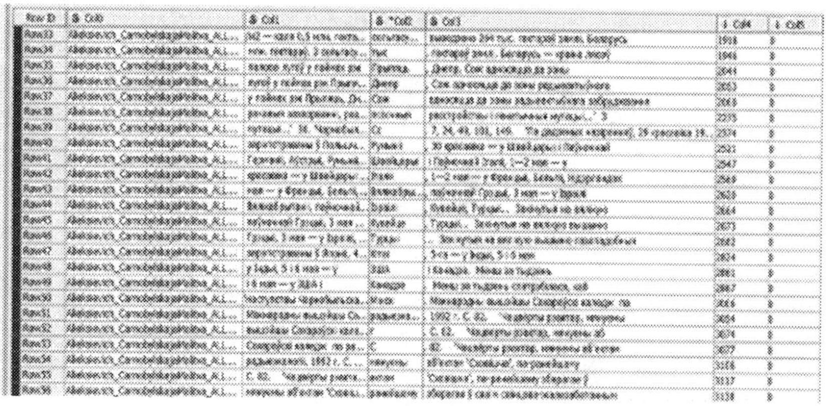

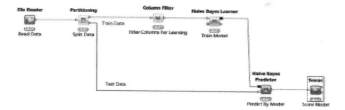

Fig. 1. The excerpt of the NLP system database with data from NooJ

2. The following algorithms are being applied:
   - Decision Tree;
   - Clustering;
   - Neural Network.
3. Firstly, the dictionary [5, 6] of known wordforms was downloaded into the system[1]. This dictionary was meant to "train" all possible word paradigms by the above-named algorithms. In other words, the algorithms' *learning* is realized, and 30 % of known wordforms were taken for *its* realization. (As is seen from Fig. 2.)

Fig. 2. Train model

Then, 70 % of checked remaining data were realized by the derived model of machine-learning algorithms to verify the proficiency of the model estimated as rather high.

4. After that, the existing dictionary of unknown wordforms (UNKNOWNS.dic) was "passed" through the machine-learning model. The results produced rather high degree of correct assignment of unknown wordforms to one or another part of speech.

---

[1] The Part-of-Speech Tagging process can be realized not only in one particular NLP system but also in many others (including integrated interactive systems), where these three algorithms, mentioned above, can be applied.

And that, even at the elementary level (here, the main wordform attribute for the realization of Part-of-Speech Tagging process, i.e. *three ending letters* of each wordform, is meant), confirms the effectiveness of the given machine-learning model. (As is seen from Figs. 3, 4 and 5.)

Fig. 3. Unknown data

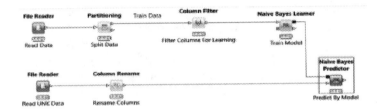

Fig. 4. POS prediction

Fig. 5. Predicted POS results

5. There are possible variants of data check results by using the aforementioned model (through the example of VERB; other parts of speech are considered as OTHER) (Table 2).

Table 2. Possible variants of data check results

Variants	Actual	Model prediction
True positive	VERB	VERB
True negative	OTHER	OTHER
False positive	OTHER	VERB
False negative	VERB	OTHER

4   Part-of-Speech Tagging Countercheck

The Part-of-Speech Tagging Countercheck on unknown words was realized with the help of Levenshtein algorithm (on basis of the file UNKNOWNS.dic).

One more task was to work out the dictionary of unknown words usage. The assignment for developers is the maximum reduction of the dictionary sizes and determination of unknown words values for their further correction and inclusion in the dictionary of the one-million Belarusian corpus. (As is seen from Fig. 6.)

Fig. 6. Unknown words in the summary table of the Part-of-Speech Tagging Countercheck

The main feature of the algorithm applied to the Belarusian one-million corpus is that the algorithm does not change the words in texts after editing, but makes it possible for users to see comments on various mistakes made in the texts incorporated in the Belarusian one-million corpus.

The words included in the dictionary were classified in groups of the unknown for various reasons:

- The words written in the Latin alphabet or having some Latin letters (**a bavyazkov, atrgml_vayutsets, an akhoplepa**);
- The words written by a tarashkevitsa, i.e. substandard spelling which, however, is used by a rather large number of people, especially the Internet users. The existence of alternative spelling is caused by the historical reasons (**абараназдольнасьці, абвешчаньня, абвясьцілі**);
- Words with spelling errors (**абслўгоўванню, абяцаюдь**);

– Words with recognition errors after scanning (**магілёўскага, встагоддзем**);
– Words of foreign languages (**perfekt, deutsche, eine**);
– Proper nouns (**Дзятлава, Анатолія**), etc.

The main objective at the stage of unknown words recognition is the definition of their morphological characteristics, i.e. assignment of parts of speech value to 49 749 wordforms. The algorithm of Levenshtein revealed parts of speech of unknown words, picked up a possible correct form of the usage, and also gave an index of probability of correct forms. (As is seen from Figs. 7 and 8.)

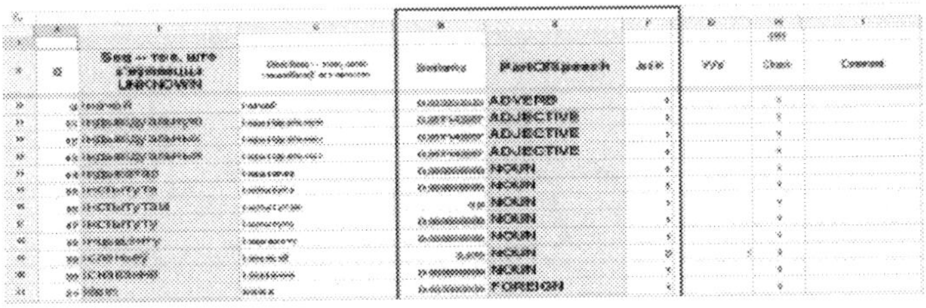

Fig. 7. Linguists' checkout of wordforms recognized by Levenshtein algorithm in the summary table of the Part-of-Speech Tagging countercheck

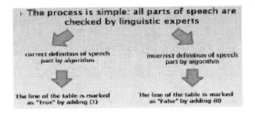

Fig. 8. The process of Parts-of-Speech tagging countercheck

The stage of manual editing is carried out after computer-assisted Part-of-Speech definition, i.e. the algorithm can correctly reveal all parts of speech on formal grounds. The algorithm is simple: all parts of speech are checked by linguistic experts. In case of the correct Part-of-Speech definition by the algorithm this line of the table is marked as "truly" (1). In an opposite case – "lie} (0). (As is seen from Figs. 9 and 10.)

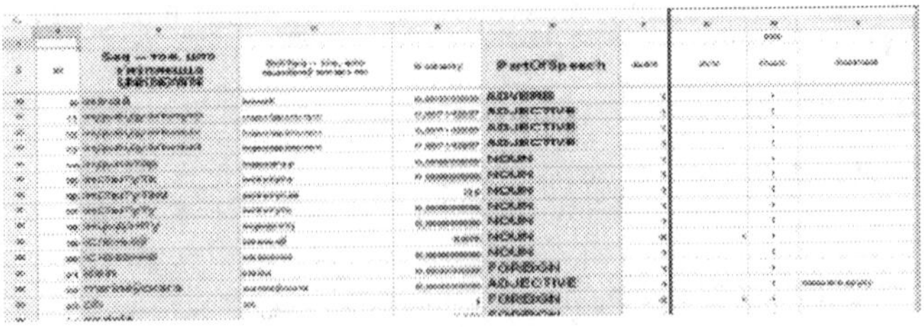

Fig. 9. Editing the results of linguist's checkout of wordforms recognized by Levenshtein algorithm in the summary table of the Part-of-Speech Tagging countercheck

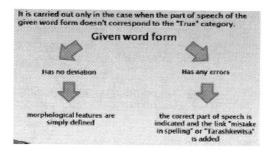

Fig. 10. The process of editing

If the part of speech of a specified wordform doesn't correspond to the validity, the editing stage comes, namely indications of the correct part of speech. If the corresponding wordform has no deviations (without spelling errors, unclear symbols, and also not foreign-language words), in this case morphological features are simply defined. If a word has a wrong spelling, the correct part of speech is indicated and the link "mistake in spelling" is specified. The same happens to the words written in a tarashkevitsa only with another link: "Tarashkevitsa".

The parts of speech noted by the "NULL" category are mainly proper names and therefore are defined by the algorithm described above: indication of the correct part of speech and assignment to this line of "true" value. (As is seen from Fig. 11.)

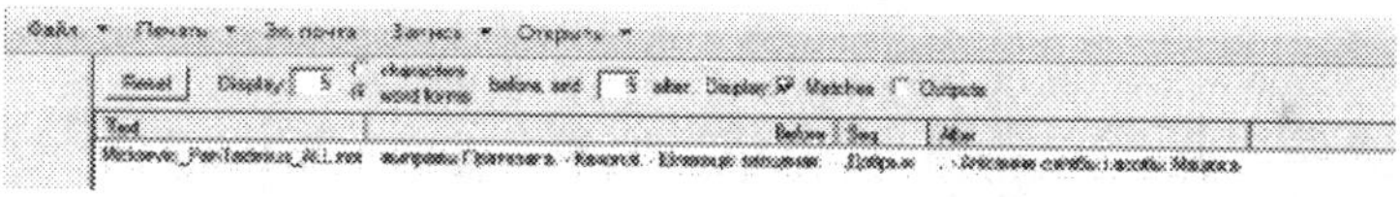

Fig. 11. Addressing to the context

In case the word meaning is not clear or causes doubts, it is necessary to address to a context, namely to the corpus.

At the end of this stage the quantity of unknown words was decreased that allowed to pass to the following stages of the first Belarusian one-million corpus improvements. (As is seen from Fig. 12.)

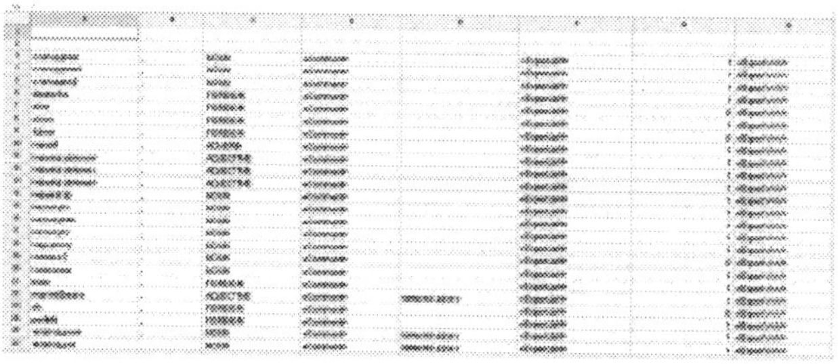

Fig. 12. The Concatenation-in-Paradigm results

According to the resulting data, the special Concatenation-in-Paradigm list was made after the countercheck of recognized by the Levenshtein algorithm unknown words (previously exported from the NooJ-dictionary file UNKNOWNS.dic)) in order to create the additional NooJ general_be.nod dictionary. (As is seen from Fig. 13.)

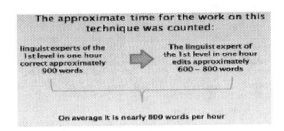

Fig. 13.   The approximate time count for the work on the technique

This calculation allows to predict the work on this technique in the future and to estimate degree of overall performance in comparison with other techniques.

5   Comparison of Lexical and Grammatical Base of the Belarusian N-Corpus [6] with Dictionary Properties' Definition File of the Belarusian NooJ Module

In a similar manner a comparison of lexical and grammatical base of a Belarusian N-corpus with dictionary properties' definition file of the Belarusian NooJ module was made. The Belarusian N-korpus is the first widely available general Belarusian corpus. The Belarusian N-korpus currently contains ~50,000 texts (~30,000,000 tokens) taken from fiction, newspapers, journals and on-line editions. The texts of the corpus are grammatically annotated and contain metatextual information.

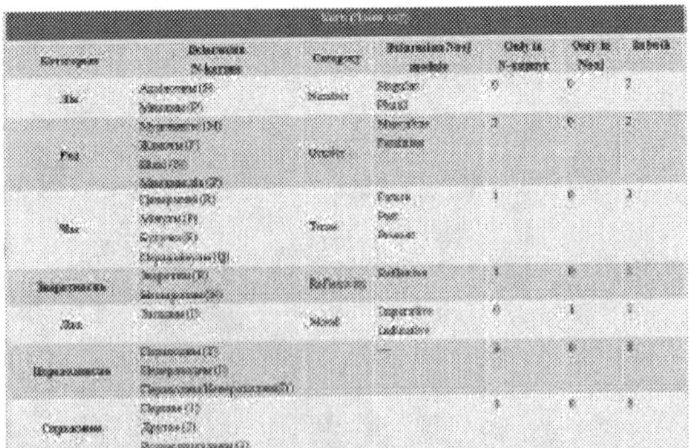

Fig. 14.   Morphological characteristics of verb

The comparative analysis was performed on the morphological characteristics of different parts of speech listed in dictionaries of both programs. After the structure analysis of both Belarusian N-corpus and the Belarusian NooJ module, it can be concluded that the programs have quite developed system of characteristics of speech parts, but nevertheless some categories need to be improved, what was found out in the process of comparing lexical and grammatical bases. Comparison of the morphological characteristics of Verb is presented on Fig. 14.

6   Conclusion

In conclusion, the first one-million corpus for the Belarusian NooJ module is suitable for research in the following aspects:

1. *Words polysemy processing in texts of different subjects;*
2. *Polysemic punctuation marks processing;*
3. *New lexical items search.*

Besides, the one-million corpus is valuable for solving other important tasks:

- Conduction of several experiments in order to specify the **syntactic and morphological grammar use efficiency** of texts of each subject in the corpus, at minimum as well as maximum level.
- Taking thorough measures in order to create the *subject domain generator.* (This will be then very useful for the formation of special subject-oriented NooJ dictionaries.)
- The usage of the given corpus (in the most extent) in the process of Text-to-Speech synthesis with the help of available programs [7], required for such a process, and also when testing newly created applications.
- Carrying-out of a comparative analysis of this corpus with the same corpora in other languages (taking into account all necessary rules, language features in texts of each current corpus, various possible emerging issues, while building syntactic and morphological grammars, etc.).

Thus, it is essential that the first one-million corpus for The Belarusian NooJ Module has practical application in any line of linguistic research. In the near future the corpus is planned to be expanded up to approximately 5–10 million words.

Acknowledgements.   Many thanks to T. Okrut, J. Baradzina, A. Fiodarau for their help in revising the language of this paper.

A Appendix

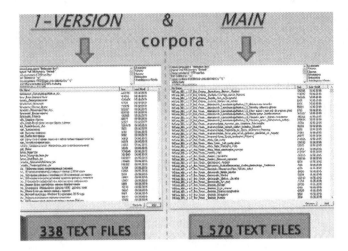

Fig. 15. 1-VERSION and MAIN corpora

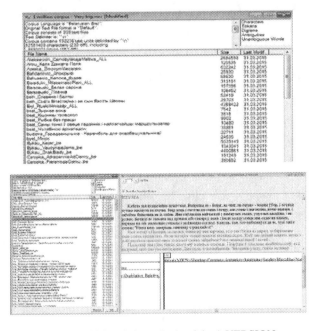

Fig. 16. Realized Linguistic analysis of the 1-VERSION corpus

References

1. NooJ: a linguistic development environment [Electronic resource] (2015). http://www.NooJ4nlp.net/. Accessed 08 May 2015
2. The Levenshtein-Algorithm [Electronic resource] (2015). http://www.levenshtein.net/. Accessed 24 Sept 2015
3. Taylor, P.: Text-to-Speech synthesis. In: Taylor, P. (ed.) Text Decoding, pp. 89–92. Cambridge University Press, Cambridge (2009). Chapter 5
4. Hetsevich, Y.: Overview of Belarusian and Russian dictionaries and their adaptation for NooJ. Hetsevich, Y., Hetsevich, S. In: Vučković, K., Božo, B., Max, S. (eds.) Automatic Processing of Various Levels of Linguistic Phenomena: Selected Papers from the NooJ 2011 International Conference, pp. 29–40. Cambridge Scholars Publishing, Newcastle (2012)
5. Hetsevich, Y.: Accentual expansion of the Belarusian and Russian NooJ dictionaries. Hetsevich, Y., Hetsevich, S., Lobanov, B., Skopinava, A., Yakubovich, Y. In: Donabédian, A., Khurshudian, V., Max, S. (eds.) Formalising Natural Languages with NooJ : Selected Papers from the NooJ 2012 International Conference, pp. 24–36. Cambridge Scholars Publishing, Newcastle (2013)
6. Аўтаматызаваная апрацоўка сімвальных выразаў у тэкстах для сістэмы сінтэзу беларускага маўлення. Беларускі N-корпус [Electronic resource] (2015). http://bnkorpus.info/. Accessed 17 May 2015
7. Corpus.by. Corpus.by [Electronic resource] (2015). http://www.corpus.by/. Accessed 08 May 2015

A Large Terminological Dictionary of Arabic Compound Words

Dhekra Najar, Slim Mesfar[✉], and Henda Ben Ghezela

RIADI, University of Manouba, Manouba, Tunisia
Dhekra.najar@gmail.com, mesfarslim@yahoo.fr,
hhbg.hhbg@gmail.com

Abstract. NooJ is a linguistic development environment that allows formalizing complex linguistic phenomena such as compound words generation, processing as well as analysis. We will take advantage of NooJ's linguistic engine strength in order to create a new large coverage terminological compound word's dictionary for Modern Standard Arabic language. Classifying and annotating Arabic compound words would have a major impact on the disambiguation of applications working with Arabic texts. The diverse analyzers, based on morphological aspect, are not able to recognize multiword expressions. Morphological analyzers usually separate compound expressions into single terms. Therefore recognizing the entire compound words is essential to preserve the semantic of texts and to provide a crucial resource for a better analysis and understanding of Arabic language.

Our work is composed of three sections. First, we will deal with a literature review on Arabic compound expression's categories which aims to dress a detailed topology. The structural variability of multiword expressions in Arabic language will be studied in order to measure the degree of morphological, lexical and grammatical flexibility of multiword expressions. Then, we will discuss the electronic thematic dictionary of compound Arabic expressions and give detailed description of our methodology and guidelines.

Keywords: Compound expressions · Natural language processing · NooJ · Arabic language

1 Introduction

Natural Language Processing (NLP) is known as the ability of systems to process natural languages. There are some steps that are considered standard in NLP. In order to process texts, usually computers divide textual documents into sets of units, known as terms. Within, there are many technical terms that often take form of Multiword expressions (MWE), particularly in specialized articles such us biomedical domain, economical domain, ect. Recent developments in the field of Natural Language Processing have shown the need for recognizing MWEs in a text in order to avoid context ambiguities. For instance, (Nakagawa and Mori 2002) show that more than 85 % of domain-specific terms are multi-word terms. These MWE are combinations of single terms expressing different meaning compared to basic term's meaning. Of course

© Springer International Publishing Switzerland 2016
T. Okrut et al. (Eds.): NooJ 2015, CCIS 607, pp. 16–28, 2016.
DOI: 10.1007/978-3-319-42471-2_2

humans can easily identify multi-word expressions while processing natural languages, but for digital systems, MWEs will be semantically seen and analyzed as separate units. As a result, semantics is lost because generally the meaning of the MWE is different from the meanings of the components.

Table 1. Example of MWE

Compound word	Components	Comments
كأس العالم world cup	كأس: cup العالم: world	Disambiguating meanings

As it can be seen from Table 1, the lemma "world" has ten different senses, in Wordnet 1.6, and the lemma "cup" has four different senses (While the MWE "world cup" has only one sense). Morphological analyzers generally separate MWEs into single terms and this would have a negative effect on the accuracy of all applications working with textual documents. Therefore recognizing the entire compound expressions is essential to constitute a better representation of text semantic content than single word terms. The main purpose of the paper is to build a large multi-genre coverage MWE's dictionary for Modern Standard Arabic (MSA) using NooJ's linguistic engine. The remainder of the paper is organized as follows: Sect. 2 describes a literature review on Arabic MWE's categories and topology. Also, the structural variability of multiword expressions in Arabic language will be studied in order to measure the degree of morphological, lexical and grammatical flexibility. The proposed thematic dictionary of MWEs is discussed in Sect. 3. Section 4 shows the experimental results. Section 5 summarizes the results of this work and draws conclusions.

2   Related Work and Typology of Arabic MWE

A multi-word expression is a consecutive sequence of at least two simple forms and blocks of separators (Silberztein 1993). There are three main approaches for extracting MWEs:

- Linguistic approach that makes use of lexicons and language rules such as morphological or syntactic information;
- Statistical approach that uses a set of standard statistical scores to estimate the degree of association between the words and their frequency in texts;
- Hybrid approach that combines the statistical and linguistic approach.

The majority of the latest MWE extraction systems have adopted the hybrid approach especially on Arabic. Statistical methods could not be applied straight since Arabic is a highly agglutinative language. The development of a terminology extraction system for Arabic language requires linguistic specifications of terms and should be associated to its specific rules. However, to our best knowledge, very few publications can be found in the literature that discusses this issue in Arabic language.

For example, (Bounhas and Slimani 2009) have followed a hybrid method to extract compound terms. First, they detect compound noun boundaries and identify sequences that are likely containing compound nouns. Then, they use syntactic rules to handle MWEs. These rules are based on linguistic information: a morphological analyzer and a POS tagger. (Attia 2008) presented a pure linguistic approach for handling Arabic MWEs. It is based on a lexicon of MWEs constructed manually. Then the system tries to identify other variations using a morphological analyzer.

Based on an analysis of the literature (Attia 2008), MWEs cover expressions that are traditionally classified as:

- idioms (e.g. the cold war), (الحرب الباردة);
- prepositional verbs (e.g. to come near to), (إقترب من);
- verbs with particles (e.g. to give up);
- compound nouns (e.g. a book cover),(غلاف الكتاب);
- collocations (e.g. howling of a wolf), (عواء الذئب);
- Conjunctive expression (assistance and cooperation), (التعاون والتآزر);

With regard to syntactic and morphological flexibility, MWEs are classified into three types: fixed, semi-fixed and syntactically flexible. Fixed compound nouns are entered in the lexicon as a list of words with spaces with no morphological variation allowed. This category contain unambiguous compound expressions such us (Middle East, الشرق الأوسط) and frozen sentences such us pragmatically fixed expressions (مَدَى الحياة, forever) and proverbs. The variations that can effect semi-fixed expressions include graphical variants, which are the graphic alternations between the letters (ى, ي) and the letters (ة, ه), as the following illustrates (Fig. 1).

Fig. 1. Example of graphical variants.

In fact, graphical variants depend on the author origins. They are processed using some low priority morphological grammars (Mesfar 2008).

As well, many morphological variants can effect semi-fixed expressions. Specifically, we mention variations that express person, number, tense, gender, and the definite article that is carried out by the fixed morpheme (ال, Al). Figure 2 shows an example of inflectional variants of an entry in Arabic language.

While MWEs that are Syntactically Flexible allow new external elements (components) to intervene between the MWE components.

In the next section, we will define the linguistic specifications of Arabic MWEs and present the implementation steps of our dictionary.

Fig. 2. Example of inflectional variants.

3 Arabic MWEs Dictionary

3.1 Linguistic Specifications of Arabic MWE

Arabic words are characterized by its complex structure. In comparison with Semitic languages, Arabic language presents distinctive features, namely the vocalization that causes a lexical ambiguity in texts. Also, Arabic is an agglutinative language (the prefix (definite article (the, الـ), prepositions (for, لـ) and (with, بـ), conjunctions (and, و), suffixes (her, ـها)).

Arabic language has a complex MWEs structure (up to 5 units) and a lot of Arabic language has a complex MWEs structure (up to 5 units) and a lot of possible variations and derivations (dual forms, multiple irregular plurals…). The recognition of all potential inflected and agglutinated forms attached to each entry needs a special tokenization that depends on their linguistic specificities. However, we used to make some specific tools to be able to deal with the specificities of the Arabic language (Mesfar 2010).

3.2 Specifications of Our Lexicon

Many researches on MWE recognition in literatures have especially focused on biomedical domain. In our approach, we will organize the multi-words entries, composed of 2, 3, 4 units and more, of our lexicon into 20 semantic fields.

Our lexicon is covering: Fixed expressions except proverbs; semi-fixed expressions and their Inflectional variants that will be processed using morphological grammars. These grammars will be recognizing all the morphological variants of the related forms:

- Gender (female, male);
- Number (dual, plural);
- Definite article: the fixed agglutinated morpheme (الـ, Al);
- Personal agglutinated pronouns;
- Agglutinated conjunctions and prepositions (for, لـ), (with, بـ), (and, و).

Our lexicon covers the different types of MWEs such as expressions that are traditionally classified as idioms, prepositional verbs, collocations, etc.

Table 2. The semantic fields of our Lexicon

Religious terms	Educational terms	Medical terms	Journalistic terms	Politic terms
Social terms	Technical terms	Administrative terms	Financial terms	Economic terms
Transport terms	Weather terms	Sportive terms	Restaurant and touristic terms	Engineering terms
Agricultural terms	Computer sciences terms	Military terms	Press terms	Industrial terms
Psychological terms	Legal terms	Media terms	Organisation terms	BioMedical terms

3.3 Proposed Approach

NooJ linguistic engine is based on large coverage dictionaries and grammars. It uses Finite State Transducers (FSTs) to parse text corpora made up of hundreds of text files in real time and associate each recognized entry with its related information, such as morpho-syntactic information (POS - Part Of Speech, Gender, Number, etc.), syntactic and semantic information (e.g. transitive, Human, etc.). NooJ is a well known linguistic environment that is already used to formalize more than 20 languages.

The recognition process consists on identification of lexical entities using dictionaries and grammars, and the transformation of grammars into transducers.

NooJ[1] is a linguistic development environment that allows formalizing complex linguistic phenomena such as compound words generation, processing as well as analysis. However, in Nooj, "simple words and multi-words units are processed in a unified way: they are stored in the same dictionaries, their inflectional and derivational morphology is formalized with the same tools and their annotations are undistinguishable from those of simple words" (Silberztein 2005)

We will take advantage of NooJ's linguistic engine strength in order to create a new large coverage terminological MWEs dictionary for Modern Standard Arabic language.

Firstly, a lexicon of MWEs is collected manually and associated with a set of semantic information. Data were gathered from various online Arabic linguistic websites. This morphological lexicon contains lexical entries divided into more than 20 domains. Most of these entries belong to scientific and technical terminology. The rest

---

[1] http://www.nooj4nlp.net/.

Fig. 3. Example of a part of MWE

of entries are extracted semi automatically from Arabic corpus using NooJ's linguistic engine. A list of thematic relevant terms that frequently occur as part of an MWE in a specialized text is built. For example and as shown in Fig. 3, we state the term "freedom" in a legal corpus.

Using local grammars, these terms are then tracked by other units in a concordance and the output is added to our MWEs lexicon. Secondly, noisy data will be manually eliminated or rectified in the lexicon:

- Common typographical errors such as confusion between Alif and Hamza or the substitution of (ة ,ه) and (ى ,ي) at the end of the word;
- The false writing of Hamza;
- The addition or omission of a character in a word;
- The lack of white between two terms

Thirdly, all the entries of the lexicon are set in the base form: "indefinite singular form" in order to automatically generate the flexional and derivational forms using NooJ's local grammars that we will implement.

Then, all the listed MWEs were voweled manually so that NooJ would be able to recognize unvoweled, semi-voweled as well as fully voweled MWEs. In some cases of Arabic words, we can find a word that has different way of vocalization and different meanings. So, the manual vocalization is an extremely important step since it allows us to vowel entries depending on their semantic information. This helps reducing linguistic ambiguities in Arabic texts.

The final manual step is classifying the MWEs according to 2 criteria: the grammatical composition (N1 N2), (N1 ADJ)... and the number of elements (1, 2, 3, 4...).

Table 3. Patterns of MWEs compositions

Grammatical category	2 units Patterns	3 units Patterns
Prothetic compound (مركّب إضافيّ)	N1_N2	N1_N2_N3 N1_ADJ_N2 N1_ADJ_prepN2
Descriptive compound (مركّب نعتيّ)	N1_ADJ	ADJ1_ADJ2_ADJ3 N1_ADJ1_ADJ2 N1_ADJ1_prepADJ2
Compound verb (فعل مركب)	V_N V_prep	
Attributive compound (مركّب شبه اسنادي)	N1_prepN2 N_prepADJ	
Adjective noun	ADJ_N	

In fact, the Arabic MWE can be a combination of different forms: a verb, a noun, an adjective and a particle. Most of MWEs are composed of one or more nouns (N), adjectives (ADJ), adverbs (ADV) or simple named entities. We provide the syntactic phrase structure composition of our Arabic MWEs (only 2 and 3 units MWEs), giving each entry of our lexical resource its component elements (noun + noun, noun + adjective, verb + preposition + noun...).

We manually extract a list of about 13 patterns of MWEs compositions.

Moreover, each lexical compound entry of our lexicon is associated with a set of semantic (Semantic information where we cover semantic fields) and distributional information (see Table 2). Organizing our specialized lexical entries in semantic field format brings many practical benefits; one of those is to allow classifying textual documents by category and translating texts by themes.

Entries in our lexicon are structured as follow:

MWEentry, N+CMPD+Struct=GrammaticalComposition+Length=n+FIELDname

Example: حَق شَرْعِي,N+CMPD+Struct=N_ADJ+Taille=2+Juridique

3.4 The Structural Variability of Our MWEs Lexicon

For the following parts of this work, we will use the Electronic Dictionary for Arabic "El-DicAr" resources (Mesfar 2008) as the basis of our local grammars for MWEs variations recognition using NooJ's morphological analyzer. Our approach is essentially based on a manually constructed lexicon of MWEs. Then the system tries to identify other variations of the MWEs which concern semi-fixed compound words. A semi-fixed multiword expression is a frequent combination of two words or more, characterized by high degree of morphological and syntactic flexibility.

So, how can we recognize all the variations and the agglutinated forms of the lexicon's semi-fixed MWEs?

Fig. 4. Variations and the agglutinated forms of an entry

To illustrate, we present the different variations and derivations of the psycho-logical MWE (تعبير وجهي, facial expression) as shown in Fig. 4.

With the new NooJ's V5 there is no more need to create inflectional paradigms for compound words since NooJ can reuse the inflectional paradigms for existing simple words. For example, the MWE (طبيب شَرْعي, forensic pathologist) has as Inflexional paradigm:

طبيب, N+Job+FLX=Atibbea26c
شَرْعِي, ADJ+FLX=AdjDesc1
شَرْعِ طبيب,N+CMPD+Struct=N_ADJ+Taille=2+FLX=AdjDesc1<P>Atibbea26c

And it recognizes the variations below:

Fem.Sing	طَبِيبة شَرْعِيّة	Forensic pathologist
Masc.Plu	أَطبّاء شَرْعِيّون	Forensic pathologist
Fem.Dual	طَبِيبَتَيْن شَرْعِيّتَيْن	Two Forensic pathologists
Masc.Dual	طَبِيبيْن شَرْعِيّيْن	Two Forensic pathologists

As we notice, the example respect gender and number because it's a human noun. Unfortunately, this solution could not be used for the whole Arabic MWEs flexions. Arabic MWEs do not always respect gender and number agreement when generating the associated forms like in Latin languages, especially for irregular plural forms. To illustrate, we give the example of (Fig. 5):

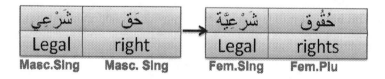

Fig. 5. Example of irregular MWE variation

In comparison with the singular form, the MWE do not respect the gender and number agreement while generating the plural. Hence, identifying the morphological flexibility and variations (graphical variants, inflectional variants…) they may have in the plural and dual forms should be either trough the generation method (1) or the recognition method (2);

Solution 1: Generation Method. It is based on building new appropriate flexional and derivational descriptions that are manually implemented for each MWE entry to

Fig. 6. Number of units in our lexicon (+CmpdElem)

generate the list of associated forms. This first approach obtains an exponential complexity due to the multiple derived forms (Exponential complexity when checking gender and number agreements manually). Also, it is time consuming to build the flexional and derivational descriptions.

Solution 2: Recognition Method. It is based on local grammars that recognize the MWE's variations and related forms without generating them. With this solution, we can process agglutinated forms as well. However, a number of limitations need to be considered. Particularly, the heavy linguistic analysis since NooJ will check the lexical constraints for each bigram, trigram....

Solution 2 bis (Extended Version): We opt for implementing a system based on the recognition method associated with some enhancements to reduce heavy linguistic analysis. In order to restrict the analysis into the units who are attested to be a part of a MWE, all the units (simple words) of our MWEs lexicon were separately extracted and annotated in El_DicAr with the distributional information (+CmpdElem). As shown in the figure, we have extracted about 28870 different units from our lexicon (Fig. 6).

Then, we develop a local grammar containing all the identified grammatical patterns (see Table 3). This grammar would be able to recognize the duals and plural forms (regular and irregular forms) of a MWE as well as its different agglutinated forms. For example, we present the grammar of the 2 units pattern N1_ADJ (Fig. 7):

If the grammar, while processing texts, finds two or more consecutive simple words with the distributional information (+CmpdElem): it will put each word in a variable $Var_ tracked by "_" to set them to their base form (indefinite Singular form). All the stored variables will be concatenated < $Var1_ $Var2_..... > to get the same multi-word expression but in the base form. Then, the grammar will try to find a similar entry of the MWE in our lexicon using the annotation:

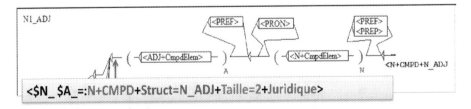

Fig. 7. MWEs variations local grammar

<$Var1_$Var2_….. =: N + CMPD + Struct = Structural Composition + lenght = n+FIELD >.

Once the MWE is found, it will be recognized and considered as a variation of an existing MWE in our lexicon.

We have built a large compound word's dictionary covering multiple domains for Modern Standard Arabic using NooJ's linguistic engine that is able to:

- Recognize all the potential inflected forms.
- Annotate MWEs in texts.
- Improve the lexical coverage of the Electronic Arabic dictionary El_DicAr.
- Get a better semantic representation.
- Reduce the lexical ambiguity.

4   Evaluation and Results

Several obstacles make the analysis of Arabic MWEs so complicated: the high inflectional nature (uses internal patterns for its grammatical processes), the agglutinated form of pronouns and prepositions, the variant sources of ambiguity (unvowled texts…), the dual forms for pronouns and verbs. These specificities of Arabic language represent the most challenging problems for Arabic NLP researchers. Compared to the big amount of available resources and MWEs lexicons in Latin languages, particularly English, the Arabic language is still immature.

We have collected about 63500 MWEs (base form) associated to 20 different fields, as shown in Table 4. We believe that these rates are high especially considering all the variations (inflectional and agglutinated forms) that can have each entry of the lexicon.

We note that 2 units MWEs represent more than half of all entries in the lexicon (66 %) followed by 3 units MWEs (21.8 %). The rest of entries are considered as fixed expressions and do not undergo MWEs variations recognition.

To test the lexical coverage of our dictionary, we launch the linguistic analysis of our corpora. We present preliminary experiments on a corpus containing 150 heterogeneous journalistic articles (Fig. 8).

The table above presents the recall and precision obtained by testing the coverage of our lexicon on the test corpus. The results, as seen in Table 5, indicate that we have reached high quality results of recognition. Our results in term of precision (0.97 of precision) are better than other existing approaches.

These are several possible explanations for the low rate of the recall:

- False vocalization of words such as (misplaced vowels);
- Common typographical errors such as confusion between Alif and Hamza or the substitution of errorsand (ة ,ه) at the end of the word;
- Lexical ambiguity of some agglutinated forms in test corpus;
- Some delimitation problems related to some incomplete MWEs in our lexicon;
- Lack of entries in our dictionary.

Table 4. The lexicon's MWEs entries

Semantic category	2 units	3 units	4+ units	Total
Economical	2253	960	563	3776
Media	540	184	103	827
Educational	1564	334	163	2061
Religious	1682	653	293	2628
Organization	1624	1083	992	3699
Touristic	2384	481	416	3281
Computer	2241	690	455	3386
Weather	339	145	69	553
Transport	2433	844	474	3751
Engineering	1230	439	116	1785
Technical	2129	655	347	3131
Biomedical	3888	1217	483	5588
Sportive	1447	619	326	2392
Financial	2393	879	553	3825
Agriculture	2411	750	106	3267
Political	3351	750	292	4393
Press	44	45	48	137
Military	2354	933	596	3883
Social	2628	812	384	3824
Psychological	2121	602	259	2982
Administrative	587	168	89	844
Total	41906	13886	7640	63432

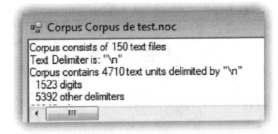

Corpus Corpus de test.noc

Corpus consists of 150 text files
Text Delimiter is: "\n"
Corpus contains 4710 text units delimited by "\n"
1523 digits
5392 other delimiters

Fig. 8. Corpus of Test

Table 5. Results

Precision	Recall
0.97	0.88

5 Conclusion and Perspectives

To sum up, multi-word terms have a great importance since they constitute domain relevant candidate terms. The study has shown that recognizing the entire compound words is essential to preserve the semantic of texts and to provide a crucial resource for understanding Arabic language. We believe that this semi-automatic method has reduced linguistic ambiguities and has improved the precision of the results. Our results in term of precision are better than other existing approaches.

More research is needed to better understand the topology of MWEs in different languages. To improve the effectiveness of an information retrieval system, further research should be done to investigate the possibility to match our MWEs lexicon with a view to ontology construction. A further point is to identify semantic relations between the concepts of the linguistic ontology to get a better semantic analysis of texts.

Annex :

NooJ's syntactic categories:

Syntactic codes	
<ADJ>	Adjective
<V>	Verb
<N>	Noun
<ADV>	Adverb
<CONJ>	Conjunction
<PREP>	Preposition
<PREF>	Prefix
<PRON>	Pronoun
<REL>	Relative pronoun
<PART>	Particle
<E>	Empty caracter
<P>	Ponctuation
Inflectional codes	
<s>	Singular
<p>	Plurial
<m>	Male
<f>	Female
Semantic codes	
<CmpdElem>	Component of a MWE

References

Nakagawa, H., Mori, T.: A simple but powerful automatic term extraction method. In: COLING-02 on COMPUTERM 2002: Second International Workshop on Computational Terminology, vol. 14, pp. 1–7. Association for Computational Linguistics (2002)

Silberztein, M.: Les groupes nominaux productifs et les noms composés lexicalizes. In: Lingvisticae Investigationes XVII: 2. John Benjamins B.V., Amsterdam (1993)

Bounhas, I., Slimani, Y.: A hybrid approach for Arabic multi-word term extraction. In: International Conference on Natural Language Processing and Knowledge Engineering, NLP-KE 2009, pp. 1–8. IEEE (2009)

Attia, M.: Handling Arabic morphological and syntactic ambiguity within the LFG framework with a view to machine translation. Thèse de doctorat, University of Manchester (2008)

Mesfar, S.: Analyse Morpho-syntaxique Automatique et Reconnaissance Des Entités Nommées En Arabe Standard. Thesis, Graduate School—Languages, Space, Time, Societies, Paris, France (2008)

Mesfar, S.: Towards a cascade of morpho-syntactic tools for Arabic natural language processing. In: Gelbukh, A. (ed.) CICLing 2010. LNCS, vol. 6008, pp. 150–162. Springer, Heidelberg (2010)

Silberztein, M.: NooJ's dictionaries. In: The Proceedings of the 2nd Language and Technology Conference, Poznan (2005)

Mesfar, S.: Analyse morpho-syntaxique et reconnaissance des entités nommées en arabe standard. Thèse, Université de franche-comté, France (2008)

The Annotation of Compound Suffixation Structure of Quechua Verbs

Maximiliano Duran[✉]

Université Franche-Comté, Besançon, France
duran_maximiliano@yahoo.fr

Abstract. In the Quechua language we find less than 1400 simple verbs. But, the language has several strategies to increase this verb lexicon generating new verbs by derivation, making use of a particular set of suffixes. First we construct a Boolean matrix showing the valid compounds of the suffixes doing this job. Then we show how we have programmed certain number of morpho-syntactic NooJ grammars to generate the corresponding compound verbs (over 43160). As a result we present a dictionary of the lexicalized compound verbs, including their Spanish and French translations. We have applied both the dictionary and some grammars for automatically annotate a Quechua text obtaining near 90 % of successful matches.

Keywords: Quechua · Compound suffixation · Nooj grammars · Compound verbs · Quechua morphology · Verb morphology · NLP applications · Verb inflection and derivation

1 Introduction

The inventory of Quechua verbs, carried out on the existing paper dictionaries, shows us a lexicon of less than 1400 simple verbs.

In a previous article[1] we have reported that we have been able to increase this list to near 2000 by the addition of some hundreds of verbs, obtained them by parsing some NooJ grammars on our corpus in which they were imbedded in the form of derivations using compound suffixations.

For example the form *asirichiy* appears in the corpus translated as: "make him smile". We notice that it contains the compound suffix *-ri-chi-* which can be analyzed as follows. *chi*: factitive, make someone do something *ri*: dynamism, to start doing the action defined by the verb. The remaining morpheme *asi-* is the lemma of the quechua verb to laugh. Thus *asiy*: to laugh has been derived by the suffixes *-ri-*, *-chi-* to give the new verb to smile.

Let us see another example: the form *rantikuy* appears translated in the corpus as: to sell. We notice that it contains the suffix *-ku-*. It can be analyzed as follows: The suffix *-ku-*: auto benefic, has induced on the original lemma *ranti-* to buy (acquiring something), a change of semantic field into to sell (get rid of something).

---

[1] Morphological and syntactic grammars for recognition of verbal lemmas in Quechua. To appear in Proceedings of the 2014 International Nooj Conference. Sassari. Italy.

© Springer International Publishing Switzerland 2016
T. Okrut et al. (Eds.): NooJ 2015, CCIS 607, pp. 29–40, 2016.
DOI: 10.1007/978-3-319-42471-2_3

2 Generation of Quechua Verbs

We might be inclined to think that the fact of having less than 1400 simple verbs could have been a handicap for the production of any kind of extensive literature like French for instance, which has several thousands of verbs. For this language, Dubois, Jean et Dubois-Charlier, Françoise (D&D) have inventoried more than 25000 entries in their dictionary[2] «Dictionnaire électronique des verbes (français)»

But, Quechua presents a remarkable strategy for generating new verbs by derivation of the simple ones as we have just seen. For this, it makes use of a set of 26 interposition suffixes IPS[3]. To illustrate this, let us take the simple verb *llamkay* (to work), which is formed by the verbal lemma *llamka-* and the infinitive suffix *-y*. Interposing the suffix *-isi-* between them we obtain the derived verb *llamka-isi-y* (to help someone to work). Joining to the same lemma the suffix *–chka-* (the action is being executed, it's similar to the role of the progressive particle ing in English), we obtain the new verb llamka-chka-y (to keep working). The parsing of the NooJ grammar of Fig. 1 or its algebraic expression V_SIP1_INF[4] on the set of 1400 verbs generates 364000 compound Quechua verbs. Besides the examples, some of these are lexicalized well known verbs like the ones appearing in Table 1.

We might be inclined to think that, the fact of having less than 1400 simple verbs could have been a handicap for the production of any kind of extensive literature like French for instance, which has several thousands of verbs. For this language, Dubois, Jean et Dubois-Charlier, Françoise (D&D) have inventoried more than 25000 entries in their dictionary[5] «Dictionnaire électronique des verbes (français)»

But, Quechua presents a remarkable strategy for generating new verbs by derivation of the simple ones as we are going to see. For that, it makes use of a set of 26 interposition suffixes IPS[5]. To illustrate this, let us take the simple verb *llamkay* (to work), which is formed by the verbal lemma *llamka-* and the infinitive suffix *–y*. Interposing the suffix *-isi-* between them we obtain the derived verb *llamka-isi-y* (to help someone to work). Joining to the same lemma the suffix *-chka-* (the action is currently executed, it is similar to the role of the progressive particle ing in English), we obtain the new verb *llamka-chka-y* (to keep on working). The parsing of the NooJ grammar of Fig. 1 or its algebraic expression V_SIP1_INF[6] on the set of 1400 verbs generates 36 4000 compound

---

[2] Jean Dubois et Françoise Dubois-Charlier (2007).

[3] **IPS** = (*chi, chka, ikacha, ikachi, ikamu, ikapu, ikari, iku, isi, kacha, kamu, kapu, ku, lla, mpu, mu,naya, pa, paya,pu,raya, ri, rpari,rqu,ru,tamu*).

[4] V_SIP1_INF = <B>(chi/FACT|chka/PROG|ikacha/DISP |ikachi/POL1 |ikamu/PREAT | ikapu/SOIT3 |ikari/PONC |iku/COURT |isi/COLL |kacha/ARO |kamu/AOL |kapu/RAS |ku/ AUBE |lla/POL1 |mpu/INSP |mu/ACENT |naya/ENV |pa/PEAU |paya/FREQ |pu/APT | raya/DUR |ri/DYN |rpari/ASUR |rqu/PAPT |ru/PRES |tamu/AEP)(y/INF);

[5] **IPS** = (*chi, chka, ikacha, ikachi, ikamu, ikapu, ikari, iku, isi, kacha, kamu, kapu, ku, lla, mpu, mu, naya, pa, paya,pu,raya, ri, rpari,rqu,ru,tamu*).

[6] V_SIP1_INF = <B>(*chi/FACT|chka/PROG|ikacha/DISP |ikachi/POL1 |ikamu/PREAT| ikapu/SOIT3 |ikari/PONC |iku/COURT |isi/COLL |kacha/ARO |kamu/AOL |kapu/RAS |ku/ AUBE |lla/POL1 |mpu/INSP |mu/ACENT |naya/ENV |pa/PEAU |paya/FREQ |pu/APT | raya/DUR |ri/DYN |rpari/ASUR |rqu/PAPT |ru/PRES |tamu/AEP)(y/INF);*.

Quechua verbs. Some of these are lexicalized well known verbs like the ones appearing in the following table.

Table 1. Lexicalized compound Quechua verbs

Lexicalized V	English V	V Lemma	IPS
rimaikuy	greet	*rima* (talk)	*-iku-*
amichiy	bore	*ami* (tired of N)	*-chi-*
atipay	win	*ati* (can)	*-pa-*
aiqiriy	start fleeing	*ayqi* (flee)	*-ri-*
aysariy	tow	*aysa* (carry)	*-ri-*

But most of them are relatively unknown ones as we will see soon.

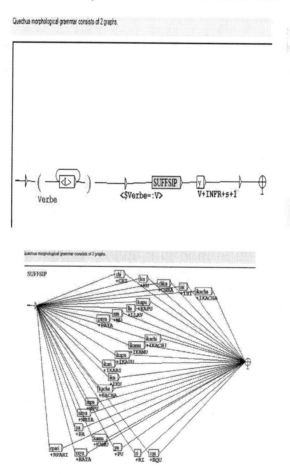

Fig. 1. The NooJ grammar that generates one dimension compound verbs using the 26 inter positioned suffixes IPS

2.1 Combinations of Two Interposed Suffixes

The Quechua grammar allows agglutinations of IPS and consequently to obtain more new verbs. We can have combinations of two or more of them. For instance the combination -*chka-isi*- which can be added to the lemma *llamka*- to obtain the new verb *llamka-chka-isi-y* (to keep helping someone to work). However the permutated combination *–isi-chka*- is not grammatically correct. To answer the question of which two-fold combinations are grammatical, we have built manually the matrix of Fig. 2 based on field work. There, the valid combination is noted by 1 and the invalid ones by 0.

Matrix binaire avec suffixes interposés

	CHI	CHKA	IKACHA	IKACHI	IKAMU	IKAPU	IKARI	IKU	ISI	KACHA	KAMU	KAPU	KU	LLAV	MPU	MU	NAYA	PA	PAYA	PU	RAYA
CHI	1	1	0	1	1	1	0	1	1	0	1	0	1	1	0	1	0	0	0	1	0
CHKA	0	0	0	1	1	1	0	0	1	0	0	0	0	0	0	0	0	0	0	1	0
IKACHA	1	1	0	0	0	0	0	0	1	0	1	0	1	1	0	1	0	0	0	1	0
IKACHI	0	1	0	0	1	1	1	0	1	0	1	1	1	1	0	0	1	0	1	1	1
IKAMU	0	1	1	1	0	1	1	0	1	1	0	0	0	1	0	0	1	0	1	0	1
IKAPU	1	1	1	1	0	0	1	0	1	1	0	0	1	1	0	1	0	0	1	0	1
IKARI	1	1	0	0	0	0	0	1	1	0	0	0	1	1	0	1	0	0	1	1	0
IKU	1	1	0	0	0	0	0	0	1	0	0	1	1	1	0	1	0	0	1	1	0
ISI	1	1	0	0	0	0	1	1	0	0	0	0	0	1	1	1	0	0	1	1	1
KACHA	1	1	0	0	1	1	0	1	0	0	1	1	1	1	0	1	1	0	1	1	1
KAMU	0	1	1	1	1	1	1	0	1	1	0	0	1	1	0	0	1	0	1	0	1
KAPU	1	1	1	1	1	1	0	1	1	0	0	0	0	1	0	1	0	0	0	0	0
KU	0	1	0	0	1	1	0	0	0	0	1	1	1	1	0	0	0	0	1	0	0
LLAV	1	1	1	0	0	0	0	1	1	0	0	0	0	0	0	1	0	0	0	0	1
MPU	0	0	0	0	0	0	0	0	0	0	1	1	0	0	0	0	0	0	0	1	0
MU	0	1	0	0	0	0	0	0	0	0	0	0	1	0	0	0	0	0	0	0	0
NAYA	1	1	0	0	0	0	0	1	0	0	0	0	0	1	0	1	0	0	0	1	1
PA	1	1	1	1	1	1	1	1	1	0	0	0	1	1	0	1	1	0	0	1	0
PAYA	1	1	1	0	0	0	1	1	1	1	1	1	1	1	0	1	1	0	1	1	0
PU	0	1	0	0	1	1	0	1	0	0	0	0	0	1	0	0	0	0	0	1	0
RAYA	1	1	1	1	1	1	0	0	1	0	0	0	1	1	0	1	1	0	0	1	0
RI	1	1	1	1	1	1	1	1	1	0	1	1	1	1	0	1	1	0	1	1	0
RPARI	1	1	0	1	1	1	0	1	1	0	1	1	1	1	0	1	0	0	0	1	0

Fig. 2. Boolean matrix of two-fold IPS combinations

We have verified that at least 292 are grammatically correct new verb generators. Here is a sample of the resulting agglutination of 2 dim IPS compounds:

CHIMU = :CHI :MU;
CHIPU = :CHI :PU;
CHKAIKAMU = :CHKA :IKAMU;
CHKAIKAPU = :CHKA :IKAPU;
IKURQU = :IKU :RQU;
ISICHI = :ISI :CHI;

Which allows us to write Nooj grammars to generate new 2-fold IPS compound verbs:

V_SIP2_INF = < B > (:*CHICHI* |:*CHICHKA* |:*CHIIKACHI* |:*CHIIKAMU* |:*CHIIKAPU* |:*CHII-KARI* |:*CHIIKU* |:*CHIISI* |:*CHIKAMU* |:*CHIKU* |:*CHILLAV* |:*CHIMU* |:*CHIPU* |:*CHIRPARI* |:*CHITAMU* |:*CHKAIKACHI* ... |:*IKAMUCHKA* |:*IKAMUIKACHA* |:*IKAMUIKACHI* |:*IKAMUIKAPU* |:*IKAMUIKARI* |:*IKAMUISI* |:*IKAMUKACHA* |:*IKAMUKU* |:*IKAMULLAV* |:*IKAMUNAYA* |:*IKAMUPAYA*)y/INF;

	A	B	C
2931	TAMUIKAPURA= :TAMU :IKAPU :RA;		
2932	TAMURQUCHKA= :TAMU :RQU :CHKA;		
2933	TAMURQUISI= :TAMU :RQU :ISI;		
2934	TAMURQULLAV= :TAMU :RQU :LLAV;		
2935	TAMURACHI= :TAMU :RA :CHI;		
2936	TAMURAPU= :TAMU :RA :PU;		
2937	RACHICHKA= :RA :CHI :CHKA;		
2938	RACHIIKACHI= :RA :CHI :IKACHI;		
2939	RACHIIKAMU= :RA :CHI :IKAMU;		
2940	RACHIIKAPU= :RA :CHI :IKAPU;		
2941	RACHIIKARI= :RA :CHI :IKARI;		
2942	RACHIIKU= :RA :CHI :IKU;		
2943	RACHIISI= :RA :CHI :ISI;		
2944	RACHIKAMU= :RA :CHI :KAMU;		
2945	RACHIKU= :RA :CHI :KU;		
2946	RACHILLAV= :RA :CHI :LLAV;		
2947	RACHIMU= :RA :CHI :MU;		
2948	RACHIPU= :RA :CHI :PU;		
2949	RACHIRPARI= :RA :CHI :RPARI;		
2950	RACHITAMU= :RA :CHI :TAMU;		
2951	RAMUCHKA= :RA :MU :CHKA;		
2952	RAMULLAV= :RA :MU :LLAV;		

Fig. 3. 3-dimension grammatical verb-generators

Moreover, these combinations are capable of generating three fold agglutinations by adding again one IPS. The respective Boolean matrix contains 7592 entries, but not all are grammatical. Manual verification yields only 2952 "1's", i.e. grammatically correct compounds. Figure 3 shows a sample of the last 22 of this list.

V_IPS4
chi-iku-na-lla
ku-lla-chka-rqa
chi-isi-mu-chka
Agglutinations of five dimensions
V_IPS5
chi-ku-na-lla-pti
chi-ku-lla-wa-pti
chi-isi-mu-chka-pti

3   The Compound Verbs

Agglutinating these grammatical compound suffixes to the 1400 simple verb lemmas we obtain 43160 grammatically correct compound verbs. In Fig. 4 we present a sample of them.

	A	B	C	D	E	F	G	H
43141	yuyapuy	yuyay	V	TR	FR="rappele	FLX=V_SIP1_	APT	INF
43142	yuyapayay	yuyay	V	TR	FR="rappele	FLX=V_SIP1_	FREQ	INF
43143	yuyapay	yuyay	V	TR	FR="rappele	FLX=V_SIP1_	PEAU	INF
43144	yuyanayay	yuyay	V	TR	FR="rappele	FLX=V_SIP1_	ENV	INF
43145	yuyamuy	yuyay	V	TR	FR="rappele	FLX=V_SIP1_	ACENT	INF
43146	yuyampuy	yuyay	V	TR	FR="rappele	FLX=V_SIP1_	INSP	INF
43147	yuyallay	yuyay	V	TR	FR="rappele	FLX=V_SIP1_	POL1	INF
43148	yuyakuy	yuyay	V	TR	FR="rappele	FLX=V_SIP1_	AUBE	INF
43149	yuyakapuy	yuyay	V	TR	FR="rappele	FLX=V_SIP1_	RAS	INF
43150	yuyakamuy	yuyay	V	TR	FR="rappele	FLX=V_SIP1_	AOL	INF
43151	yuyakachay	yuyay	V	TR	FR="rappele	FLX=V_SIP1_	ARO	INF
43152	yuyaisiy	yuyay	V	TR	FR="rappele	FLX=V_SIP1_	COLL	INF
43153	yuyaikuy	yuyay	V	TR	FR="rappele	FLX=V_SIP1_	COURT	INF
43154	yuyaikariy	yuyay	V	TR	FR="rappele	FLX=V_SIP1_	PONC	INF
43155	yuyaikapuy	yuyay	V	TR	FR="rappele	FLX=V_SIP1_	SOIT3	INF
43156	yuyaikamuy	yuyay	V	TR	FR="rappele	FLX=V_SIP1_	PREAT	INF
43157	yuyaikachiy	yuyay	V	TR	FR="rappele	FLX=V_SIP1_	POL1	INF
43158	yuyaikachay	yuyay	V	TR	FR="rappele	FLX=V_SIP1_	DISP	INF
43159	yuyachkay	yuyay	V	TR	FR="rappele	FLX=V_SIP1_	PROG	INF
43160	yuyachiy	yuyay	V	TR	FR="rappele	FLX=V_SIP1_	FACT	INF

Fig. 4. A sample of the generated dictionary of 43000 compound verbs

4 The Semantics of the Agglutinations

But, grammatically correct forms do not necessarily mean meaningful forms. For instance what is the precise meaning of the verb *llamkarachitamuy*? or *tiyarachitamuy*, where *llamka-*: to work and *tiya-*: to sit are the lemmas and *rachitamuy* is the valid combination of the suffixes *-ra-*, *-chi-*, *-tamu-*.

Table 2. Neologisms proposed instead of loans in use

Generated compound verb	Originating simple verb	neologism	may avoid the Spanish loan word
aysariy,V + FR = “remorquer, traîner un petit bout de chemin”	aysay : to pull, to drag	aysariy: to tow	rimulkay < remorcar(to tow)
yapariy,V + FR = “rajouter un peu de quelque chose”	yapay : to add	yapariy: to award a prise	premiay < premiar (to award a prise)
kausariy,V + FR = “revenir à la vie, revenir à soi”	kausay : to live	kausariy: to revive	resusitay < resucitar (to revive)
qipariy,V + FR = “se retarder un peu lentement”	qipay : to delay a little	qipariy : to get delayed	tardiyaruy < tardarse(to get delayed)
utiriy,V + FR = “devenir fou”	utiy : to go crazy	utiriy : to go crazy	lukuyay < alocarse (to go crazy)

Table 3. Semantic values for suffixes IPS

```
#Suffixes inter posées entre le lemma verbal et la désinence de personne

chi,SIP+FACT+"VS=invite FACT_2 autorise FACT_3 pousse  l'objet du verbe à  réaliser l'action
chka,SIP+PROG+"VS=en train deréaliser l'action
ikacha,SIP+DISP+"VS=en désordre DISP_2 desorienté réalise l'action
ikachi,SIP+POLI+"VS=poliment POLI_2 concrètement POLI_3 précisément POLI_4 courtoisement
ikamu,SIP+PREAT +"VS=vers le sujet PREAT _2 en prévoyant PREAT _3 attentionné PREAT _4 de haut en bas
ikapu,SIP+SOIN3+"VS=avec attention SOIN3_2 soigneusement SOIN3_3 concernant un tiers SOIN3_4 recommençant
ikari ,SIP+APRP+"VS= ponctuelle et rapidement APRP_2 à la hâte mais avec précision réalise l'action
iku,SIP+COURT +"VS=courtoisement COURT _2 soigneusement COURT _3 amicalement COURT _4 vers le sujet
isi,SIP+COLL +"VS=collabore COLL _2 aide réalise l'action
kacha,SIP+ARO +"VS=collabore ARO_2 aide réalise l'action
kamu,SIP+AAR+"VS=aller àréaliser l'action
kapu,SIP+RAS +"VS=auto bénéfice réalise l'action
ku,SIP+AUBE+"VS=se responsabilisant AUBE_2 affectueusement AUBE_3 s'impliquant réalise l'action
lla,SIP+POLI+"VS=gentiment POLI_2 poliment POLI_3 doucement POLI_4 emphatiquement
mu,SIP+ACENT +"VS=se déplaçant ACENT_2 sous contrainte réalise l'action
mpu,SIP+INSP+"VS=inopinément réalise l'action
na,SIP+OBL +"VS=obligé POLI_2 potentiellementréaliser l'action
naya,SIP+ENV+"VS=envié de ENV_2 souhaiteréaliser l'action
pa,SIP+PEAU+"VS=peaufine PEAU_2 réitère PEAU_3 réalise l'action
paya,SIP+FREQ+"VS=répétition fréquente FREQ_2 persaiste réalise l'action
pu,SIP+APT+"VS=en substitution APT_2 en action centrifuge réalise l'action
ra,SIP+PASS+"VS=avais réalise l'action
raya,SIP+DUR+"VS=demeure un temps pour réalise l'action
ri,SIP+DYN+"VS=commence à DYN_2 recommence à réalise l'action
rpari,SIP+ASUR+"VS=action surprise ASUR_2 impulsivement réalise l'action
rqu,SIP+PAPT+""VS=accompli en peu de temps APT_2 en action centrifuge réalise l'action"
ru,SIP+PRES+"VS=pressantle_sujetPRES_1en_peu_de_tempsPRES_2 de_façon_pressante réalise_l_action
tamu,SIP+AEP+""VS=en passant réalise_l_action"
```

What are the actual meanings of this amazing quantity of the generated new verbs? Are they really currently used by the native speakers? Which ones are really meaningful in the language?

Many are certainly candidates to become neologisms like in the following table:

But many others seem not to have a plausible meaning.

We are aware that the only way to answer these questions is by hand verification on the field, nevertheless to ease this task we have written some NooJ grammars which give us, as a first step, the corresponding annotations of the suffixes contained in the verbal form, like in Fig. 5. Then, it proposes automatically the glossed translation. For this, we

```
#use grammaire_Verbs_SIP_INF.nof
#
kuyaramullay, kuyay, V+FR="to love"+FLX=V_SIP3_INF+PASS+ACENT+POL1+INF
kuyaramuchkay, kuyay, V+FR="to love"+FLX=V_SIP3_INF+PASS+ACENT+PROG+INF
kuyarachitamuy, kuyay, V+FR="to love"+FLX=V_SIP3_INF+PASS+FACT+AEP+INF
kuyarachirpariy, kuyay, V+FR="to love"+FLX=V_SIP3_INF+PASS+FACT+ASUR+INF
kuyarachipuy, kuyay, V+FR="to love"+FLX=V_SIP3_INF+PASS+FACT+APT+INF
kuyarachimuy, kuyay, V+FR="to love"+FLX=V_SIP3_INF+PASS+FACT+ACENT+INF
kuyarachillay, kuyay, V+FR="to love"+FLX=V_SIP3_INF+PASS+FACT+POL1+INF
kuyarachikuy, kuyay, V+FR="to love"+FLX=V_SIP3_INF+PASS+FACT+AUBE+INF
kuyarachikamuy, kuyay, V+FR="to love"+FLX=V_SIP3_INF+PASS+FACT+AOL+INF
kuyarachiisiy, kuyay, V+FR="to love"+FLX=V_SIP3_INF+PASS+FACT+COLL+INF
kuyarachiikuy, kuyay, V+FR="to love"+FLX=V_SIP3_INF+PASS+FACT+COURT+INF
kuyarachiikariy, kuyay, V+FR="to love"+FLX=V_SIP3_INF+PASS+FACT+PONC+INF
kuyarachiikapuy, kuyay, V+FR="to love"+FLX=V_SIP3_INF+PASS+FACT+SOIN3+INF
kuyarachiikamuy, kuyay, V+FR="to love"+FLX=V_SIP3_INF+PASS+FACT+PREAT+INF
kuyarachiikachiy, kuyay, V+FR="to love"+FLX=V_SIP3_INF+PASS+FACT+POLI+INF
kuyarachichkay, kuyay, V+FR="to love"+FLX=V_SIP3_INF+PASS+FACT+PROG+INF
kuyatamurapuy, kuyay, V+FR="to love"+FLX=V_SIP3_INF+AEP+PASS+APT+INF
kuyatamurachiy, kuyay, V+FR="to love"+FLX=V_SIP3_INF+AEP+PASS+FACT+INF
```

Fig. 5. Annotated 3-dim 2931 verbs derived from the verb to love

have first inventoried the IPS suffixes and their corresponding main semantic values as it appears in Table 3.

Where for the first one CHI, we have three factitive values (in English and French for this suffix but only in French for the rest)

FACT_1 : the subject aids, helps le_sujet_assiste, aide

FACT_2 : the subject invites, authorizes, incites le_sujet invite, authorise, incite

FACT_3 : the subject forces, commands a third party to do the action; le sujet oblige, commande à un tiers à réaliser l'action.

5   Proposing Automatic Transductors from Quechua Compound Verbs into French

Using Table 2 we have written some NooJ grammars to annotate the 3-dim 2931 verbs derived from the verb to love *kuyay* as we see in the sample of Fig. 5.

We have searched plausible meanings for the generated compound verbs by applying on the annotated forms the semantic values of Table 2. We show some results of this approach in Fig. 6 for the derivations of the verb *rimay* to talk:

```
#use grammaire_Verbs_26feb15.nof
#
rimatamurquy,rimay,V+FR="parler"+FLX=V_SIP2_INF
    +le_sujet_en_passant_réalise_l'action
    +le_sujet_accompli_en_peu_de_temps
    +APT_2_en_action_centrifuge_réalise_l_action+INF
rimatamuikapuy,rimay,V+FR="parler"+FLX=V_SIP2_INF
    +le_sujet_en_passant_réalise_l'action
    +le_sujet_avec_attention_SOIN3_2_soigneusement
    +SOIN3_3_concernant_un_tiers_SOIN3
    +4_recommençant_l_action_interrompu_réalise_l_action+INF
rimatamuikamuy,rimay,V+FR="parler"+FLX=V_SIP2_INF
    +le_sujet_en_passant_réalise_l'action+le_sujet_vers_le_sujet
    +PREAT_2_en_prévoyant_PREAT_3_attentionné
    +PREAT_4_de_haut_en_bas_réalise_l_action+INF
rimatamuikachiy,rimay,V+FR="parler"+FLX=V_SIP2_INF
    +le_sujet_en_passant_réalise_l'action+le_sujet_poliment
    +POLI_2_concrètement_POLI_3_précisément
    +POLI_4_courtoisement_réalise_l_action+INF
rimatamuikachay,rimay,V+FR="parler"+FLX=V_SIP2_INF
    +le_sujet_en_passant_réalise_l'action+le_sujet_en_désordre
    +DISP_2_desorienté_réalise_l_action+INF
rimatamuchkay,rimay,V+FR="parler"+FLX=V_SIP2_INF
    +le_sujet_en_passant_réalise_l'action
    +le_sujet_en_train_de_réaliser_l_action+INF
rimatamuchiy,rimay,V+FR="parler"+FLX=V_SIP2_INF
    +le_sujet_en_passant_réalise_l'action+le_sujet_invite
    +FACT_2_autorise_FACT_3_pousse_l'objet_du_verbe_à_réaliser_l_action+INF
rimarullay,rimay,V+FR="parler"+FLX=V_SIP2_INF
    +le_sujet_en_peu_de_temps
    +PRES_2_de_façon_pressante_réalise_l_action+le_sujet_gentiment
```

Fig. 6. Glossed meanings for some compound verbs derived from *rimay* to talk

After verification of the pertinence of these glossed outputs we may propose the possible meaning for the compound verb, like in the following examples:

ayqiriy,ayqiy,V + FR ="échapper" + FLX = V_SIP_INF + le_sujet_commence_à_D YN_2_recommence_à_réalise_l_action + INF *aisariy,aisay*,V + FR = "tirer" + FLX = V_SIP_INF + le_sujet_commence_à_ DYN_2_recommence_à_réalise_l_action + INF

which could be interpreted as: the subject starts towing something, and so *aisariy* should be: to tow, as it has been actually lexicalized.

rimaikuy,rimay,V + FR = "parler" + FLX = V_SIP_INF+le_sujet_courtoise-ment_COURT_2_soigneusement_COURT_3_amicalement_COURT_4_vers_le_sujet_réalise_l_action + INF

which means (the subject) talks someone courteously, carefully, friendly, which could in fact has been lexicalized as: to greet

These meanings may be opposed to the existing lexicalized entries that we have gathered out of our corpus. We see that for the three first ones, they match well:

aiqiriy,V + FR = "commencer à fuir, entreprendre un retrait" + SP = "comenzar a huir, emprender la retirada" + FLX = V_TR

rimaikuy,V + FR = "adreser la parole à qqn avec courtoisie" + SP = "dirigir la palabra a alguien atentamente" + FLX = V_TR

amichiy,V + FR = "faire qqn s'ennuyer" + SP = "hacer aburrir a alguien" + FLX = V_TR

aiqiriy,V + FR = "se retirer lentement à une petite distance" + SP = "retirarse lentamente a pequeña distancia" + FLX = V_TR

asiriy,V + FR = "sourire" + SP = "sonreír" + FLX = V_TR

asnariy,V + FR = "commencer à sentir (la viande)" + SP = "comenzar a oler (carne)" + FLX = V_TR

Table 4. Automatic glossed translation compared to lexicalized entries

Automatic glossed translation	Lexicalized entries translated into FR
rimariy,rimay, V + FR = "parler" + FLX = V_SIP_INF + le_sujet_commence_à_DYN_2_recom-mence_à_réalise_l_action + INF	*rimariy*,V + FR = " commencer à parler" + EN = "to start talking" + FLX = V_TR
rimapamuy,rimay, V + FR = "parler" +FLX = V_SIP_INF + le_sujet_peau-fine_PEAU_2_réitère_PEAU_3_réalise_l_action + le_sujet_se_dépla-çant_ACENT_2_sous_contra-inte_réalise_l_action + INF	*rimapamuy*,V + FR = " parler à la place de quelqu'un" + EN = "to talk in behaf of someone" + FLX = V_TR
rimaikachay,rimay, V + FR = "parler" + FLX = V_SIP_INF + le_sujet_en_désordre_DISP_2_desorienté_réalise_l_action + INF	*rimaikachay*,V + FR = " parler constamment, sans arrêt" + EN = " to talk constantly" + FLX = V_TR
rimanayay,rimay, V + FR = "parler" + FLX = V_SIP_INF + le_sujet_envié_de_ENV_2_souhaite_réal-iser_l_action + INF	*rimanayay*,V + FR = "avoir envie de parler" + EN = "to have the desire to talk" + FLX = V_TR

yaikuriy,V + FR = "entrer un peu, un moment, et aussi, entrer en étant de passage" + SP = "entrar un poco, y también: entrar estando de paso" + FLX = V_TR

In the next table we show some more comparisons for other verbs (Table 4).

6   Results

As a result of this hand verifications carried out on some hundreds of cases, we have elaborated a trilingual dictionary (Qu, Fr, Sp) of Quechua compound verbs. It contains 1600 entries which can be added to our 1400-simple verbs lexicon. It includes their Spanish and French translations. We present below a sample of the entries of this dictionary (Fig. 7):

huqariy,V+FR=" lever, hausser, ramasser"+ SP="levantar, alzar, recoger"+FLXV_TR

qapariy ,V+FR=" crier"+SP=" gritar"+FLXV_TR

paqariy,V+FR=" commencer à faire jour, lever du jour, naissance du jour"+SP="amanecer, nacer"+FLXV_TR

anchichiy,V+FR=" aimer quelqu'un"+SP="quejarse a alguien"+FLXV_TR

aiqichiy,V+FR=" laisser échapper"+SP="dejar escapar"+FLXV_TR

aysachiy,V+FR=" tirer avec force"+SP="tirar con fuerza"+FLXV_TR

akllachiy,V+FR="ordonner de choisir ou le permettre"+SP="ordenar escoger, o permitirlo"+FLXV_TR

amichiy,V+FR=" causer du dégoût"+SP="causar asco"+FLXV_TR

allqachiy,V+FR=" entraîner une faute"+SP="causar una falta"+FLXV_TR

anchuchiy,V+FR=" appeler quelqu'un quelque part"+SP="llamar a alguien a un lado"+FLXV_TR

apachiy,V+FR=" commander de porter quelqu'un"+SP="mandar llevar a alguien"+FLXV_TR

asichiy,V+FR=" faire rire"+SP="hacer reír"+FLXV_TR

asirichiy,V+FR=" faire sourire"+SP="hacer sonreír"+FLXV_TR

Fig. 7. A sample of the entries of the dictionary of compound Quechua verbs

7   Text Annotations

With the help of this dictionary and some NooJ grammars like V_SIP1_INF presented before we may automatically annotate a Quechua text. We applied them on a collection of eight Quechua tales. We show in Fig. 8 the annotated correspondences obtained. We have found around 90 % of successful matches, 6 % of partial matches and 4 % are incorrect matches, mainly because of ambiguities.

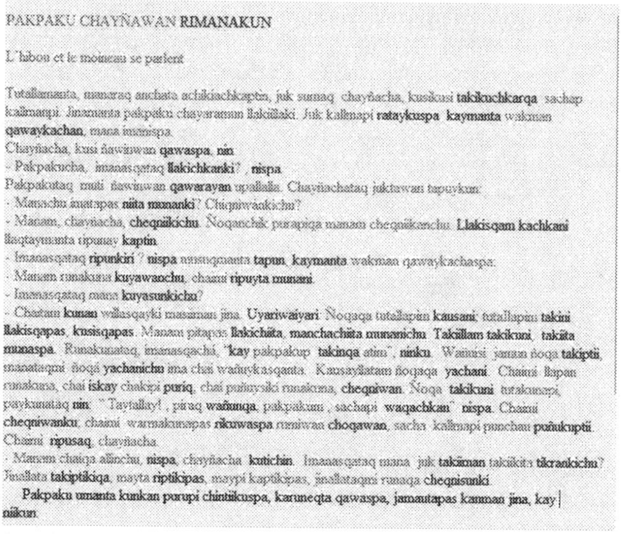
PAKPAKU CHAYÑAWAN **RIMANAKUN**

L'hibou et le moineau se parlent

Tutallamanta, manaraq anchata achikiachkaptin, juk sumaq chayñacha, kusikusi **takikuchkarqa** sachap kallmanpi. Jinamanta pakpaku chayaramun llakillaki. Juk kallmapi **rataykuspa kaymanta** wakman **qawaykachan**, mana imanispa.
Chayñacha, kusi ñawiwan **qawaspa, nin**:
- Pakpakucha, imanasqataq **llakichkanki**? , **nispa**.
Pakpakutaq mulli ñawinwan **qawarayan** upallalla. Chayñachataq juktawan tapuykun:
- Manachu imatapas **niita munanki**? Chiqniwankichu?
- Manam, chayñacha, **cheqnikichu**. Ñoqanchik purapiqa manam cheqnikanchu. **Llakisqam kachkani** llaqtaymanta ripunay **kaptin**.
- Imanasqataq **ripunkiri**? **nispa** nimuqmanta **tapun**, **kaymanta** wakman qawaykachaspa.
- Manam runakuna **kuyawanchu**, chaymi **ripuyta munani**.
- Imanasqataq mana **kuyasunkichu**?
- Chaytam **kunan** willasqayki mayman jina. **Uyariwaiyari**. Ñoqaqa tutallapim **kausani**; tutallapim **takini llakisqapas, kusisqapas**. Manam pitapas **llakichiita, manchachiita munanichu**. **Takillam takikuni**, **takiita munaspa**. Runakunataq, imanasqachá, "**kay** pakpakup **takinqa** atim", **ninku**. Wakinsi jamam ñoqa **takiptii**, manataqmi ñoqa **yachanichu** ima chai wañuykasqanta. Kausayllatam ñoqaqa **yachani**. Chaimi llapan runakuna, chai **iskay** chakipi **puriq**, chai puñuysiki runakuna, **cheqniwan**. Ñoqa **takikuni** tutakunapi, paykunataq **nin**: "Taytallay!, piraq **wañunqa**, pakpakum, sachapi **waqachkan**" **nispa**. Chaimi **cheqniwanku**, chaimi warmakunapas **rikuwaspa** rumiwan **choqawan**, sacha kallmapi punchau **puñukuptii**. Chaimi **ripusaq**, chayñacha.
- Manam chaiqa allinchu, **nispa**, chayñacha **kutichin**. Imanasqataq mana juk **takiinan** takiikita **tikrankichu**? Jinallata **takiptikiqa**, mayta **riptikipas**, maypi kaptikipas, jinallataqmi runaqa **cheqnisunki**.
Pakpaku umanta kunkan purupi chintiikuspa, karuneqta qawaspa, jamautapas kamnan jina, kay niikun.

Fig. 8. Recognition of compound verbal forms in one text of the corpus

8 Conclusion

We have studied the key role of inter positioned suffixes IPS, for the generation of new Quechua verbs. After the study of thousands of combinations we have found altogether 3249 valid compounds of up to three IPS suffixes which will generate that amount of new verbs out of a single one. This considerably increases the verb lexicon. In fact parsing the NooJ grammar V_SIP_INF on our dictionary of around 1400 simple verbs gives us 43160 new compound Quechua verbs. With the help of morpho-syntactic NooJ grammars and the use of the semantic annotations corresponding to the IPS suffixes we propose a glossed form in order to figure out the meaning of these verbs.

Perspectives
Increase the compound verb bilingual dictionary.
Improve our grammars to obtain less ambiguous translations

References

1. Bogacki, K., Gwiazdecka, E.: Derivational structure of polish verbs and the expansion of the dictionary. In: Automatic Processing of Various Levels of Linguistic Phenomena. Selected Papers from the NooJ 2011 International Conference, pp. 50–62. Cambridge Scholars Publishing, New Castle upon Tyne (2012)
2. Dubois, J., Dubois-Charlier, F.: Le verbes français (le « dictionnaire électronique des verbes français (DEV). In: 1992 Diffusé à partir de septembre 2007 par MoDyCo dans un format Excel (2007)
3. Duran, M.: Dictionaire Quechua-Français-Quechua. Éditions HC, Paris (2009)

4. Duran, M.: Morphological and syntactic grammars for recognition of verbal lemmas in quechua. In: Proceedings of the 2014 International Conference and Workshop, Sassari (2014). (at Print)
5. Silberztein, M.: NooJ Manual (2003). www.nooj4nlp.net (220 pages updated regularly)
6. Silberztein, M.: Syntactic parsing with NooJ. In: Proceedings of the NooJ 2009 International Conference and Workshop, 177–190. Centre de Publication Universitaire, Sfax (2010)
7. Silberztein, M.: Automatic transformational analysis and generation. In: Proceedings of the 2010 International NooJ Conference, pp. 221–231. Democritus University Editions, Komotini (2011)
8. Silberztein, M.: Variable unification in nooj V3. In: Automatic Processing of Various Levels of Linguistic Phenomena: Selected Papers from the NooJ 2011 International Conference, pp. 50–62. Cambridge Scholars Publishing, New Castle upon Tyne (2011)
9. Vietri, S.: The annotation of the predicate-argument structure of transfer nouns. In: Formalising Natural Languages wih NooJ, pp. 88–99. Cambridge Scholars Publishing, New Castle upon Tyne (2013)

Morphological Relations for the Automatic Expansion of Italian Sentiment Lexicons

Serena Pelosi[✉]

Department of Political, Social and Communication Science,
University of Salerno, Via Giovanni Paolo II, 132, Fisciano, SA, Italy
spelosi@unisa.it

Abstract. This paper introduces a morphological method for the expansion of Italian Sentiment Lexicons. The purpose of the work is to exploit the existing resources of Nooj in order to make unknown words automatically inherit the semantic information associated to the known items, tanks to derivation phenomena. The research did not focused only on the propagation of the semantic tags, but explored also the reversion, the intensification and the weakening of the words by the effect of special kinds of morphemes.

1 Introduction

The present research proposes a morphological strategy for the enlargement of electronic dictionaries of sentiment in the Italian language. The paper will show the possibility to double the dimension of existing sentiment dictionaries, thanks to derivational phenomena. The inputs are SentIta, a manually built Nooj lexicon of Italian words that, among other part of speech, includes more than 5,000 adjectives of sentiment (Maisto 2014); a list of prefixes and suffixes and a set of Nooj morphological grammars, able to put in relation sentiment words and affixes and to modify, in many different ways, the grammatical category, the semantic orientation (positive/negative), or the intensity (strong/weak) of the starting lemmas.

In detail, our work takes advantage of derivation linguistic clues that put in relation semantically oriented adjectives with quality nouns (e.g. *bello* "beautiful", *bellezza* "beauty") and with adverbs in *-mente* (e.g. *dolce* "sweet", *dolcemente* "sweetly"). The purpose is making new words automatically derive the semantic information associated to the adjectives which they are morpho-phonologically related with.

Furthermore, we use as morphological Contextual Valence Shifters (mCVS) a list of prefixes able to negate (e.g. *anti-*, *non-*, ect...) or to intensify/downtone (e.g. *arci-*, *semi-*, ect...) the orientation of the words with which they occur. Thus, if the just mentioned suffixes can interact with pre-existing dictionaries of the Italian module of Nooj, in order to automatically tag them with new semantic descriptions; the cited prefixes can directly work on opinionated documents, so Nooj can "understand" the actual orientation of the words occurring in real texts.

The evaluation of the precision reached by the automatically built dictionaries and the error analysis will be discussed in detail in the next paragraphs.

T. Okrut et al. (Eds.): NooJ 2015, CCIS 607, pp. 41–51, 2016.
DOI: 10.1007/978-3-319-42471-2_4

We clarify in advance that the morphological method could have been applied also to Italian verbs, but we chose to avoid this solution because of the complexity of their argument structures. We decided, instead, to manually evaluate all the verbs described in the Italian Lexicon-grammar binary tables, so we could preserve the different lexical, syntactic and transformational rules connected to each one of them (Pelosi 2015, Pelosi et al. 2015).

The paper is structured as follows: Section 2 introduces Sentiment Analysis, focusing on the state of the art sentiment lexical databases for the Italian language; Sect. 3 rapidly explores the literature on sentiment lexicon propagation; Sect. 4 describes the rules on which the derivation of adverbs has been performed in this research; Sect. 5 goes in depth in the derivation of quality nouns from qualifiers adjectives; Sect. 6 clarifies the ways in which mCVS can be used in real text occurrences and, in the end, Sect. 7 concludes the work and introduces the improvements that the research still needs.

2   Sentiment Analysis Grounded on Lexicons

Among the most used approaches in the Sentiment Analysis field the lexicon-based methods emerge for popularity. The basic assumption on which they are grounded consists in the idea that the text orientation comes from the semantic orientations of words and phrases occurring in it.

Although hand-built lexicons are more precise than the automatically built ones; to manually draw up a dictionary is a strongly time consuming activity (Taboada et al. 2011; Bloom 2011). That is why the presence of a large number of studies on automatic polarity lexicons creation and propagation can be noticed in literature. Among the most popular lexicons for the sentiment analysis, at least *WordNet-Affect* (Strapparava et al. 2004), *SentiWordNet* (Esuli and Sebastiani 2006) and *SentiFul* (Neviarouskaya et al. 2011) deserve to be cited.

Because the largest part of the state of the art lexicons focuses on the English language, Italian lexical databases are mostly created by translating and adapting the English ones. Steinberger et al. (2012), for example, verified a triangulation hypothesis for the creation of sentiment dictionaries in many languages (namely English, Spanish, Arabic, Czech, French, German, Russian and also Italian).

Baldoni et al. (2012) proposed an ontology-driven approach to Sentiment Analysis, by selecting representative Italian emotional words and using them to query *Multi-WordNet*. The synsets connected to these lemmas were then processed with *WordNet-Affect*, in order to populate the emotion ontology only with the words belonging to synsets that represented affective information. Furthermore, thanks to the *SentiWordNet* database every synset has been associated to the neutral, positive or negative scores.

Basile and Nissim (2013) merged the semantic information belonging to existing lexical resources in order to obtain an Italian annotated lexicon of senses, *Sentix*. They used *MultiWordNet* (Pianta et al. 2002) to transfer polarity information associated to English synsets in *SentiWordNet* to Italian synsets, thanks to the multilingual ontology *BabelNet* (Navigli and Ponzetto 2012).

In the end, Hernandez-Farias et al. (2014) achieved good results in the *SentiPolC 2014* task by semi-automatically translating in Italian different sentiment lexicons; namely, *SentiWordNet, AFINN Lexicon* (Hansen et al. 2011), *Whissel Dictionary* (Whissel 1989), etc...

2.1   The SentIta Database

SentIta, is an Italian sentiment lexicon that has been semi-automatically generated at the Department of Political, Social and Communication Science, on the base of the richness of the Italian module of Nooj (Silberztein 2003; Vietri 2014) and the Italian Lexicon-grammar (LG) resources (Elia et al. 1981; Elia 1984). The tagset used for the Prior Polarity annotation (Osgood 1952) of the lexical resources is composed of four tags (POS "positive"; NEG "negative"; FORTE "intense" and DEB "weak"), that combined together generate an evaluation scale that goes from -3 (+NEG+FORTE) to +3 (+POS+FORTE) and a strength scale that ranges from -1 (+DEB) to +1 (+FORTE). Neutral words have been excluded from the lexicon. In detail, the *SentIta* adjectives and bad words have been manually extracted and evaluated starting from the Nooj databases, preserving their inflectional (FLX) and derivational (DRV) properties. Compound adverbs (Elia 1990), idioms (Vietri 1990; Vietri 2011), psych verbs and other LG verbs (Elia et al. 1981; Elia 1984), instead, have been weighted starting from the Italian LG tables, in order to maintain the syntactic, semantic and transformational properties connected to each one of them.

In this paper we just used a fraction of *SentIta*, that in whole contains more than 15,000 sentiment items. In the next paragraphs we will explain the details concerning the rules used to automatically enlarge this lexical database.

3   State of the Art on Sentiment Lexicon Propagation

The literature on lexicon propagation can be easily grouped into three main research lines. The first one is grounded on the richness of the already existent thesauri, *WordNet*, among others. Although *WordNet* does not include semantic orientation information for its lemmas; semantic relations, such as synonymy or antonymy, are commonly used in order to automatically propagate the polarity, starting from a manually annotated set of seed words (Hu and Liu 2004; Kim and Hovy 2004; Esuli and Sebastiani 2006; Maks and Vossen 2011).

The second line of research is based on the hypothesis that the words that convey the same polarity should appear close in the same corpus, so the propagation can be performed on the base of co-occurrence algorithms (Turney 2002; Baroni and Vegnaduzzo 2004; Kanayama and Nasukawa 2006; Qiu et al. 2009; Wawer 2012).

In the end, the morphological approach is the one that employs morphological structures and relations for the assignment of the prior sentiment polarities to unknown words, on the base of the manipulation of the morphological structures of known lemmas (Ku et al. 2009; Moilanen and Pulman 2008; Wang et al. 2011, Neviar-ouskaya 2010).

4 Deadjectival Adverbs in -*Mente*

As anticipated, this research aims to enlarge the size of *SentIta* on the base of the morphological relations that connect the words and their meanings. In a first stage of the work, more than 5,000 labeled adjectives have been used to predict the orientation of the adverbs which were morphologically related with them. This paragraph will go through the rules exploited to perform the task.

Adverbs are morphologically invariable and, consequently, they do not present any infection. As exemplified below, the great part of them is characterized by a complex structure that includes an adjective base and the derivational morpheme -*mente* "-ly" (Ricca 2004).

[[*veloce*]A -*mente*]AVV "fastly"
[[*fragile*]A -*mente*]AVV "delicately"
[[*rapido*]A -*mente*]AVV "rapidly"

Therefore, all the adverbs contained in the Italian dictionary of simple words have been put in a Nooj text and the FSA shown in Fig. 1 has been used to quickly populate the new dictionary by extracting the words ending with the suffix -*mente* and by making such words inherit the adjectives' polarity.

The Nooj annotations consisted in a list of adverbs that, at a later stage, has been manually checked, in order to adjust the grammar's mistakes and to add the Prior Polarity to the adverbs that did not ended with the suffixes used in the grammar (e.g. *volentieri*, "gladly"; *controvoglia*, "unwillingly").

Other mistakes concerning the annotation of the adjectives regard the adverbs that change the SO of the base adjectives (e.g. *vigorosamente*, "vigorously", and *pazza-mente*, "madly", that respectively come from the positive adjective "vigorous" and the negative adjective "mad", as adverbs, become intensifiers) and also the exceptions that were not enough productive to deserve a specific path in the local grammar (e.g. adjectives ending in -*lento* that, although have the -*o* as last vowel, do not require the thematic vowel -*a*-, but the -*e*-, such as *violento* "violent" that becomes *violent-e-mente* rather than **violent-a-mente* "violenty").

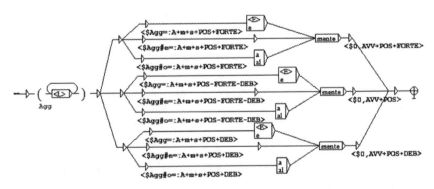

Fig. 1. Extract of the FSA for the population of the sentiment adverbs lexicon.

The manual check produced a set of 3600+ adverbs. The Precision achieved in this task is 0.99 and the Recall is 0.88.

In detail, the word recognition is anchored to the localization of an adjective stem (see the first node on the left, in the variable Agg). Then, the automaton continues the word analysis by checking that the adjective stem belongs to the sentiment dictionary (e.g. $Agg=:A+m+s+POS+FORTE).

It can be noticed, in the center of the FSA, a multiplication of paths. This depends on the different inflectional classes of adjectives on which it is attached. The rules used in the grammar to derive the adverbs are the following:

- first path: nothing in the adjective changes, e.g. *veloc-e* "fast", *veloce-mente* "fastly";
- second path: in the adjectives ending in *-re*, *-le* the *-e* is deleted [#e], e.g. *debol-e* "weak", *debol-mente* "weakly";
- third path: the *-o* is deleted [#o] and substituted by the thematic vowel *-a*, e.g. *rapid-o* "rapid", *rapid-a-mente* "rapidly".

Actually, in the FSA almost nothing about the inflection of the base adjectives has been specified. Because the adverbs of sentiment must be identified among the whole list of Nooj adverbs and semantically annotated (and not generated from scratch), we did not find necessary to recall all the inflectional classes of the derived adjectives: just the deletion or the conservation of the final vowels in the male singular adjectives (A+m +s) was used to select the correct derivational rule.

As concern the superlative form of the adverbs in *-mente*, it must be underlined that they have been treated as adverbs derived from the superlative form of the adjectives. In fact, the rule for the adverb formation is selected by the inflectional paradigm of the superlative form and not by the adjective inflection. Moreover, the semantic orientation inherited by the superlative adverb is, again, the one belonging to the superlative adjective and not the one of the adjective itself. Therefore, the superlative adverbs FSA is almost the same of the one shown in Fig. 1; the only difference is in the recognition of the base adjective, that is A+SUP rather than only A.

5 Deadjectival Nouns of Quality

Furthermore, we took advantage of other derivation phenomena connected to nouns: the derivation of quality nouns from qualifier adjectives. These kind of nouns let us treat as entities the qualities expressed by the base adjectives.

We built a morphological FSA (Fig. 2) that, following the same idea of the adverbs grammar, matches into a list of abstract nouns the stems that are in morphophonological relation with our list of hand-tagged adjectives.

Because the nouns, differently from the adverbs, include inflectional morphemes (FLX); for simplicity, we chose to associate the inflectional paradigm directly in the electronic dictionary of quality nouns suffixes (see Table 1). This way, when the FSA in Fig. 2 recalls all the syntactic properties of the nouns ($0,N$2S), the inflectional paradigms are automatically assigned to the words derived by a specific derivational morpheme.

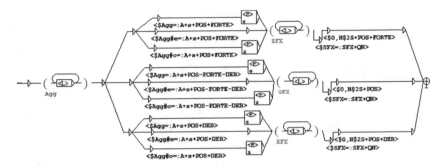

Fig. 2. Extract of the FSA for the population of the sentiment nouns lexicon

The Precision achieved in the general task is 0.93, while the Precision performances of the automatic tagging of the QN evaluated on every single suffix is summarized in Table 1.

As regards the suffixes used to form the quality nouns (Rainer 2004), it must be said that they generally make the new words simply inherit the orientation of the derived adjectives. Exceptions are *-edine* and *-eria* that almost always shift the polarity of the

Table 1. Error analysis of the automatic QN annotation

SFX	FLX	Correct	Errors	Precision
-edine	N46	0	0	–
-età	N602	0	0	–
-izie	N602	0	0	–
-ela	N41	0	1	0
-udine	N46	5	2	0.71
-ore	N5	36	9	0.80
-(z)ione	N46	359	59	0.86
-anza	N41	57	9	0.86
-itudine	N46	13	2	0.87
-ura	N41	142	20	0.88
-mento	N5	514	58	0.90
-izia	N41	14	1	0.93
-enza	N41	148	10	0.94
-eria	N41	71	4	0.95
-ietà	N602	27	1	0.96
-aggine	N46	72	2	0.97
-ia	N41	145	3	0.98
-ità	N602	666	13	0.98
-ezza	N41	305	2	0.99
-igia	N41	3	0	1
-(z)a	N41	2	0	1
Tot	–	**2579**	**196**	**0.93**

Table 2. Annotation Performances

	Precision	Recall	F-score
nouns	0.93	0.72	0.81
adverbs	0.99	0.88	0.93
average	0.96	0.8	0.87

quality nouns into the weakly negative one (−1), e.g. *faciloneria* "slapdash attitude. Also the suffix *-mento* differs from the others, in so far it belongs to the derivational phenomenon of the deverbal nouns of action (Gaeta 2004). It has been possible to use it into our grammar for the deadjectival noun derivation by using the past participles of the verbs listed in the adjective dictionary of sentiment (e.g. V:*sfinire* "to wear out", A: *sfinito* "worn out", N:*sfinimento*; "weariness"). Basically, we chose to include *-mento* in our list of suffixes because of its productivity. That caused an overlap of nouns derived by both the psychological predicates and the qualifier adjectives of sentiment.

Less than 200 psych nominalizations exceeded the coverage of our morphological FSA, proving the power of our methodology also in terms of Recall (0.72).

In about half the cases the annotations differed just in terms of intensity, the other mistakes affected the orientation also (see Table 2).

6 Morphological Semantics

Our morphological FSA can, moreover, interact with a list of prefixes able to negate (*non-, mis-, a-, dis-, in-, s-, anti-, contra-, contro-, de-, di-, es-*), to intensify (*iper-, bis-, macro-, maxi-, mega-, multi-, oltre-, pluri-, poli-, sopra-, sovra-, stra-, super-*), or to downtone (*fra-, infra-, intra-, ipo-, micro-, mini-, para-, semi-, sotto-, sub-, sur-, ultra-*) the orientation of the words in which they appear (Iacobini 2004).

If the suffixes for the creation of Quality Nouns can interact with the pre-existing dictionaries of the Italian module of Nooj, in order to automatically tag them with new semantic descriptions; the prefixes treated in this Section directly work on opinionated documents, so the machine can understand' the actual orientation of the words occurring in real texts, also when their morphological context shifts the polarity of the words listed in the dictionaries. These prefixes are endowed with special tags that specify the way in which they alter the meaning of the sentiment words with which they occur:

- FORTE: "strong", intensifies the Semantic Orientation of the words, making their polarity increase their score in the evaluation scale;
- DEB: "weak", downtones the Semantic Orientation of the words, making their polarity decrease their in the evaluation scale;
- NEGAZIONE: "negation", works following the same rules of the syntactic negation (Maisto 2014);

Figure 3 shows the morphological FSA that combines the polarity and intensity of the adjectives/adverbs of sentiment with the meaning carried on by the mCVS. The shifting rules, in terms of polarity score, are the same exploited in the syntactic

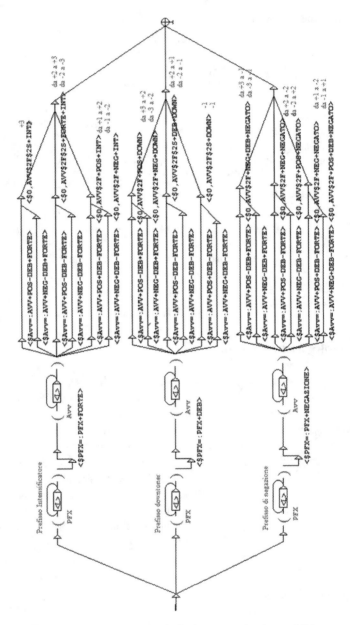

Fig. 3. FSA for the morphological contextual valence shifting

grammar net (Maisto 2014). They are summarised in the green comments on the right side of Fig. 3. As regards the manipulation of the annotations of the resulting words we followed three parallel rules:

- when the score doesn't change, the resulting word simply inherits the inflectional ($2F) and syntactic and semantic ($2S) information of the original word;
- when the intensity changes and the polarity remains steady, the resulting word inherits the inflectional and syntactic and semantic in formation of the original word, but also obtains the tags FORTE/DEB;
- when both the intensity and the polarity change, the resulting word just inherits the inflectional information, while the semantic tags are added from scratch.

We used the list of the sentiment adjectives and adverbs as Nooj text in order to check the performances of this grammar. The discovery that the words containing the mCVS lemmatised in the dictionary are very few (just 29 adjectives, e.g. *straricco*, "very rich", *ultraresistente*, "heavy duty", *stramaledetto*, "damned", and 9 adverbs, e.g. *strabene*, "very well", *ultrapiattamente*, "very dully"), increases the importance of a FSA like the one described in this Paragraph. It is also important to underline that all the synonyms of *poco* "few", also the ones that take the shape of morphemes, e.g. *ipo-*, *sotto-*, *sub-* seem not to be proper downtoners, but resemble the behaviour of the negation words that transform the sentiment words with which they occur into weakly negative ones, e.g., *ipodotato*, "subnormal" *ipofunzionante*, "hypofunctioning" (Maisto 2014). Therefore, we excluded it from the dictionary of mCVS and we included it into a dedicated metanode of the morphological FSA, able to compute its meaning in the right way.

7   Conclusion

This paper introduced a morphological strategy for the enlargement of electronic dictionaries of sentiment in the Italian language. The research has been divided into two main subtask: the semantic annotation of adverbs in *-mente* and of nouns of quality. The starting point, in both the cases, is the information connected to the adjectival bases from which new words are derived.

A large part of the contributions on sentiment lexicon expansion exploited a thesaurus based approach; while our method is morphology based. With it has been possible to automatically create, from a manually built dictionary of 5,000 sentiment adjectives, a dictionary of more than 3,200 sentiment adverbs and a dictionary of more than 3,500 nouns of quality. Moreover, we collected and used into a FSA a set of able to negate or to intensify/downtone the orientation of the words in which they appear.

Future improvement of our lexicon expansion task include the extension of the syntactic categories on which the morphological method can be applied and a systematic evaluation of the performances of the mCVS grammar on large corpora.

References

Maisto, A., Pelosi, S.: A lexicon-based approach to sentiment analysis. The Italian module for Nooj. In: Book of Proceedings of the International Nooj 2014 Conference, 3–5 June, University of Sassari, Italy (2014)

Pelosi, S.: SentIta and Doxa: italian databases and tools for sentiment analysis purposes. In: Book of Proceedings of the second Italian Conference on Computational Linguistics (CLiC-it 2015), Trento, 3–4 December 2015

Neviarouskaya, A.: Compositional Approach for Automatic Recognition of Fine-Grained Affect, Judgment, and Appreciation in Text. Doctoral Dissertation, University of Tokyo (2010)

Pelosi, S., Elia, A., Maisto, A., Guarasci, R.: Towards a lexicon-grammar based framework for NLP: an opinion mining application. In: Book of Proceedings of Recent Advances in Natural Language Processing 2015, RANLP 2015, Hissar, Bulgaria, 5–11 September. Incoma Ltd., Shoumen (2015). ISSN 1313-8502

Taboada, M., Brooke, J., Tofiloski, M., Voll, K., Stede, M.: Lexicon-based methods for sentiment analysis. Comput. Linguist. **37**(2), 267–307 (2011)

Bloom, K.: Sentiment analysis based on appraisal theory and functional local grammars. Doctoral Dissertation, Illinois Institute of Technology (2011)

Strapparava, C., Valitutti, A., et al.: Wordnet affect: an affective extension of wordnet. In: LREC, vol. 4, pp. 1083–1086 (2004)

Esuli, A., Sebastiani, F.: Determining term subjectivity and term orientation for opinion mining. In: EACL, vol. 6, p. 2006 (2006)

Basile, V., Nissim, M.: Sentiment analysis on italian tweets. In: Proceedings of the 4th Workshop on Computational Approaches to Subjectivity, Sentiment and Social Media Analysis, pp. 100–107 (2013)

Pianta, E., Bentivogli, L., Girardi, C.: Multiwordnet: developing an aligned multilingual database. In: Proceedings of the First International Conference on global WordNet, vol. 152, pp. 55–63 (2002)

Navigli, R., Ponzetto, S.P.: BabelNet: the automatic construction, evaluation and application of a wide-coverage multilingual semantic network. Artif. Intell. **193**, 217–250 (2012)

Steinberger, J., Ebrahim, M., Ehrmann, M., Hurriyetoglu, A., Kabadjov, M., Lenkova, P., Steinberger, R., Tanev, H., Vázquez, S., Zavarella, V.: Creating sentiment dictionaries via triangulation. Decis. Support Syst. **53**(4), 689–694 (2012)

Hernandez-Farias, I., Buscaldi, D., Priego-Sánchez, B.: Iradabe: Adapting English lexicons to the Italian sentiment polarity classification task. In: First Italian Conference on Computational Linguistics (CLiC-it 2014) and the Fourth International Workshop, EVALITA 2014, pp. 75–81 (2014)

Hansen, L.K., Arvidsson, A., Nielsen, F.A., Colleoni, E., Etter, M.: Good friends, bad news - affect and virality in twitter. In: Park, J.J., Yang, L.T., Lee, C. (eds.) FutureTech 2011, Part II. CCIS, vol. 185, pp. 34–43. Springer, Heidelberg (2011)

Whissel, C.: The dictionary of affect in language, emotion: theory, research and experience. In: Plutchik, R., Kellerman, H. (eds.) The Measurement of Emotions, vol. 4. Academic, New York (1989)

Baldoni, M., Baroglio, C., Patti, V., Rena, P.: From tags to emotions: ontology-driven sentiment analysis in the social semantic web. Intelligenza Artificiale **6**(1), 41–54 (2012)

Silberztein, M.: Nooj manual (2003). www.nooj4nlp.net

Vietri, S.: The Italian module for Nooj. In: Proceedings of the First Italian Conference on Computational Linguistics, CLiC-it 2014. Pisa University Press (2014)

Elia, A., Martinelli, M., D'Agostino, E.: Lessico e Strutture sintattiche. Introduzione alla sintassi del verbo Italiano. Liguori, Napoli (1981)

Elia, A.: Le verbe italien: les complétives dans les phrases à un complément. Schena; Nizet (1984)

Osgood, C.: The nature and measurement of meaning. Psychol. Bull. **49**(3), 197 (1952)

Elia, E.: Chiaro e tondo: lessico-grammatica degli avverbi composti in Italiano. Segno Associati (1990)

Vietri, S.: On some comparative frozen sentences in Italian. Lingvisticæ Investigationes **14**(1), 149–174 (1990)

Vietri, S.: On a class of italian frozen sentences. Lingvisticæ Investigationes **34**(2), 228–267 (2011)

Hu, M., Liu, B.: Mining and summarizing customer reviews. In: Proceedings of the Tenth ACM SIGKDD International Conference on Knowledge Discovery and Data Mining, pp. 168–177. ACM (2004)

Kim, S.M., Hovy, E.: Determining the sentiment of opinions. In: Proceedings of the 20th International Conference on Computational Linguistics, p. 1367. Association for Computational Linguistics (2004)

Maks, I., Vossen, P.: Different approaches to automatic polarity annotation at synset level. In: Proceedings of the First International Workshop on Lexical Resources, WoLeR, pp. 62–69 (2011)

Turney, P.D.: Thumbs up or thumbs down? Semantic orientation applied to unsupervised classification of reviews. In: Proceedings of the 40th Annual Meeting on Association for Computational Linguistics, pp. 417–424. Association for Computational Linguistics (2002)

Baroni, M., Vegnaduzzo, S.: Identifying subjective adjectives through web-based mutual information. In: Proceedings of KONVENS, vol. 4, pp. 17–24 (2004)

Kanayama, H., Nasukawa, T.: Fully automatic lexicon expansion for domain-oriented sentiment analysis. In: Proceedings of the 2006 Conference on Empirical Methods in Natural Language Processing, pp. 355–363. Association for Computational Linguistics (2006)

Qiu, G., Liu, B., Bu, J., Chen, C.: Expanding domain sentiment lexicon through double propagation. In: IJCAI, vol. 9, pp. 1199–1204 (2009)

Wawer, A.: Extracting emotive patterns for languages with rich morphology. Int. J. Comput. Linguist. Appl. **3**(1), 11–24 (2012)

Ku, L.W., Huang, T.H., Chen, H.H.: Using morphological and syntactic structures for Chinese opinion analysis. In: Proceedings of the 2009 Conference on Empirical Methods in Natural Language Processing, vol. 3, pp. 1260–1269. Association for Computational Linguistics (2009)

Moilanen, K., Pulman, S.: The good, the bad, and the unknown: morphosyllabic sentiment tagging of unseen words. In: Proceedings of the 46th Annual Meeting of the Association for Computational Linguistics on Human Language Technologies: Short Papers, pp. 109–112. Association for Computational Linguistics (2008)

Wang, X., Zhao, Y., Fu, G.: A morpheme-based method to chinese sentence-level sentiment classification. Int. J. Asian Lang. Proc. **21**(3), 95–106 (2011)

Ricca, D.: Derivazione avverbiale. In: La formazione delle parole in Italiano, pp. 472–489 (2004)

Rainer, F.: Derivazione nominale deaggettivale. In: La formazione delle parole in Italiano, pp. 293–314. Max Niemeyer Verlag (2004)

Gaeta, L.: Nomi d'azione. In: La formazione delle parole in Italiano, pp. 314–351. Max Niemeyer Verlag (2004)

Iacobini, C.: Prefissazione. In: La formazione delle parole in Italiano, pp. 97–161 (2004)

Syntax and Semantics

Joe Loves Lea: Transformational Analysis of Direct Transitive Sentences

Max Silberztein[✉]

ELLIADD, Université de Franche-Comté, Besançon, France
max.silberztein@univ-fcomte.fr

Abstract. NooJ is capable of both parsing and producing any sentence that matches a given syntactic grammar. We use this functionality to describe direct transitive sentences, and we show that this simple structure of sentence accounts for millions of potential sentences.

Keywords: Nooj · Syntactic analysis · Transformational analysis · Transformational grammar

1   Introduction

NooJ allows linguists to formalize various types of linguistic description: orthography and spelling, lexicons for simple words, multiword units and frozen expressions, inflectional and derivational morphology, local, structural and transformational syntax. One important characteristic of NooJ is that all the linguistic descriptions are reversible, i.e. they can be used both by a parser (to recognize sentences) as well as a generator (to produce sentences). (Silberztein 2011) and (Silberztein 2016) show how, by combining a parser and a generator and applying them to a syntactic grammar, we can build a system that takes one sentence as its input, and produce all the sentences that share the same lexical material with the original sentence.

Here are two simple transformations[1]:

- [Pron-0] Joe loves Lea = He loves Lea
- [Passive] Joe loves Lea = Lea is loved by Joe

The second one can be implemented in NooJ via the following grammar:

This graph uses three variables $NO, $V and $N1. When parsing the sentence *Joe loves Lea*, the variable $N0 stores the word *Joe*, $V stores the word *loves* and $N1 stores *Lea*. The grammar's output "$N1 is $V_V+PP by $N0" produces the string *Lea is loved by Joe*.

Note that morphological operations such as "$V_V+PP", operate on NooJ's Atomic Linguistic Units (ALUs) rather than plain strings; in other words, NooJ knows that the word form *loves* is an instance of the verb *to love* and it can produce all the conjugated

---

[1] I am using the term *transformation* as in (Harris 1968): an operator that links sentences that share common semantic material, as opposed to (Chomsky 1957) whose transformations link deep and surface structures.

© Springer International Publishing Switzerland 2016
T. Okrut et al. (Eds.): NooJ 2015, CCIS 607, pp. 55–65, 2016.
DOI: 10.1007/978-3-319-42471-2_5

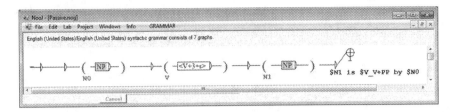

Fig. 1. The [Passive] transformation

and derived word forms from this ALU (e.g. "loving", "lovers"). Here, $V_V+PP takes the value of variable $V (*loves*), lemmatizes it (*love*), produces all its verb forms and selects the ones that have property +PP (i.e. Past Participle) to get the result *loved*.

One application of this rewriting system is Machine Translation, whereas one grammar recognizes sentences in one input language, and produces the corresponding "rewritten" sentences in another language, see for instance (Barreiro 2008) for Portuguese-English translation, (Fehri et al. 2010) for Arabic-French translation and (Ben et al. 2015) for Arabic-English translation.

As (Silberztein 2016) has shown, any serious attempt at describing a significant part of a language will involve the creation of a large number of elementary transformations (Fig. 2):

[Pron-0]	*Joe loves Lea = He loves Lea*
[Pron-1]	*Joe loves Lea = Joe loves her*
[Pron-2]	*Joe gives an apple to Lea = Joe gives her an apple*
[Preterit]	*Joe loves Lea = Joe loved Lea*
[Impfct]	*Joe loves Lea = Joe has loved Lea*
[Futur]	*Joe loves Lea = Joe will love Lea*
[Cond]	*Joe loves Lea = Joe should love Lea*
[Passive]	*Joe loves Lea = Lea is loved by Joe*
[Negation]	*Joe loves Lea = Joe does not love Lea*
[Cleft-0]	*Joe loves Lea = It is Joe who loves Lea*
[Cleft-1]	*Joe loves Lea = It is Lea that Joe loves*
[Question-0]	*Joe loves Lea = Who loves Lea?*
[Question-1]	*Joe loves Lea = Who does Joe love?*
[Nom-0]	*Joe loves Lea = Joe is in love with Lea*
[Nom-V]	*Joe loves Lea = Joe feels love for Lea*
[Nom-1]	*Joe loves Lea = Lea is Joe's love*
...	

Fig. 2. Elementary transformations

Previously, each of these transformations would have to be described by two NooJ grammars, because each pair of sentences involve two opposite computations: we want to produce not only *Lea is loved by Joe* from the sentence *Joe loves Lea*, but also the sentence *Joe loves Lea* from the sentence *Lea is loved by Joe*, and the grammars that can perform the reverse operation is different, as we can seen in the following figure (Fig. 3):

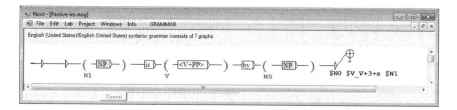

Fig. 3. The [Passive-inv] transformation

(Silberztein 2016) shows that it is not always possible to combine elementary transformations with each others in order to take account of all complex sentences. For instance, it would not be possible to use the elementary graphs [Cleft-1], [Passive] and [Neg] to produce the sentence *It is Lea who is not loved by Joe* from the original sentence *Joe loves Lea* without modifying them profondly, as the graph in Fig. 1 would not parse the intermediary sentence *Joe does not love Lea*.

The solution described by (Silberztein 2016) is based on the fact that all NooJ's linguistic resources are reversible, i.e. they can be used both to parse texts and also to produce them. For instance, NooJ's morphological grammars can be used to recognize and analyze word forms, but also to produce lists of forms in the form of a dictionary, see following figure (Fig. 4).

NooJ's command GRAMMAR > Generate Language automatically constructs the dictionary that contains all the word forms recognized by the morphological grammar,

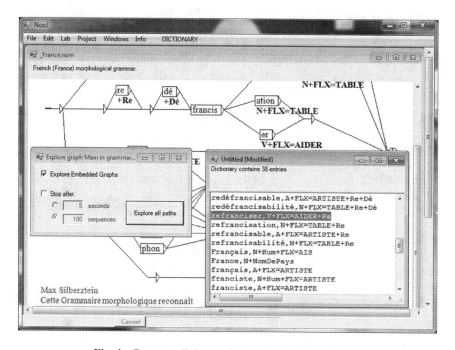

Fig. 4. Generate all the word forms derived from *France*

and associates each of the word forms with the corresponding grammar output. In the resulting dictionary, the linguistic information associated with each lexical entry corresponds in a sense to its linguistic analysis: analyzing the word form *refranciser* as a verb with the **+Re** (repetition) feature is similar to analyzing the sentence *Joe does not love Lea* with the **+Neg** (negation) operator. Our goal is then to construct a syntactic grammar that represents all the sentences transformed from the elementary sentence *Joe loves Lea*.

2   A Simple Grammar

I have constructed a simple grammar that contains three sub-grammars:

- a grammar that recognizes declarative sentences, e.g. *Joe cannot stop loving Lea*
- a grammar that recognizes interrogative sentences, e.g. *Does Joe love Lea?*
- a grammar that recognizes noun phrases, e.g. *Joe's love for Lea*.

2.1   Declarative Sentences

The graph **Declarative** shown in Fig. 5 recognizes the simple sentence *Joe loves Lea* (in the path at the very top), as well as over 1 million variants.

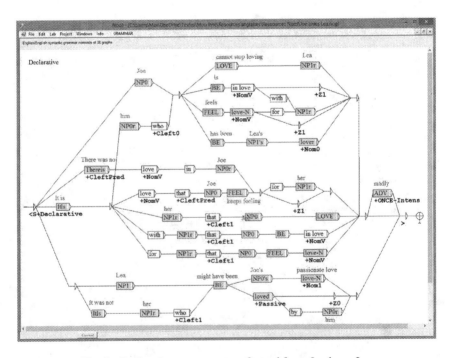

Fig. 5. Declarative sentences transformed from *Joe loves Lea*

– Three nominalizations:

Joe was in love with Lea (+NomV), *Joe did no longer feel any love for Lea* (+NomV), *Joe is Lea's lover* (+Nom0), *Lea has been Joe's love* (+Nom1)

– Three extractions:

It is not Joe who loves Lea (+Cleft0), *It is Lea that Joe loved* (+Cleft1), *It was love that Joe felt for Lea* (+CleftPred)

– Three pronouns:

He loves Lea (+Pron0), *Lea is loved by him* (+Pron0), *Joe is in love with her* (+Pron1), *She is loved by Joe* (+Pron1), *Joe feels something for Lea* (+PronPred).

– Three elisions:

Lea is loved (+Z0), *Joe is in love* (+Z1), *Joe feels for Lea* (+ZPred).

– Five intensive adjectives and adverbs:

Joe feels little love for Lea (+Intens0), *Joe loves Lea a lot* (+Intens1), *Joe loved Lea very much* (+Intens2), *Lea was Joe's passionate love* (+Intens3), *Joe is madly in love with Lea* (+Intens4)

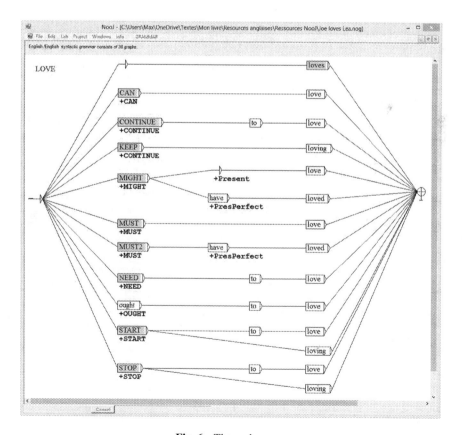

Fig. 6. The verb group

– Two aspectual adverbs:

Joe no longer loves Lea (+STOP), *Joe still loves Lea* (+CONT),

– In the graph **LOVE** shown in Fig. 6, the embedded graph **loves** recognizes all conjugated forms of *to love* (*loves, loved, has loved, was loving*) as well as the corresponding negative (*doesn't love*) aspectual (*is still loving*) and emphasis (*does love*) sequences.

– The graphs **CAN, MIGHT, MUST, MUST2, NEED** recognize modal sequences such as *could no longer love, must have loved, needs to love*, etc. The embedded graphs **CONTINUE, KEEP, START** and **STOP** are used to recognize aspectual sequences such as *kept on loving, started to love*, did not *stop loving*, etc.

By exploring all the paths in the Declarative graph, NooJ produces over 1 million declarative sentences (Fig. 7).

Similarly, the graph **NounPhrase** represents over 500,000 noun phrases such as *Lea's lover* (+Nom0), *Joe's mad love for Lea* (+NomV) and *Joe's love* (+Nom1), etc.

The graph **Interrogative** represents over 3 million questions such as: *Who used to love Lea? When did Joe's love for Lea end? Why could Joe no longer love Lea? How come Joe still loves Lea?*, etc.

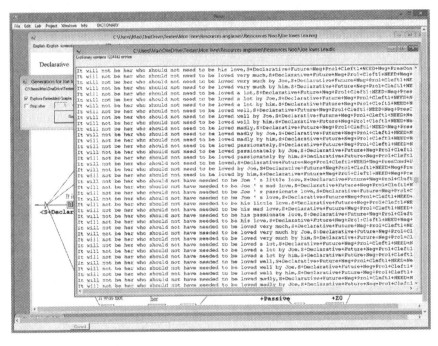

Fig. 7. The **Declarative** grammar represents over 1 million sentences

3   Generalizing the Grammar

If we want to construct a syntactic grammar that recognizes all direct transitive sentences such as *My cousin ate an apple*, we can start by replacing *Joe* and *Lea* with a description of Noun Phrases, and *love* with any direct transitive verb.

Such a grammar would indeed recognize any sentence of structure NP V NP successfully; however it would be useless as a transformational grammar because it would not restrict the elements of the sentence. For instance, it would recognize the three sentences:

Lea is seen by Joe. The busy teacher dropped the broken pen. Joe saw Lea.

but it would not be able to tell that the first and the third sentences are linked by a transformation, whereas the second one is unrelated. Moreover, we want the grammar to process the two following sentences as two unrelated sentences:

Joe loves Lea. Joe is loved by Lea.

In order to produce the sentence *Lea is loved by Joe* (and reject sentence *Joe is loved by Lea*) from the first one, we need to index the elements of the sentence:

$NP_0 \ V \ NP_1 = NP_1 \ is \ V\text{-}pp \ by \ NP_0$

and then set NP_0, V and NP_1 respectively to *Joe*, *love* and *Lea*. To do that, we use NooJ's global variables.

The new grammar is very similar to original grammar *Joe loves Lea*. As a matter of fact, the main Declarative graph in the new grammar is almost identical to the one shown

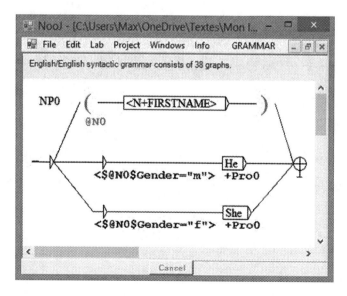

Fig. 8. A generic grammar to represent the main verb of a direct transitive sentence.

in Fig. 5[2]. However, we modified the graphs that contain the actual lexical material, as seen in Figs. 8 and 9.

The new version of the **NP0** graph sets the global variable @N0 and uses a lexical contraint on the gender of @N0 in order to produce the correct pronoun (i.e. *He* for *Joe* and *She* for *Lea*). The corresponding **NP0r** graph produces the pronouns *him* (instead of *He*) and *her* (instead of *She*) to take account of the object complements.

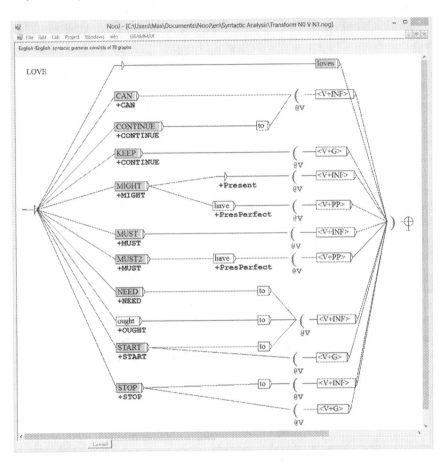

Fig. 9. A generic grammar to represent the main verb of a direct transitive sentence.

Similarly, the new version of the **LOVE** graph sets the global variable @V and replaces all conjugated forms of the verb to love with a syntactic symbol such as <V>, <V+PP>, <V-G>, etc.

---

[2] We have just replaced the regular nodes labeled with the word form "love" with auxiliary nodes that call embedded graphs in which the conjugated forms of *to love* are replaced with syntactic symbols such as <V>.

Nominalizations. Remember that the original grammar takes account of three nominalizations:

> *Joe was in love with Lea* (+NomV), *Joe did no longer feel any love for Lea* (+NomV), *Joe is Lea's lover* (+Nom0), *Lea has been Joe's love* (+Nom1)

In the original grammar, these three nominalized forms were described in graphs **love-N**, **lover** and **love-0**. The same graphs have been modified as follow (Fig. 10):

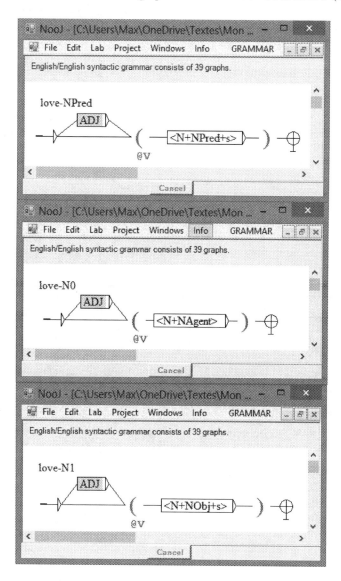

Fig. 10. Three nominalizations

Note that the variable @V is used to store the predicate of the sentence, whether it is a verb or if it has been derived as a noun. In order for each of these graphs to be activated, the initial verb needs to have the corresponding derivational property: +NPred (Predicate is nominalized), +NAgent (Subject is nominalized) and +NObj (Object is derived); these three properties are produced by the corresponding derivational DRV paradigms applied to lexical entry, e.g.:

love+FLX=LOVE+DRV=PRED_ID+DRV=AGENT_R:TABLE
+DRV=OBJECT_ID:TABLE
PRED_ID = <E>/N+NPred;
AGENT_R = r/N+NAgent;
OBJECT_ID = <E>/N+NObj;

Reciproquely, if a given verb does not accept one of these derivations, then the sentences that contain this derivation will just not be produced. For instance, if we start from sentence: *Mary sees Helen*, only 600,000 declarative sentences will be produced, because the verb to see does not accept any of the three derivations:

Mary sees Helen = *Mary is a seer*
Mary sees Helen = *Mary (does | feels) some seing for Helen*
Mary sees Helen = *Helen is Mary's see*

The list of features produced with each transformed sentence represents its transformational analysis. For instance, the resulting sentence "Mary couldn't see Helen" is associated with the features S+Declarative+CAN+Preterit+Neg (Fig. 11).

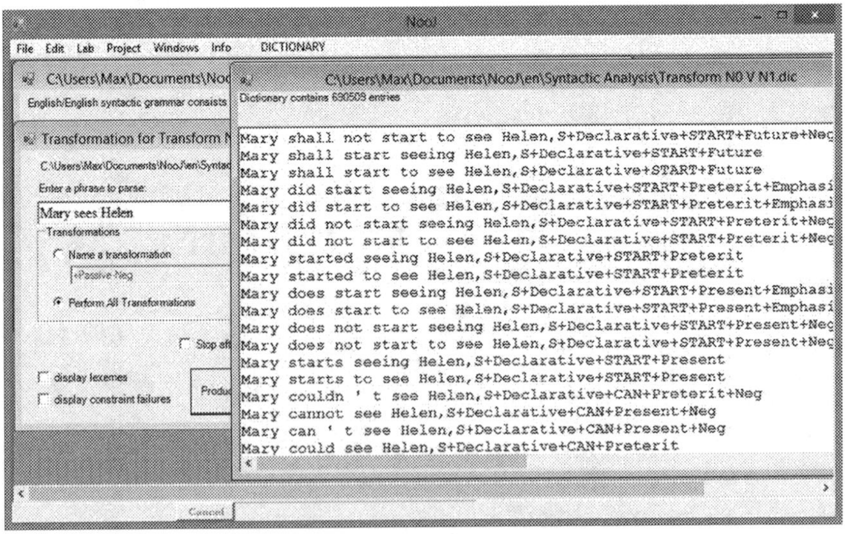

Fig. 11. Produce all the sentences transformed from *Mary sees Helen*

4 Conclusion

In this paper, I have presented a simple grammar capable of recognizing and producing a large number of sentences that are derived by transformations from the initial elementary sentence *Joe loves Lea*. This accounts for approximately 4 million sentences, including over 1 million declarative sentences, 500,000 noun phrases and over 3 million questions.

Modifying this grammar so that it can recognize any direct transitive sentence and produce the corresponding transformed sentences is suprisingly easy: it involves the replacement of word forms with more general syntactic symbols (e.g. replace *loved* with <V+PP>) and global variables that store the three elements of the sentence @N0, @V and @N1 and then provide the reference for the arguments, wherever they are located in the sentence.

As opposed to the traditional point of view on transformational grammars, the system presented here does not require linguists to implement a new level of linguistic description that would be different from the syntactic structural level: no need to implement specific transformational operators nor design a complex set of mechanisms to process chains of transformations.

References

Barreiro, A.: ParaMT: a paraphraser for machine translation. In: Teixeira, A., de Lima, V.L.S., de Oliveira, L., Quaresma, P. (eds.) PROPOR 2008. LNCS (LNAI), vol. 5190, pp. 202–211. Springer, Heidelberg (2008)

Ben, A., Fehri, H., Ben, H.: Translating Arabic relative clauses into English using NooJ platform. In: Monti, J., Silberztein, M., Monteleone, M., di Buono, M.P. (eds.) Formalising Natural Languages with NooJ 2014, pp. 166–174. Cambridge Scholars Publishing, Newcastle (2015)

Fehri, H., Haddar, K., Ben Hamadou, A.: Integration of a transliteration process into an automatic translation system for named entities from Arabic to French. In: Proceedings of the NooJ 2009 International Conference and Workshop, pp. 285–300. Centre de Publication Universitaire, Sfax (2010)

Harris, Z.: Mathematical Structures of Language. Interscience, New York (1968)

Silberztein, M.: Automatic transformational analysis and generation. In: Gavriilidou, Z., Chatzipapa, E., Papadopoulou, L., Silberztein, M. (eds.) Proceedings of the NooJ 2010 International Conference and Workshop, pp. 221–231. Univ. of Thrace, Komotini (2011)

Silberztein, M.: Language formalization: the NooJ's Approach. Wiley Eds. (2016)

A Hierarchy of Semantic Labels for Spanish Dictionaries

Xavier Blanco[(✉)]

Universitat Autònoma de Barcelona, Cerdanyola del Vallès, Spain
Xavier.Blanco@uab.cat

Abstract. We present a hierarchy of semantic labels for the Spanish language. Each semantic label corresponds to the *genus proximum* (the next kind) of the lexical units that it describes. After having chosen ALGO 'something' as the head of our hierarchy, we distinguish between HECHO 'fact' and ENTIDAD 'entity', each of which are further partitioned into around twenty subclasses. Facts correspond to predicates while entities can correspond either to semantic names (objects) or to quasi-predicates. For disambiguation of predicates and quasi-predicates, we use the notion of an actantial formula (a linguistic expression that specifies the actants of a predicative form). The implementation of this hierarchy in the Spanish electronic dictionary of NooJ would allow us to foresee diverse applications.

Keywords: Semantic label · Actantial formula · Quasi-predicate · Spanish lexicography

1 Introduction

In the frame of the Labelsem project (FFI-2013-44185-P funded by the Spanish Ministerio de Economía y Competitividad), the research group fLexSem (Phonetics, Lexicology and Semantics, Autonomous University of Barcelona) is developing a comprehensive hierarchy of semantic labels for dictionaries of Spanish. A "semantic label" of a dictionary's entry is a lexical unit (simple or complex) or (more rarely) a syntagm that corresponds to the genus proximum (the next kind) of the entry in question. For example, the semantic label for *arañazo* ('scratch'), *corte* ('cut') and *herida* ('wound') in contexts such as *Mi hijo se hizo un arañazo en la cara* ('My son got a scratch on his face'), *¿Cómo evitar que mis padres vean los cortes que llevo en la muñeca?* ('How to hide cuts on my wrist from my parents?') or *Lamerse una herida es una respuesta instintiva en los humanos y en otros muchos animales* ('Wound licking is an instinctive response in humans and many other animals') would be LESIÓN ('injury', 'lesion') because the definitions of *arañazo*, *corte* and *lesión* would begin with *lesión que...* More precisely, the semantic label is a minimal paraphrase for a given lexical unit that corresponds to

This research has been funded by the *Ministerio de Economía y Competitividad* (Spain) in the frame of the project FFI-2013-44185-P *Jerarquía de etiquetas semánticas (español y francés) para los géneros próximos de la definición lexicográfica*.

the communicatively dominant component of its (Aristotelian) definition. Note that we will use capital letters for the labels.

The semantic label constitutes the syntactic head of the entry's formal definition. It must be noted that the *definiendum* almost never corresponds with the entry form (the lemma) but with a propositional form or actant structure that includes all the semantic actants of the lemma. For instance, we do not define *herida* ('wound') but *herida de X por parte de Y en Z con W* ('wound of W from Y in Z with W') (X and Y being animates, Z a part of X, and W a physical object). Other propositional forms accepted by *herida* would be the objects of different definitions.

Let us stress that these labels are actual linguistic signs of Spanish and not a meta-linguistic device. This implies that the regular semantic, syntactic and restricted lexical co-occurrence of a given label with the *definiendum* can and must be controlled before attributing a lemma to it. This control plays a key role in the elaboration of the hierarchy as it is the central criterion for the attribution of a label. Moreover, it is a distinctive trait of our hierarchy of labels since most sets of semantic labels are made up of metalinguistic entities. Labelling in this way we obtain both a minimal paraphrase of the lemma's signified and a syntactical substitute in any context [2].

At present, our hierarchy comprises approximately 700 labels (only nominal ones). The total number of labels in the hierarchy cannot be fixed in advanced since we cannot arbitrarily restrict ourselves to particular sets of hyperonyms. The hierarchy is (mainly) inductively built, so we need the *genus* or next kind for each lema in the dictionary. Of course, the usual inheritance mechanism can be used to form quantitatively manipulable sets of lemmas.

The label with the greatest semantic extension is ALGO ('something'), followed by HECHO ('fact') and ENTIDAD ('entity'). An HECHO [1] is always a semantic predicate, while an ENTIDAD can be a semantic name or a predicate (quasi-predicate). In this paper, we will restrict ourselves to discussing the semantic labels of a sample containing 1,000 lemmas corresponding to facts and 1,000 lemmas corresponding to entities.

It is worth emphasising that the hierarchy of semantic labels is language-dependent. As a result, it cannot be directly used for translation or for multilingual search operations. However, different mechanisms of connections or equivalences between hierarchies can be proposed in order to consider translinguistic applications. That is relatively straight-forward between Spanish and French, since we are building our hierarchy according to the methods and results obtained for the French language by the researchers of the ATILF Laboratory (*Analyse et Traitement Informatique de la Langue Française, Université de Lorraine*) and of the OLST (*Observatoire de Linguistique Sens-Texte, Université de Montréal*) [5, 9, 10]. Moreover, up until now we have kept the same number of classes for the first two levels of the hierarchy.

2   Facts *vs* Entities

First of all, we have to choose a label for the root of our hierarchy. This label has to be the most extensive meaning in Spanish. As indicated above, we choose the label ALGO ('something') since every Spanish lexical unit can accept (stylistic considerations aside)

ALGO as a *genus* (*un armario es algo que...* 'a cupboard is something that...', *un roble es algo que...* 'an oak is something that...'). Note that even for humans the replacement by *algo* is possible and even natural in some contexts (*Un abogado es algo distinto* 'A lawyer is something different', *Ese tío es algo especial* 'This guy is something special') even if, obviously, replacing ALGO by ALGUIEN ('someone') would dramatically improve acceptability when defining lexical units denoting humans.

Next, a basic distinction must be drawn between HECHO ('fact') and ENTIDAD ('entity') [1]. A fact 'takes place', whereas an entity 'is'. A lexical unit of Spanish denoting a fact can be embedded under *Sé que...* or *Creo que...* (*Sé que Juan tiene cáncer* 'I know that John has cancer', *Sé que Juan dio un paseo* 'I know that John went for a walk', *Sé que Juan dio una charla* 'I know that John gave a talk'...). *Cáncer, paseo* and *charla*, in these contexts, are facts.

Facts are inscribed in time and, consequently, they combine with grammatical meanings as 'present', 'past', 'future', 'simultaneous', 'previous', etc. They also combine with aspectual meanings like 'semelfactive', 'iterative', 'distributive', 'punctual', 'durative', 'habitual', 'perfective', 'progressive', etc. Moreover, they accept other grammatical meanings such as 'intensive', 'negative', 'causative', 'inchoative', 'interrogative', etc.

By contrast, entities are inscribed in space and they present dimensional values (length, weight...). The grammatical meanings applied to entities are different to those applied to facts. Entities, for instance, accept size ('augmentative', 'diminutive'), and sometimes (if they are living beings) sex ('masculine', 'feminine'), etc. An important point to be taken into account is that an entity always corresponds to a noun, whereas the opposite is not true. A noun can certainly correspond to a fact (see above the examples of *cáncer, paseo, charla*), and adjectives and verbs are often facts (never entities), while adverbs are facts that select only other facts in their actant structure (see Sect 3).

2.1 Subclasses of Facts

At the moment, our hierarchy comprises sixteen subclasses of facts, namely (in alphabetical order): ACCIÓN ('action'), ACONTECIMIENTO ('event'), ACTITUD ('attitude'), ACTIVIDAD ('activity'), CANTIDAD ('quantity'), CARACTERÍSTICA ('feature'), COMPORTAMIENTO ('behaviour'), CONJUNTO DE HECHOS ('set of facts'), COSTUMBRE ('habit'), ESTADO ('state'), FENÓMENO ('phenomenon'), PERÍODO ('period'), PARÁMETRO ('parameter'), RELACIÓN FACTUAL ('factual relationship'), PROCESO ('process') and SITUACIÓN ('condition'). The English translations of these labels are not to be taken as labels themselves. They are approximative and are only given for the convenience of the reader.

To a certain extent, it is possible to resort to linguistically motivated criteria in order to distinguish these subclasses. So, for instance, lexical units labelled as GOLPE 'blow' can be viewed as facts with a puntual character that occur at a given moment, and do not present an internal temporal structure. States would be atelic, since they do not have an inherent limit. Therefore, sentences such as *Está sabiendo la respuesta*, *He is knowing the answer* are ungrammatical. Actions are performed by an agent and thence they can be volitional: *Juan me dio un golpe (a propósito, sin querer)*, 'John hit me (on purpose, unintentionally)' but *Juan sabe la respuesta a propósito, *'John knows the answer on purpose'.

However, even if these criteria can prove useful in many circumstances, specific contextual effects often blur the applicability of the linguistic tests on which they are based. Not only metaphorical or idiomatic uses, but also technical ones can indeed modify the acceptability of a sentence. Therefore, the main criterion for the attribution of a semantic label to a given lexical unit remains the possibility or impossibility of using the label in a question as *genus proximum* in the lexicographical definition. Another possible formalisation of this lexical relation is the lexical function **Gener** (generic concept) [5]. For instance, the **Gener** value of *incremento* 'increase' is PROCESO 'process'. Note that **Gener** is not the same as hyperonymy, because hyperonymy is a semantic relation while **Gener** is a lexical one. The former will resist translation to another language, whereas the latter may not. The value of **Gener** for a given keyword must accept the attributive construction: *(un) incremento es un proceso (que)* … 'increase is a process (that)…'.

Each one of these subclasses of facts has, in turn, its own subclasses. For example, PROCESO includes PROCESO FÍSICO 'physical process', PROCESO FISIOLÓGICO 'physiological process' and PROCESO SOCIAL 'social process'. The noun *regeneración* (in a context as *La regeneración de los tejidos periodontales* 'Regeneration of periodontal tissues') would be labelled PROCESO FISIOLÓGICO.

2.2 Subclasses of Entities

Our hierarchy comprises twenty subclasses of entities, namely (in alphabetical order): ACUMULACIÓN 'accumulation', ALGO QUE ESTÁ EN DETERMINADA RELACIÓN CON ALGO 'something that stands in a certain relation with', ALGO QUE ESTÁ EN DETERMINADO ESTADO 'something that is in a certain state', ALGO QUE SE CONSUME 'something that is consumed', ÁMBITO DE ACTIVIDAD 'area of activity', BIEN 'property', CONJUNTO 'set', CREACIÓN 'creation', ENTIDAD GEOLÓGICA 'geological entity', ENTIDAD INFORMACIONAL 'informative entity', ENTIDAD SOCIAL 'social entity', ENTIDAD VISUAL 'visual entity', LUGAR 'place', LUGAR ABSTRACTO 'abstract place', MATERIA 'matter', OBJETO FÍSICO 'physical object', OCUPACIÓN SOCIAL 'social occupation', SER IMAGINARIO 'imaginary being', SER VIVO 'living being' and SUMA DE DINERO 'amount of money'.

Some of these classes encompass a very large number of lexical units. Such is the case of SER VIVO 'living being' that includes the labels HUMANO 'human', ANIMAL 'animal' and VEGETAL 'vegetal'. Even leaving aside terminology, the number of lexical units referring to humans is very large. Subclasses of humans can be precisely characterized by means of predicates that select them in a specific way. We observe, for example, that *(Contratar, despedir) a un camarero* ('To hire, to fire a waiter') is acceptable, but not *(Contratar, despedir) a un sacerdote* (*'To hire, to fire a priest'). *Camarero* and *sacerdote* will then be in two different subclasses of INDIVIDUO QUE PRACTICA UN OFICIO 'individual that has a profession'. The methodology of the "classes of objects" [3, 7] is based upon this property of some predicates.

The label OBJETO FÍSICO 'physical objet' is another example of a class that subsumes a considerable number of subclasses. The larger of these subclasses is ARTE-FACTO 'artefact', which introduces the important difference between natural objects and artificial ones. Interestingly, artefacts often present verbs of realization or fulfillment as specific collocational values: **Real**$_1$ (*coche*) = *conducir* 'to drive a car', **Prepar-Fact**$_0$ (*coche*) = *poner gasolina* 'to fill up the car', **Real**$_2$ (*bus*) = *ir en* 'to ride on a bus', **PreparReal**$_2$ (*taxi*) = *parar* 'to hail a taxi', etc.

3   Semantic Apparatus

It is important to highlight that a semantic label is not attributed to a form (that can be ambiguous and, therefore, require more than a semantic label) but to a lexical unit. Several methods can be used in order to individualize a lexical unit in a dictionary. In our case, we resort to an actantial formula accompanied by an example.

The actantial formula of a lexical unit is a linguistic expression that includes the form of this lexical unit and its actants (identified by variables: X, Y, Z... and semantically labelled if necessary). For instance, the actantial formula of *acusación* corresponds to *ENUNCIADO que la PERSONA X emite* contra la PERSONA Y a propósito del HECHO Z 'STATEMENT that the PERSON X makes against the PERSON Y concerning the FACT Z'. An example could be: *Se tomó mi observación como una acusación personal* 'He took my remark as a personal accusation'. In the example *El fiscal retiró la acusación contra el ex-diputado* 'The prosecutor withdrew the accusation against the congressman', the actantial formula would be *ACTO JURÍDICO de la PERSONA X contra el INDIVIDUO Y debido a su ACCIÓN Z presentada ante la AUTORIDAD JUDICIAL W* 'JURIDICAL ACT of the PERSON X against the INDIVIDUAL Y because of his ACTION Z'. For the sentence *El Ayuntamiento se personó como acusación particular en aquel caso* 'The city council entered its appearance as private prosecutor in this case', the actantial formula would be *PERSONA X que presenta la acusación Z (contra el INDIVIDUO Y debido a su ACCIÓN Z)* 'PERSON X who presents the accusation Z (against the INDIVIDUAL Y because of his ACTION Z)'. Since our description has a semantic nature, we do not specify in the actantial formula the syntactic actants of the described lexical unit.

In principle only predicates (that denote facts) can have actantial formulae, "pure" semantic names (that denote entities) are accompanied only by an example: *avena, La avena ayuda a adelgazar* 'Oats help one to lose weight'. However, many lexical units denoting entities do have an actantial formula that they inherit from the particular situations to which they are related. For example, *tripulación* 'crew' denotes a set of human beings but inherits the semantic actants of *tripular* 'to crew' and has then the actantial formula: *CONJUNTO DE INDIVIDUOS X del MEDIO DE TRANSPORTE Y* 'SET OF INDIVIDUALS X of the MEANS OF TRANSPORT Y'. *Bocadillo* 'sandwich' presents the formula *PREPARACIÓN ALIMENTÍCIA del INDIVIDUO X hecha con el pan Y y el ALIMENTO Z* 'ALIMENTARY PREPARATION of the INDIVIDUAL X made with the bread Y and the NOURISHMENT Z' that it inherits from the fact that it is prepared in a certain way for the purpose of nourishing X.

4   Methodology and Results

In order to build our hierarchy we are applying a top-down approach as well as a bottom-up one.

We use a top-down approach because our concept of the semantic label is based on the Meaning-Text Theory [4, 6] (more precisely, on the Explanatory and Combinatorial Lexicology) and on its lexicographical developments, such as the DiCo (*Dictionnaire de Combinatoire*) [11] and the *Réseau Lexical du Français* (RLF) [8]. The French hierarchy of semantic labels developed in the frame of these projects is a great advantage when outlining the general structure of our Spanish hierarchy, at least until the third level of labels.

Nevertheless, even when working with closely related languages, such as French and Spanish, the top-down approach cannot reach a satisfactory degree of precision. As a result, we need to adopt a bottom-up strategy that consists mainly of the manual labelling of a large number of Spanish lexical units. By "manual" labelling we mean the assignment, by a lexicographer, of an actantial formula and a semantic label to a disambiguated lexical unit. We plan to label 20,000 Spanish lexical units extracted from our Spanish Electronic Dictionary of Spanish (integrated in the NooJ linguistic development environment [12]), of which we have labelled approximately 8,000 up to the present day. This labelling of assorted and relatively usual Spanish lexical units allows us to progressively build up the different levels of our hierarchy (up to eight at this moment) and postulate the necessary labels.

Labelling is performed without previously ordering the lexical units. Peer-to-peer revisions (especially overall revisions of the lemmata attributed to a given semantic label until a precise moment, as well as revisions that focus on overrepresented labels) ensure, from our point of view, a fair degree of accuracy and homogeneity. Nevertheless, only systematic tests performed when our quantitative goal is attained will be able to ensure real robustness.

It is worth highlighting that our methodology is, by no means, the quickest way to semantically label a dictionary. It could even be said that it is a particularly arduous one. But it is important to bear in mind that our final goal is not only (and not mainly) the labelling of the dictionary but the development of a hierarchy of classes that accurately represent the lexical semantics of Spanish. In our opinion, that can only be done by a team of trained lexicographers applying their know-how to a large sample of the lexicon. Subsequently, there would be no need to continue with this procedure.

One way to significantly increase the lexical coverage would be simply to look for lexical units that correspond to a certain label. If *clavel* 'carnation', *dalia* 'dahlia' and *gardenia* 'gardenia' are labelled FLOR 'flower', nothing would prevent us compiling a list of flowers and then checking for their presence in the dictionary. This strategy is particularly suited for populating the hierarchy with multiword lexemes, since they are normally unambiguous. Of course, it will work much better for deep classes belonging to technical domains than for shallow classes or for labels incorporating evaluative meanings.

5   Further Applications

The obvious field of application for a hierarchy of semantic labels, as we conceive it, is the electronic lexicography. By itself, the mere implementation of an extensive system of semantic labels inside a large coverage electronic dictionary opens the field to a large range of applications. This is especially true when working with a fully-fledged linguistic development environment like NooJ. The possibility to annotate semantically very large corpora, to combine this information with the available morphological and syntactic descriptions, and to include it, when needed, in finite-state machines and regular grammars offers a world of possibilities for the processing of natural language. Let us point out that semantic labels are very often the only real semantic information that PLN systems can access. And semantic information is crucial for so many applications.

It goes without saying that semantic information is particularly relevant for search engines and for machine translation. In this latter field, the combined use of semantic labels and actantial formulae can be a reliable method of disambiguation and, therefore, of precise translation.

Let us return to the example of *acusación*. In the sentence *El Ayuntamiento se personó como acusación particular en aquel caso* the subject of *personarse* can only be a human being. The selected actantial formula for acusación will be then: *PERSONA X que presenta...*', which is linked to the translation equivalent 'prosecutor'. In this context, *acusación* can be safely translated by 'prosecutor': 'The city council entered its appearance as private prosecutor in this case'. However, 'prosecutor' would be completely inappropriate for translating forms associated with the two other formulae of *acusación*, that do not correspond to human beings but to ENUNCIADO and ACTO JURÍDICO respectively: *'He took my remark as a personal prosecutor'. *'The prosecutor withdrew the prosecutor against the congressman'. The combined use of the actantial formula of *personarse* and of the semantic label (next kind) of *acusación* allows us to select the appropriate translation equivalent.

Finally, from a more theoretical point of view, we think that the hierarchy of semantic labels can be used to accurately describe a variety of diachronic semantic changes that have up to now been referred to in a rather loose way. We are currently working in this direction.

6   Conclusion

We firmly believe that research in the area of semantic labels can be profitable for different areas of linguistics. Moreover, the more a hierarchized set of semantic labels is used in a varied range of applications, the more robust and reliable it will become. Of course, we are still far from having reached the point at which we can contemplate full-fledged real-world applications. Aside from achieving much better lexical coverage, we have to solve a number of procedure problems.

One of the questions that we need to address is how to adapt our hierarchy to label not only nouns but the other parts of speech as well [2]. Let us remember that the semantic label is a *genus proximum*. As a consequence, it is necessary that the semantic label could replace in any context (stylistic considerations aside) the lexical units labelled by it. Since a noun cannot replace an adjective, nor a verb or an adverb, we need the corresponding sets of adjectival, verbal and adverbial labels. This sets are not to be rebuilt from scratch, but rather to be derived from the nominal labels resorting to the derivational paradigmatic lexical functions A_0, e.g. A_0 (*fuerza* 'strength') = *fuerte* 'strong'; V_0, e.g. V_0 (*muerte* 'death') = *morir* 'to die'; Adv_0 e.g. Adv_0 (*cuidado* 'care') = *cuidadosamente* 'carefully' [9, 11].

Finally, let us mention that semantic granularity is a question that requires further investigation, especially when considering particular applications. At the same level of depth, there are labels that represent semantic contents much more intuitively than others. For instance, DEPORTE 'sport' or COLOR 'colour' are perceived as more natural and easier to work with than DISPOSITIVO 'device' or ALGO DE CARÁCTER NEGATIVO 'something having a negative character'. While considering bilingual applications, it is worth asking if these perceptions will always be similar for both languages.

References

1. Blanco, X.: Etiquetas semánticas de HECHO como género próximo en la definición lexicográfica. In: Calvo, C., Lépinette, B., Anscombre J.-C. (eds.) Lexicografía en el ámbito hispánico, pp. 159–178. Universitat de València (2010)
2. Blanco, X.: Les étiquettes sémantiques comme genre prochain : le cas des verbes. Verbum **XXIX**(1–2), 113–125 (2007)
3. Gross, G.: Manuel d'analyse linguistique. Approche sémantico-syntaxique du lexique. Presses universitaires du Septentrion, Villeneuve-d'Ascq (2012)
4. Mel'čuk, I., Milićević, J.: Introduction à la linguistique. Hermann, Paris (2014). vol. 1
5. Mel'čuk, I., Polguère, A.: Lexique actif du français. L'apprentissage du vocabulaire fondé sur 20 000 dérivations sémantiques et collocations du français. De Boeck & Larcier, Bruxelles (2007)
6. Mel'čuk, I.: Semantics. From Meaning to Text. John Benjamins Publishing Company, Amsterdam (2012)
7. Lepesant, D.: Principles for a Semantic Classification of Verb Predicates. Language Research, Special Issue December 2003. Language Education Institute, Seoul National University, pp. 21–38 (2003)
8. Polguère, A.: From Writing Dictionaries to Weaving Lexical Networks. Int. J. Lexicography **27**(4), 396–418 (2014)
9. Polguère, A.: Classification sémantique des lexies fondée sur le paraphrasage. Cahiers de lexicologie **98**, 197–211 (2011)
10. Polguère, A.: Étiquetage sémantique des lexies dans la base de données DiCo. Traitement Automatique des Langues (TAL) **44**(2), 39–68 (2003)
11. Polguère, A.: Towards a theoretically-motivated general public dictionary of semantic derivations and collocations for French. In: Heid, U., Evert, S., Lehmann, E., Rohrer, C. (eds.) Proceedings of EURALEX 2000, pp. 517–528. Institut für Maschinelle Sprachverarbeitung, Universität Stuttgart, Stuttgart (2000)
12. Silberztein, S.: La formalisation des langues. L'approche de NooJ. ISTE Editions, London (2014)

Grammars for Sentence into Phrase Segmentation: Punctuation Level

Yuras Hetsevich[(✉)], Tatsiana Okrut, and Boris Lobanov

United Institute of Informatics Problems of the National Academy
of Sciences of Belarus, Minsk, Belarus
yury.hetsevich@gmail.com

Abstract. This paper deals with so-called punctuational phrases that make up sentences and with their marking according to intonation type in Belarusian electronic texts using NooJ. Such markings may be used for the implementation of an algorithm for intonationally-coloured text-to-speech synthesis in order to obtain expressive synthetic speech.

Keywords: Punctuational phrases · Intonation-type marking · Belarusian language · Expressive text-to-speech · NooJ

1 Introduction

To date, text to speech (TtS) systems have reached a certain level of development and are now used in a number of practical applications. But under real operational conditions, the way synthesized speech is perceived is not always fully satisfactory. As our verbal experiences show, depending on the degree of speech expressiveness, the same text read by two different speakers may have different effects on an audience. The global trends of speech technology development have created a real demand for expressive TtS systems.

Therefore, this paper aims to give an overview of the initial step in formal representation of the expressive speech phenomena using NooJ.

The concept of expressive speech was formed as an interdisciplinary concept characterizing one of the human speech functions [1–3]. The main components of oral speech expressiveness include speech prosody and, in particular in speech synthesis, correctness and quality of prosodic marking [4]. Within this work, prosodic marking involves the segmentation of sentences into punctuational phrases and the determination of their intonation type.

In speech synthesis, such markings make it possible to avoid frequent repetition of similar intonation constructions, which in turn promotes better intelligibility and naturalness of synthesized speech.

Apart from the application in TtS, prosodic marking may be used for educational purposes. The authors have also developed an algorithm aimed to visual prosodic marking for practical training of intonation.

© Springer International Publishing Switzerland 2016
T. Okrut et al. (Eds.): NooJ 2015, CCIS 607, pp. 74–82, 2016.
DOI: 10.1007/978-3-319-42471-2_7

2   Sentence and Phrase Segmentation

Speech synthesis is carried out sentence by sentence, with each sentence prosodically independent from another sentence in a text.

A sentence is regarded as a text passage separated by punctuation marks such as a full stop {.}, a question mark {?}, an exclamation mark {!}, an exclamation/question mark combination {!?}, several exclamation marks {!!!}. Ellipses {…} may also serve as an end-of-sentence punctuation mark, provided the word after the ellipsis starts with a capital letter.

Then each sentence is separated into punctuational phrases by using the following punctuation marks:

- semicolon {;},
- colon {:},
- comma {,},
- dash {–},
- left bracket {(},
- right bracket {)},
- combination of comma and dash {,–}.

Thus, if a sentence contains n punctuation marks (including the end-of-sentence mark), it is divided into n punctuated phrases ($n = 1, 2, 3,…$).

It is obvious that phrases may be different in length (where length is regarded as a number of words). If the phrase length is too large (for instance, more than four words), you must determine whether the phrase contains any simple lexical signs (certain words or word combinations) allowing it to be divided into smaller phrases.

Experimental studies show that, in many cases, such lexical signs may include:

- coordinate conjunction "i" (*and*) – phrase segmentation before "i";
- disjunctive conjunction "цi" (*or*) – phrase segmentation before "цi";
- proper names – phrase segmentation after the last in a list of proper names;
- abbreviations – phrase segmentation after abbreviations;
- digit position names – phrase segmentation after each digit position name;
- names of months, the words "гадзіна, хвіліна" (*hour, minute*) when writing dates and times in full unabbreviated form – phrase segmentation after dates and times.

This list is not complete and may be expanded through the analysis of increasingly more large-scale text and speech corpora.

3   Intonation Types of Phrases

Based on the punctuational phrase segmentation described above, four main categories of punctuational phrase intonation types may be identified: finality (P), non-finality (C), interrogation (Q) and exclamation (E).

The category of a declarative sentence is characterized by final intonation. There are following types of final intonation:

- "full stop" intonation - {.},
- "ellipsis" intonation - {...},
- "title" intonation - {*},
- "paragraph" intonation - {$}.

Apart from these types of final intonation, characteristic of end-of-sentence phrases, there are two additional punctuational types of intonation with different degrees of finality:

- "semicolon" intonation – {;},
- parenthetical intonation – {)}, {,–}, {–}.

Parenthetical intonation presupposes that the marks specified should be preceded by the following marks respectively: {(}, {,–}, {–}.

There may also be four punctuational subtypes of intonation with different degrees of non-finality in a sentence:

- "comma" intonation - {,},
- "dash" intonation - {–},
- "colon" intonation - {:},
- pre-parenthetical intonation - {(}, {,–}, {–}.

Pre-parenthetical intonation presupposes that the marks specified should be followed by the {(}, {,–}, {–} marks.

Punctuational phrases may in turn contain lexical phrases with three types of non-final intonation:

- intonation of conjunction "i" (*and*)
- intonation of conjunction "цi" (*or*),
- intonation of lexical phrases with proper names, abbreviations, digit position names and date and time names.

Interrogation and exclamation intonations are identified respectively by question and exclamation marks.

4   Realization of Phrase Segmentation and Intonation Type Marking with NooJ

Based on the segmentation techniques proposed above, the authors have developed a NooJ syntactical grammar (Fig. 1) representing the initial stage of prosodic processing in a speech synthesizer.

The grammar carries out marking of the following intonation types:

- Non-finality (C) – 11 types;
- Finality (P) – 11 types;
- Exclamation (E) – 2 types;
- Interrogation (Q) – 2 types.

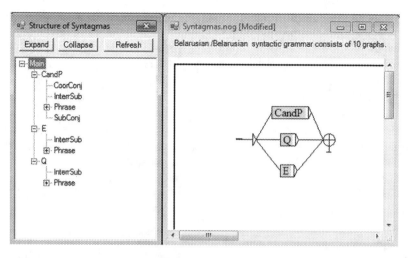

Fig. 1. General view of the grammar for marking phrases at punctuation level

As punctuational phrases may be different in length, in the grammar, by punctuational phrase, we mean any sequence of word forms or phonetic words separated by punctuation marks (Fig. 2).

When marking the intonation type of a phrase, not only punctuation marks are taken into account but also the nearest context in a text. For example, the intonation type "C31" corresponds to each second phrase in a line of consecutive "C3"-phrases – phrases with non-final "comma" intonation (Fig. 3).

In general, depending on the nearest context, there are six types of non-final "comma" intonation:

- C3 - simple "comma" intonation (C3),
- C7 - "comma" intonation with a comma followed by a coordinate conjunction (which indicates the beginning of P7 phrase with a "full-stop" final intonation),

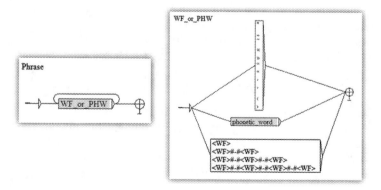

Fig. 2. Phrase

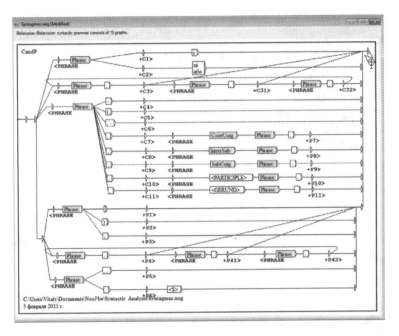

Fig. 3. Non-finality and finality

- C8 - "comma" intonation with a comma followed by an interrogative word (which indicates the beginning of P8 phrase with a "full-stop" final intonation),
- C9 - "comma" intonation with a comma followed by a subordinating conjunction (which indicates the beginning of P9 phrase with a "full-stop" final intonation),
- C10 - "comma" intonation with a comma followed by a participle (which indicates the beginning of P10 phrase with a "full-stop" final intonation),
- C11 - "comma" intonation with a comma followed by a gerund (which indicates the beginning of P11 phrase with a "full-stop" final intonation).

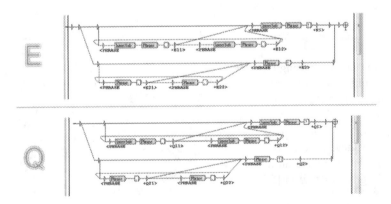

Fig. 4. Exclamation and interrogation

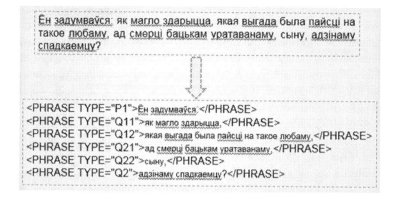

Fig. 5. Applying the grammar to a text

Figure 4 shows sub-graphs for marking exclamation and interrogation. Depending on whether there is an interrogative word starting an exclamation or interrogation phrase, there are two types of exclamation intonation and two types of interrogation intonation.

After applying the grammar to a text, we obtain a text annotated with corresponding intonation indexes (Fig. 5).

In Fig. 5, phrases in the sentence are annotated with the following indexes:

- "P1" – final "colon"-intonation,
- "Q11" and "Q12" – interrogative intonations corresponding respectively to each uneven and each even phrase in a line of consecutive "Q1"-phrases - interrogative non-final phrases containing an interrogative word,
- "Q21" and "Q22" – interrogative intonations corresponding respectively to each uneven and each even phrase in a line of consecutive "Q2"-phrases – interrogative non-final phrases without an interrogative word,
- "Q2" – intonation type corresponding to an end-of-sentence interrogative phrase without an interrogative word.

5 Graphical Representation of Phrase Intonation

One more option for using the results of this grammar is for the marking of a text by graphical intonation. The idea is that each phrase in a text is represented by a particular colour and will be accompanied with a prosodic portrait (contour) corresponding to the phrase's intonation type.

By prosodic portrait, we mean a graphical representation of phrase intonation. This method was developed by one of the authors, Boris Lobanov, and is called Portraits of Accentual Units, where an accentual unit is a minimal prosodic unit in speech (discussed in greater detail in [5]).

```
while (<IN>)
    {
        s/PHRASE/FONT/g;
        s/<FONT TYPE="(.*?)"[^>]*>(.*?)</FONT>/ <FONT TYPE="$1">$2</FONT> <FONT STYLE=\"text-decoration:underline;
color:black;\">($1)</FONT><img src="..\/bd\/$1a1.jpg" width="70px">/g;
        if ($1)
        {
            s/TYPE="C1"/STYLE="text-decoration:underline; color:blue;"/g;
            s/TYPE="C2"/STYLE="text-decoration:underline; color:blue;"/g;
            s/TYPE="C3"/STYLE="text-decoration:underline; color:blue;"/g;
                s/TYPE="C31"/STYLE="text-decoration:underline; color:blue;"/g;
                s/TYPE="C32"/STYLE="text-decoration:underline; color:blue;"/g;
            s/TYPE="C4"/STYLE="text-decoration:underline; color:blue;"/g;
            s/TYPE="C5"/STYLE="text-decoration:underline; color:blue;"/g;
            s/TYPE="C6"/STYLE="text-decoration:underline; color:blue;"/g;
        }
        #s///g;
        #s///g;

    $lines++;
    print OUT $_;
    }
```

Fig. 6. Intonation marker program code

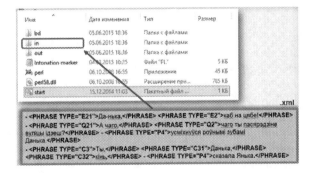

Fig. 7. Marking phrases

For the purpose described, the authors have developed a Perl program which processes texts after having been annotated with the NooJ grammar for phrase segmentation and intonation marking (Figs. 6 and 7).

When processing texts, the program highlights and marked segments of text and applies the base of intonation contours created previously within the framework for developing models of prosodic portraits. All this results in the creation of documents in HTML format, with texts marked as shown in Fig. 8. Such markings serve as instructions on how to read a text.

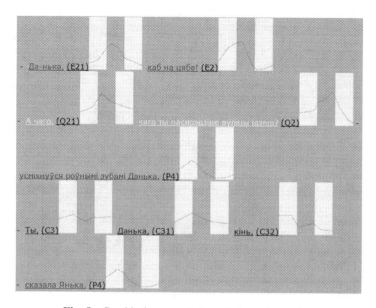

Fig. 8. Graphical representation of phrase intonation

6 Conclusion

In this paper we have presented a technique for automated phrase segmentation at the punctuational level and a system of marking types of phrase intonation in electronic Belarusian texts using NooJ.

This technique seeks to boost the prosodic performance of the Belarusian text-to-speech system and may also serve to improve the Belarusian NooJ module with so-called prosodic transcription.

Alternatively, this technique could be used for educational purposes, for example in learning Belarusian phonetics.

References

1. Pitrelli, J.F., et al.: The IBM expressive text-to-speech synthesis system for American English. IEEE Trans. Audio Speech Lang. Process. **14**(4), 1099–1108 (2006)
2. Froehlich, P., Hammer, F.: Expressive text-to-speech: a user-centred approach to sound design in voice-enabled mobile applications. Telecommunications Research Centre Vienna (FTW). (http://userver.ftw.at/ ~ froehlich/papers/JDS2004_ExpressiveTTS.pdf)
3. Leskovec, L.: Lexical Stress Assignment and Pronunciation Formalization in Expressive TTS/ Trinity College Dublin. (http://www.cs.tcd.ie/research_groups/clg/COST2102.IS2009/content/program/node61.html)

4. Kawanami, H., et al.: Designing Speech Database with Prosodic Variety for Expressive TTS system, Nara Institute of Science and Technology, Takayama-cho. (http://gandalf.aksis.uib.no/lrec2002/pdf/337.pdf)
5. Lobanov, B.M., Tsirulnik, L.I.: Computer speech synthesis and cloning. Belarussian science, p. 342 (2008). (in Russian)

NooJ Local Grammars and Formal Semantics: Past Participles vs. Adjectives in Italian

Mario Monteleone[(✉)]

Department of Political, Social and Communication Sciences,
University of Salerno, Fisciano (SA), Italy
mmonteleone@unisa.it

Abstract. As for past participles (PPs) and adjectives (As), and especially from the point of view of lexicographic descriptions, in Italian we may find a high level of categorial ambiguity. Very often, the words belonging to these two parts of speech (PsOS) are homographs and semantically contiguous. Therefore, when necessary, and in most of their occurrences, it may be useful to automatically parse their correct linguistic functions. Essentially, this is possible only by means of precise syntactic analyses, which must be focused on and applied to both the left and right contexts co-occurring with the propositions to be examined. Such analyses must also infer about all the possible verb antecedents to past participles and adjectives, be they operators, support verbs or simple auxiliary verbs. Therefore, in our article, we intend to use NooJ with the following purposes:

- Regarding Italian simple words, and at the level of lexicographical description, we will study and define the levels of categorial ambiguity existing between past participles and adjectives;
- Subsequently, we will define the syntactic pattern in which this ambiguity can be solved;
- Then, we will describe the construction of a set of local grammars to apply for the disambiguation and correct tagging of these parts of speech;
- Finally, we will determine the levels of recall and precision of these grammars.

At the end of this four-step process, we aim at creating a set of formal semantic analysis tools, to exploit in NooJ to distinguish sentences with conventional operators (verb predicates) from sentences with support verbs and predicative adjectives, that is to say, to make work our grammars as Formal Semantics processing tools.

Keywords: Lexicon-Grammar · NooJ · NooJ local grammars · NooJ finite-state automata/transducers · Formal semantics · Support verbs · Simple sentences · Passive diatheses

© Springer International Publishing Switzerland 2016
T. Okrut et al. (Eds.): NooJ 2015, CCIS 607, pp. 83–95, 2016.
DOI: 10.1007/978-3-319-42471-2_8

1 Foreword

As for past participles (PPs) and adjectives (As), and especially from the point of view of lexicographic descriptions, in Italian we may find a high level of categorial ambiguity.[1] Very often, the words belonging to these two PsOS are homographs and semantically contiguous. Therefore, when necessary, and in most of their occurrences, it may be useful to automatically parse their correct linguistic functions. Moreover, this is possible only by means of precise syntactic analyses applied to both the left and right contexts co-occurring with the propositions/sentences to examine. Such analyses must also infer about all the possible verb antecedents to past participles and adjectives, be they operators, support verbs or simple auxiliary verbs.

Therefore, in such cases, to define automatically if a given Italian word is a past participle or an adjective, it is crucial to disambiguate correctly the role of its immediate verb antecedent(s).

In the following pages, we will see how to a certain extent, especially within Lexicon-Grammar framework [2–4] which we adopt, such formal procedures may be used to define the semantics of those sentences in which homograph PPs and As occur. In order to demonstrate this and using NooJ [5–7], we will accomplish a four-step task, structured as follows:

- Regarding Italian simple words, and at the level of lexicographical description, we will study and define the levels of categorical ambiguity existing between past participles and adjectives.
- Subsequently, we will define the syntactic pattern in which this ambiguity can be solved.
- We will describe the construction of a set of local grammars to apply for the dis-ambiguation and correct tagging of these parts of speech.
- Finally, we will determine the levels of recall and precision of these grammars.

At the end of this four-step process, we aim at creating a set of formal semantic analysis tools, to exploit in NooJ to distinguish sentences with conventional operators (verb predicates) from sentences with support verbs and predicative adjectives.

Figures of the Finite-State Transducers (FSTs) used to achieve this four-step task will be presented where appropriate to support the development of content description in the paper.

---

[1] Categorial ambiguity (CA) is a linguistic phenomenon mainly pertaining to lexicon, and to lexicon entry descriptions made on the basis of all their possible concrete uses. It is widely employed in computational morphology (CM) to describe the necessity to label a given entry with two or more POS tags inside electronic lexica and/or dictionaries. As for Italian, CA is equal to 2,2 in percentage, which means that any Italian simple word is labelled with at least two different morph-grammatical tags. For more on this topic see Monteleone [1].

2 Past Participles and Adjectives in Italian

2.1 Auxiliaries, Past Participle Functions and Morph-Syntactic Constraints

As in all languages in which verb inflection contemplates them, also in Italian PP [8] forms are used to indicate the effect an action has on a given verb argument. Moreover, such forms are necessary to inflect all verb compound tenses, i.e. those tenses formed by the auxiliary verbs *essere*[2] (to be) or *avere* (to have) [9], placed before the past participle of the verb that follows. PPs[3] are also used to build passive diatheses of active simple sentences.

Furthermore, the two verbs *essere* and *avere* may be used also as non-auxiliary verbs. As for *essere*, it is possible to state that:

- It is a synonym of *esistere* (to exist) in sentences as *Dio è* (God exists);
- Also, it is a synonym of *stare* (to stay) in several *essere prep* sentences [10] as *Il pane (è + sta) nella credenza* (The bread is in the cupboard).

As for *avere*, we observe that:

- It may be used to express the notion of possess and/or property, as in the sentence *Ho una casa* (I have got a house).

Another very important aspect of *essere* and *avere* is their being support verbs when introducing predicative names and/or adjectives for the former, and predicative nouns for the latter. A brief example of such function are the following two pairs of sentences:

Max è affamato <-> Max ha fame (Max is hungry)
Max è assonnato <-> Max ha sonno (Max is sleepy)

in which we may note the morph-phonemic contiguity between the adjective *affamato* and the name *fame*, and also between the adjective *assonnato* and the name *sonno*.

Finally, as a support verb and in order to indicate a state, *avere* is also used in constructions of the type "verb + illness name". Also in these cases, the nouns introduced by *avere* have morph-phonemic correspondences with the adjectives introduced by *essere*:

Ho l'influenza <-> *Sono influenzato* (I have got the flu)

---

[2] Not all Italian verbs have PP forms, as for instance *convergere* (to converge), *distare* (to be distant), *divergere* (to diverge), or *irrompere* (to break into).

[3] In this use, and in order to reduce possible ambiguities which we will cope with in the following pages, in the building of passive diatheses the verb *essere* may often be substituted by two other verbs, namely:
Venire (to come), as in the sentence *Max è/viene spinto da Luca* (Max is pushed by Luca);
Andare (to go), as in the sentence *Il lavoro andò finito* (The work was done).
These substitutions have no syntactic value and may present some slight stylistic changes.

Auxiliaries and Past Participles in Verb Compound Tenses. Concerning the use of verb compound tenses, the only PP form allowed is masculine singular, even when a feminine noun coccurrs, as in:

*Abbiamo (*vista + **visto**) l'ultima bella **opera** di Leonardo da Vinci* (We saw the last wonderful work by Leonardo da Vinci)

However, in cleft sentences, which extrapolates direct objects to the left of the compound verb group, PPs may act as adjectives and agree in gender and number with the nouns which they refer to:

*L'ultima **opera** di Leonardo da Vinci che abbiamo (**visto** + **vista**) è molto bella* (The last work by Leonardo da Vinci which we saw is wonderful)

Besides, this morph-syntactic feature becomes compulsory when the last deictic antecedent to the PP is a pronoun:

*L'opera **la** avevano (*visto + **vista**) ed era molto bella* (They had seen the work and it was wonderful)
*Il quadro **lo** avevano (**visto** +*vista) ed era molto bello* (They had seen the picture and it was very beautiful)

The choice of auxiliaries with which PP forms complete compound tenses is subject to different morph-syntactic constraints. Essentially, the auxiliary used with transitive verbs is easily predictable: *avere* (to have) is used in active compounds diathesis tenses [11], as in:

Io ho amato Angela (I have loved Angela);
Io avrò amato Angela (I will have loved Angela).

Therefore, it is possible to state that in such constructions the auxiliary verb *avere* is always followed by a PP.

In contrast, *essere* (to be) is used in passive diatheses, as in:

Io sono amato da Angela (I am loved by Angela);
Io fui amato da Angela (I was loved by Angela).

Conversely, with intransitive verbs the prediction on the auxiliaries to use is possible only on morph-syntactic basis. In fact, no specific rule of use may be inferred from the simple fact that a verb is intransitive. Sentence semantics can help to define some trends. For instance, it is possible to state that the auxiliary *avere* seems to be more used when the subject of a given sentence is ergatively marked, while the auxiliary *essere* seems to be more used when the subject of a given sentence is not ergatively marked. In any case, as for auxiliary uses, only taxonomic studies on verb syntactic and semantic behaviors may help in detecting precise co-occurrence and selection-restriction rules.

For instance, verbs as *scendere, salire, saltare, passare, guarire, bruciare*, when transitive, use the auxiliary *avere*, and when intransitive, the auxiliary *essere*:

Ho salito le scale (I climbed the stairs) <-> *Sono salito in soffitta* (I went up to the attic);

Ho passato una notte insonne (I passed a sleepless night) <-> *Sono passato da casa di mia madre* (I went to my mother's house)

In addition, verbs as *volare, saltare, emigrare, correre* use the auxiliary *avere* when they are intransitive and do not select an indirect object. In similar cases, the sentences in which they co-occurr can be transformed into verb support sentences:

Max ha corso (Max ran)
Max ha saltato (Max jumped)

T =: Nominalization

Max ha fatto una corsa (Max has made a run)
Max ha fatto un salto (Max has made a jump)

These same verbs use the auxiliary *essere* when are intransitive and select an indirect object. In these cases, the sentences in which they co-occur cannot be transformed into support verb sentences while maintaining the verb *essere*. In fact, the choice of the auxiliary depends on the syntactic features of the support verb used:

Max è corso a casa (Max has run home)
Max è saltato dalla sedia (Max has jumped from the chair)

T =: Nominalization

Max (*è + ha) fatto una corsa a casa (*?Max has made a run home)
Max (*è + ha) fatto un salto dalla sedia (Max has made a jump from the chair)

Finally, some intransitive verbs like *vivere* (to live) o *durare* (to last) allow the use of the double auxiliary without changing their meanings or syntactic behaviors:

Max (è + ha) vissuto in America (Max has lived in the States)
Il suo isolamento (è + ha) durato a lungo (His isolation has lasted long).

2.2 Adjective and Attributive Adjectives

As in all languages, also in Italian adjectives [12–14] are used to modify semantically other PsOS, mostly the one of nouns, with which they establish morph-syntactic correlations. As an inflectional language, Italian has adjectives that vary in gender (male and female) and number (singular and plural). Also, adjectives may often be used as nouns, and equally many nouns can function as adjectives.

To cope with the main topics of this paper, we will focus mainly on the notions of attribute and attributive adjectives [15], leaving out of our descriptions definite, indicative, possessive, numeral, demonstrative, undefined, question and exclamation adjectives.

Providing specific qualifications or determinations, attributes typically accompany a name or another word that has a nominal function and with which they agree in gender and number.

As well as nouns, for instance *lampo* in *guerra lampo* (blitzkrieg), or adverbs, like *dopo* in *il giorno dopo* (the day after), in Italian both adjectives and participles can be attributes. As we will see in (3), this feature is one of the main causes of ambiguity of simple sentences in which the verb *essere* introduces an A that in the Italian lexicon is also classified as PP.

2.3   Diatheses and Ambiguity

When the auxiliary verb *essere* is used, agentless passive diatheses of transitive sentences may produce ambiguous results. For instance:

Max ama Ida (Max loves Ida)

may be passivized as follows:
T =: Passive

Ida è amata da Max (Ida is loved by Max)

Thanks to the syntactic properties of the verb *amare* that allows the use of substructures, we can delete the agent of the passive sentence, thus obtaining:
T =: Agent_Deletion

Ida è amata (*?Ida is loved + Ida is a beloved person)

In this and all similar cases in which verb operators allow the use of substructures, the results of this transformation procedure are classified as both agentless-passive and support-verb sentences. This structural ambiguity is reinforced by the fact that the PP used is also an attributive adjective and that the auxiliary functions as a support verb.

In many cases, the agentless passive sentence has even a different meaning with reference to the active simple sentence from which it derives:

Max mangia la torta (Max eats the cake)

T =: Passive

La torta è mangiata da Max (The cake is eaten by Max)

T =: Agent_Deletion

La torta è mangiata (*?The cake is eaten + The cake is chewed up)

The possibility to insert quantity adverbs strengthens the change of meaning:

La torta è completamente mangiata (The cake is completely chewed up)

The ambiguity is solved putting the verb in the present perfect, past perfect, or any other past tense. In such cases, sentences can only be interpreted as the result of an agentless passive diathesis:

La torta fu mangiata (E + da Max) (The cake was eaten (E + by Max))
La torta è stata mangiata (E + da Max) (The cake has been eaten (E + by Max))

A list of the Italian verbs with these syntactic and semantic features includes:

accelerare (to accelerate)
accrescere (to increase)
affievolire (to weaken)
affogare (to drown)
affondare (to sink)
agghiacciare (to freeze)
ammutolire (to be struck dumb)
annegare (to drown)
annerire (to blacken)
ardere (to burn)
arretrare (to draw back)
arricchire (to enrich)
arrugginire (to rust)
asfissiare (to asphyxiate)
aumentare (to increase)
avanzare (to advance)
azzittire (to silence)
bruciare (to burn)
calare (to drop)
calzare (to wear)
cambiare (to change)
centuplicare   (to
centuplicate)
cessare (to cease)

cicatrizzare (to cicatrize)
colare (to strain)
cominciare (to begin)
continuare (to continue)
convenire (to agree)
correre (to run)
crepare (to crack)
crescere (to grow)
declinare (to decline)
derivare (to result)
deviare (to divert)
diminuire (to decrease)
discendere (to descend)
evadere (to escape)
esplodere (to explode)
fallire (to fail)
finire (to end)
fuggire (to flee)
gelare (to freeze)
guarire (to heal)
importare (to import)
ingrassare (to put
on weight)
invecchiare (to grow old)
mancare (to miss)

maturare (to mature)
migliorare (to improve)
montare (to mount)
mutare (to change)
passare (to switch)
peggiorare (to worsen)
pesare (to weigh)
resuscitare (to resuscitate)
rincarare (to get expansive)
ringiovanire (to rejuvenate)
salire (to climb)
saltare (to skip)
sbarcare (to land)
scattare (to take)
scendere (to get down)
schizzare (to splash)
scorrere (to slide)
seguire (to follow)
servire (to serve)
sfumare (to vanish)
suonare (to play)
toccare (to touch)
trascorrere (to spend)
variare (to vary)

As for the verbs in the previous list, shifts of meaning due to the use of the auxiliary *essere* or *avere* are note predictable and should be studied case by case.

Furthermore, agentless passive diatheses may be derived also from intransitive verbs, by means of non-acceptable passive transformations. In such cases, the resulting sentences will not be ambiguous, due to the fact that the attribute will only be classified as adjective:

Max passeggia sul marciapiede (Max strolls on the sidewalk)

T =: Passive

*Il marciapiede è passeggiato da Max (*The sidewalk is strolled by Max)

T =: Agent_Deletion

Il marcipiede è passeggiato[4] (*?The sidewalk is strolled – People stroll on the sidewalk)

Also in these cases, the possibility to insert quantity adverbs strengthens the change of meaning:

Il marcipiede è molto passeggiato (Many people stroll on the sidewalk)

Finally, some intransitive monovalent verbs [16] accepting the use of both the auxiliaries *essere* and *avere* [17] produce ambiguous sentences when using the compound tenses of the former one, as for instance in:

Max è arretrato (Max has drawn back + Max is retrograde).

A brief list of these verbs includes:

arretrare (to draw back)
degenerare (to degenerate)
figurare (to appear, to figure out, to seem)
garbare (to suit well)
germogliare (to sprout)
inorridire (to horrify)
marcire (to rot)
migliorare (to improve)
tramontare (to set, of the sun).

3   NooJ Disambiguation Grammars

The set of NooJ local grammars we are about to present were built on the basis of all the linguistic constraints previously exposed, of which the most important ones are:

- with reference to As, PPs are categorially ambiguous;
- PPs and As may function as attributes of nouns;
- in passive diatheses *essere* introduces a PP;
- when followed by an A, *essere* may very often function as a support verb;
- very often, support verb sentences with *essere* are formally identical to agentless passive diatheses, i.e. to sentences in which *essere* introduces a PP;
- *avere* is used in compound tenses diatheses, which means that the PPs that it introduces almost never functions as As.

In addition, while building our grammars, we have being trying to consider all phenomena without forcing disambiguation. This means that in presence of ambiguous sentences, as those that follow:

---

[4] Despite the oddness of this sentence, to an average Italian native speaker it is fully comprehensible and reusable. This aspect calls into cause the concepts of speakability, linguistic analogy, anomaly, and creativity, which are indeed very interesting topics but which unfortunately fall outside the main subject of this paper.

È ferito (He/It is wounded)
È legato (He/It is tied)
É perso (He/It is lost)
È punito (He is punished)
È sospeso (He/It is suspend)
È venduto (He/It is sold)

in which it is not possible to state if the attributes are PPs or As, our grammars will consider both options. Therefore, such sentences will be tagged as belonging to the type of both "support verb + adjective" and "verb + past participle".

On the contrary, non ambiguous sentences that include the same attributes but are preceded by compound tenses, as:

È stato ferito (He/It has been wounded)
È stato legato (He/It has been tied)
È stato perso (He/It has been lost)
È stato punito (He has been punished)
È stato sospeso (He/It has been suspended)
È stato venduto (He/It has been sold)

will be tagged only as sequences of the type "verb + past participle".

Therefore, leaving space also to natural language ambiguity, such an approach will allow us to separate, automatically and in all possible cases, support verbs and support-verb extensions from pure verb operators. As stated elsewhere, the achievement of this result is what we may refer to as "formal semantics".

3.1 Grammars and Example of Disambiguation

As shown by Fig. 1 below, we used 8 graphs in order to build a comprehensive local grammar for the disambiguation of PPs and As:

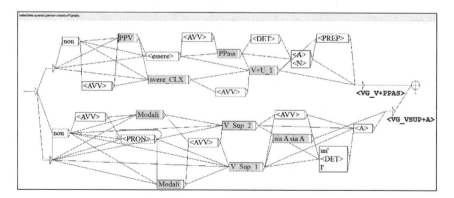

Fig. 1. Complete Auxiliaries grammar (AU.nog) (Color figure online)

As for the final tags of this graph, we observe that:

- "VG_V + PPAS" will tag all the verb groups formed by a verb and a past participle;
- "VG_VSUP + PPAS" will tag all the verb groups formed buy a support verb and an adjective.

As for the different metanodes (yellow nodes) we observe that:

- "PPV" contains pre-verbal pronoun particles;
- "Avere_clx" contains all the forms of the verb *avere* plus all its infinitive and gerund agglutinated forms[5] which may be used as auxiliary verb forms;
- "Modali" contains modal verbs;
- "sia A sia A" contains instructions to recognize disjoint attributes;
- "V_Sup_1" and "V_Sup_2" contains support verbs and support-extension verbs; "PPas" contains all the past participles allowed in the construction of past participle verb groups;
- "V + U_1" (Fig. 2) contains instructions which limit the distribution of past participle forms of the verb *essere*, blocking their occurrence after any other form of the same verb *essere* and also of the verb *avere*:

V+U_1

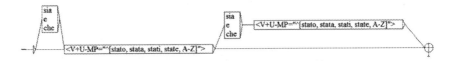

Fig. 2. Metanode "V + U_1"

As for disambiguation examples, Figs. 3, 4 and 5 show how NooJ grammar debug function allows to test the efficiency of the instructions inserted. Figure 3 shows how agentless passive diatheses are ambiguous and therefore take a double tagging:

Figure 4 shows how the ambiguity shown in Fig. 3 is solved thanks to the occurrence of the preposition *da* (by) which introduces the agent of a passive sentence:

Figure 5 shows a recursive passive diathesis in which also the discontinued conjunction *sia...che* (both...and) is recognized:

Finally, in Fig. 6 we show recursive attributes and PP occurrences recognized as both verb + past participle and verb support + adjective constructions:

---

[5] Such agglutinated (and only simtagmatically translatable) forms are: *avendoci, avendogli, avendola, avendole, avendoli, avendolo, avendomi, avendosi, avendoti, avendovi, averci, avergli, averla, averla, averle, averli, averlo, averlo, avermi, averne, aversi, averti, avervi.*

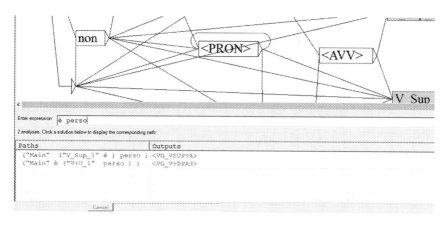

Fig. 3. First example of automatic recognition: *è perso* (he/it is lost)

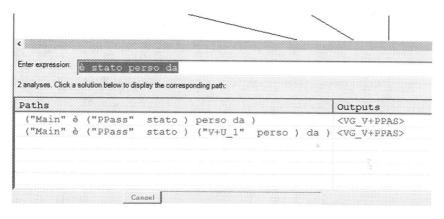

Fig. 4. Second example of automatic recognition: *è stato perso da* (he/it has been lost by)

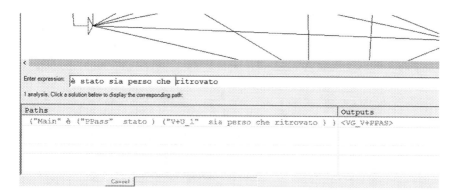

Fig. 5. Third example of automatic recognition: *è stato sia perso che ritrovato* (he/it has been both lost and found)

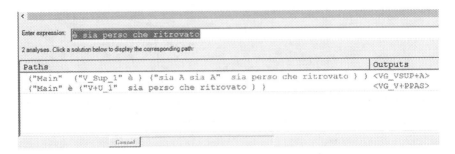

Fig. 6. Fourth example of automatic recognition: *è sia perso che ritrovato* (he/it is both lost and found)

4   Conclusions and Further Steps to Take

This grammar has been tested over a corpus of more than 1 MB. Its efficiency is quite elevate, if we consider that it can disambiguate up to a 90 % of occurrences. However, some corrections seem to be necessary, mainly inside Italian electronic dictionaries, in which specific tags could be assigned to all the verbs listed in the previuos paragraphs, be they used as auxiliaries, operators, support verbs or support verb extensions.

Also, other tests should be performed, on larger corpora, in order to further verify the efficiency of the grammar and the necessity to insert new parsing instructions. However, the experiment and the analysis that we have been achieving here show that having available an accurate NLP method (Lexicon-Grammar) and well-balanced formal means of analysis, it is possible to shorten the distance existing between formal parsing and sentence semantics of a given language.

References

1. Monteleone, M.: Grammatical disambiguation of Italian words using part of the speech of words in the context. In: Laporte, É. (ed.) Project Copernicus 621 GRAMLEX. Deliverables, October 1997–April 1998 (1998)
2. Gross, M.: Grammaire transformationnelle du français. Cantilène, Paris (1968)
3. Gross, M.: Méthodes en syntaxe. Hermann, Paris (1975)
4. Elia, A., Martinelli, M., D'Agostino, E.: Lessico e strutture sintattiche: introduzione alla sintassi del verbo italiano. Liguori, Napoli (1981)
5. Silberztein, M.: La Formalisation des Langues. L'Approche de NooJ. ISTE Edition (2015)
6. Silberztein, M.: NooJ computational devices. In: Donabédian, A., Khurshudian, V., Silberztein, M. (eds.) Formalising Natural Languages with NooJ: Selected Papers from the NooJ 2012 International Conference. Cambridge Scholars Publishing, Newcastle (2013)
7. Vietri, S.: The syntax of the Italian verb essere prep. In: Linguisticae Investigationes, vol. 20, pp. 287–363. John Benjamins Publishing, Amsterdam (1996)
8. http://www.treccani.it/enciclopedia/ricerca/participio/
9. Vietri, S.: The Italian module for NooJ. In: Proceedings of the First Italian Conference on Computational Linguistics, CLiC-it 2014. Pisa University Press (2014)

10. http://www.treccani.it/enciclopedia/verbi-ausiliari_%28Enciclopedia-dell'Italiano%29/
11. http://www.treccani.it/enciclopedia/costruzione-passiva_%28Enciclopedia-dell'Italiano%29/
12. http://www.treccani.it/enciclopedia/ricerca/aggettivi/
13. D'Achille, P.: L'italiano contemporaneo, Bologna, il Mulino (2003)
14. Dardano, M., Trifone, P.: La nuova grammatica della lingua italiana, Bologna, Zanichelli (1997)
15. http://www.treccani.it/enciclopedia/attributo_%28La-grammatica-italiana%29/
16. Tesnière, L.: Elementi di sintassi strutturale. A cura di Germano Proverbio e Anna Trocini Cerrina. Rosenberg & Sellier, Torino (2001)
17. http://cr.middlebury.edu/Italian%20Resources/progetto/grammar/more/verbi_con_doppio_ausiliare.htm

Recognizing Verb-Based Croatian Idiomatic MWUs

Kristina Kocijan[✉] and Sara Librenjak

Department of Information and Communication Sciences,
Faculty of Humanities and Social Sciences, Zagreb, Croatia
krkocijan@ffzg.hr, sara.librenjak@gmail.com

Abstract. This paper tackles the computational problems of Croatian verbal idioms. Croatian language has very rich phraseme structure, as described in Matešić (1982), Menac (2007) and Menac-Mihalić (2007), as well as many others. This work is one of the few attempts of computational analyis of idioms in Croatian language as multi-word units. We used rule-based approach and NooJ syntactic grammars in order to recognize any verb based idiom (of the ~1500 analyzed) in any syntactic position. The Croatian Dictionary of Idioms (Menac et al. 2003) was used for the initial list, which was implemented with new additions during training phase. Grammars were tested within the corpora constructed specifically for this work, and used to calculate statistical measures of recall, precision and f-measure for our grammars. With the final results of recall < 98 %, precision < 96 % and f-measure < 97 %, we consider this a successful attempt in the recognition of verb based idioms in Croatian language.

Keywords: Croatian · Idioms · Verbal phrases · NooJ · MWU · Frozen expressions · Semi-frozen expressions

1 Introduction

Idioms, or the non-literal expressions, are considered to be an important and quite large field of any language, but are believed to be especially rich in the Croatian language. They are often a topic of discussion for many linguists and Croatian language researchers. Various types of idioms are present in most styles of spoken and written language, although pertaining more to spoken and journalistic style. They can be found in many internet texts written by users, newspaper (especially sport and gossip), literature, and of course natural speech of native speakers when one tends to be more poetic or hyperbolic in their expression. On the other hand, they are rarely found in the scientific and specialized texts, since they constitute a type of speech which is not always specific and stylistically marked. The literature (Arsovski et al. 2010) cites that the first papers on Croatian idioms were written not earlier than 1970-ies covering different aspects but also different variants of Croatian (contemporary, old, dialectal).

Although the existence of idioms in most (or all) languages is a known fact, they are not always so present in the computational analysis of natural language. The idioms pose as a difficult field for computational approach. This is due to few unavoidable factors: they are mostly multi-word in nature, their meaning is hard to grasp for a computer, and

© Springer International Publishing Switzerland 2016
T. Okrut et al. (Eds.): NooJ 2015, CCIS 607, pp. 96–106, 2016.
DOI: 10.1007/978-3-319-42471-2_9

polysemy is frequent. Also, their cultural and historical nuances render them very difficult to process or translate without special preparation.

We believe that the approach for dealing with the idioms in Croatian language should be rule-based, and that NooJ is the ideal tool for the task. Provided that we assure the detailed syntactic description and categorization of idioms, NooJ can be used to construct grammars to detect any known idioms in a Croatian text. Using somewhat different approaches than we propose in this paper, NooJ has already been tried in the area of multi word expressions, including, among others, Bulgarian verbal idioms (Todorova 2008), Italian support verb constructions (Chatzitheodorou 2014), English phrasal verbs (Machonis 2010, 2012) and Greek idioms (Gavrilidou et al. 2012).

Thus, this work describes the process of categorizing and describing the idioms, writing the grammars and testing them on corpora, using NooJ as the environment. We specifically concentrate on the most complex and most numerous type of idioms, those based on a verbal phrase. Idioms based on a verbal head take up a bigger portion of idioms, not only in Croatian but in other languages as well (Wehrli 1998; Sakaeva and Nurullina 2013). It is thus of a great importance that they are analyzed and classified with care so that their identification in text may serve as a good basis for any future work (e.g. translation, information retrieval, language learning (Granger et al. 2006) etc.).

2   Methodology and Corpora

As a starting point for this work, we collected idioms from the printed Croatian Dictionary of Idioms - CDI (Menac et al. 2003). We found there many syntactically different types of idioms, such as:

(a) fixed phrase which does not change in any syntactic environment
(b) noun phrase with an attribute or apposition
(c) verbal phrase with a direct object
(d) verbal phrase with the optional direct object which can disrupt the syntactic structure
(e) comparative structure (A/V as N).

In this article, we will provide the detailed analysis of the third and fourth category, i.e. verb based idioms. This work is a continuation of the work presented in Kocijan and Librenjak (2016a) where general description of all the types is given and Kocijan and Librenjak (2016b) where we described the comparative structures in more detail. Verbal phrases are most complex of all the types and require special attention, thus we chose to concentrate our interest on this type in more detail in this article.

After consulting the CDI, we analyzed all the verb-based idioms syntactically, taking special care when it comes to structures that can be disrupted with objects, those that can be inverted or negated. Closer research yielded more sub-types which will be discussed in latter chapters. In addition to CDI, additional idioms were found while working on this project and added to the corpus of idioms. This gives the cumulative number of approximately 1500 verb-based idioms which were analyzed for the purpose of this work. All the idioms were listed in the NooJ dictionary, along with their type, sub-type and possible objects.

In the following step, we constructed syntactic NooJ grammars in order to recognize verbal idioms in all possible contexts and syntactic variations that can come to being in the Croatian language. As this is the most important part of this work, it is discussed at length in the sections that follow, along with the grammars, corpora for both training corpus and testing corpus needed to be constructed.

The training corpus was used in order to improve the grammars during their construction period, and it was constructed specifically for the purposes of our idioms research. This is a smaller corpus of approximately 60 Kw (60 000 words). It consists of sentences from Croatian newspaper articles and contemporary Croatian authors and each sentence has at least one version of the processed idioms[1].

Subsequently, finished grammars were tested on the web based Croatian corpus sample (Agić and Ljubešić 2014), and compared with manually marked results. Sentences were extracted randomly, and a corpus of approximately 100 Kw (100 000 word) was built. Each sentence was manually checked and marked if an idiom was found. This enabled us to get statistical measures of our grammars, such as recall, precision and f-measure. The results are described in the Evaluation section of the article.

3   Verb-Based Idioms

Verbs that are part of a comparative MWU (Verb as NP, Verb as PP or Verb as NP+PP) are placed into the category 5c (Kocijan, Librenjak, 2016b). Such examples are *buljiti kao tele u šarena vrata, čekati kao ozeblo sunce, govoriti kao iz knjige*.

Also, those MWUs that have a verb in a fixed position and no variation i.e. the verb never changes gender, number, person or tense, are placed in the category 1 (*nije šala, ni pas s maslom ne bi pojeo, povuci-potegni, pričam ti priču*). They are listed in the dictionary as simple entries (Kocijan, Librenjak, 2016a)[2] and belong to fixed expressions, as termed by Sag et al. (2002).

Verbs appearing as a head of an idiom that undergo any type of morphological variation as well as word order variations and short insertions belong to Type 3 and Type 4 classes of idioms. Each of these classes belongs to syntactically flexible expressions (Sag et al. 2002), thus their subtypes (7 and 8 respectively) describe different syntactic patterns.

We use the following model to describe these two classes inside the NooJ dictionary: the verb (used in the idiom) is considered to be the main entry in the dictionary while the remaining of the phrase is entered as the verb's semantic description using the notation PX, SUFX, SUFXA, SUFXB, SUFXC and SUFXV. The main entry is marked as

---

[1] An on-line version of Croatian corpus of idioms is prepared and maintained by Rittgasser and Fink-Arsovski at http://www.lingua-hr.de/phraseologie/stichwort.html.

[2] In the two papers published (Kocijan and Librenjak, 2016a, 2016b) we have used a special category NW to describe the MWUs. Since that feature is no longer supported in NooJ 5, we have decided to change the NW notation with the FXC. The remaining of our dictionaries and grammars remain the same.

a category verb (V) with additional feature PHR (short for phrase) and special feature FXC. This special feature in NooJ is associated with lexical entries "that must not result in real annotations" but remain visible to the syntactic grammar (Silberztein 2003). This way we are able to avoid the unnecessary annotations of the text if only the verb is used in a sentence. Thus, only if the entire expression is recognized (verb and its suffix part/s) the string will be annotated as an idiom. In all other cases, each word will be annotated as a single lexical unit with the lexical information that inherits from the dictionary and related grammars. Since verbs change their form (gender, number, tense, person), each dictionary entry is also provided with the FLX value so that any variation is recognized. Also, each entry has its type (Type=3|4) and subtype (SType=a|b|m|n|p|v|w and SType=a|b|c|d|e|f|g|p) defined. This classification of types and subtypes is used inside the corresponding syntactic grammars for the purposes of constraining and annotating the recognized strings. The distribution of types, subtypes and PX, SUFX, SUFXA, SUFXB, SUFXC and SUFXV used in the dictionary is given in Fig. 1.

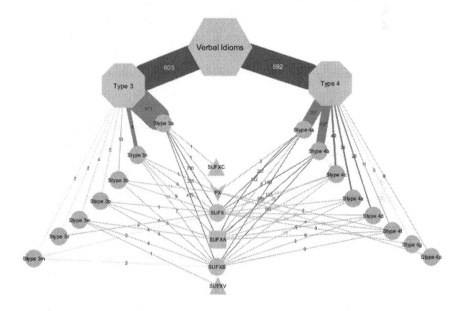

Fig. 1. Distribution of verbal idioms and their types

Although there are 605 type 3 and 592 type 4 main entries in the dictionary, there are more than 1197 verbal idioms that we recognize. This is possible since one dictionary entry may hold more than one SUFX, SUFXA and/or SUFXB values. For example, the verb *dobiti* (en. to get) forms an idiom with 17 possible SUFX endings, like: *dobiti šipak, dobiti brus, dobiti figu, dobiti nogu, dobiti krila* etc. and verb *imati* (en. to have) has 7 SUFXA values that combine with one and the same SUFXB (*ruke* – en. hands) to form 7 different idioms like: *imati krvave | slobodne | okrvavljene | dvije lijeve | odriješene | prljave | zlatne ruke* (en. to have blody|free|gory|two left|loose|dirty|golden hands) while the verb *biti* (en. to be) has one SUFXA (*na* – en. on) and 20 SUFXB values and forms idioms like *biti na aparatima | konju | izdisaju, | cijeni* (en[lit]. to be on life support | horse

| exhale | price). Majority of type 3 verbs are subtype **a** (573 main entries) and they use 730 SUFX, 328 SUFXA and 479 SUFXB values. Other subtypes in this category are quite small with 10 or less main entries but were necessary in order to raise the precision of the grammars.

The largest subtype group in type 4 verbal idioms are subtypes a and b with 267 and 197 entries respectively. These two subcategories use 457 SUFX, 233 SUFXA and 324 SUFXB values in total.

Many of our dictionary entries have more than one possible variants (ex. *staviti **bubu** u uho* = *staviti **buhu** u uho*). Regardless the fact that some are more widely used than others (Fink and Menac 2008), we have decided on including all available variants. Thus the idioms *baciti prašinu u oči* and *baciti pijesak u oči* (en[lit]: 'throw dust into the eyes' and 'throw sand into the eyes', meaning 'to deceive someone') have only one dictionary entry with two SUFXA attributes and one SUFXB attribute (since it is same for both variants):

- baciti,NW+FLX=BIRATI+Type=3+SType=a+**SUFXA=prašinu** +**SUFXA=pijesak**+SUFXB=u oči

In the following two sections we will discuss type's 3 and 4 forms, grammars used for their detection and will provide examples of both dictionary entries and concordances for each subtype.

3.1 Type 3 and Subtypes

The main difference between type 3 and type 4 idioms is that type 3 has continuous suffix section while type 4 allows discontinuity i.e. insertion of noun or prepositional phrases. In order to facilitate our grammars, we have decided on the following subcategorization of type 3 verbal idioms:

SType=**a** category allows for the verb and the suffix to be interrupted with some other word categories, but the entire suffix (if it is built from two sections like SUFXA and SUFXB) must remain uninterrupted (see Fig. 2. for the segment of 3a grammar).

- ostajati,V+PHR+FXC+Type=3+SType=a+FLX=SMIJATI+SUFX=kratkih rukava
  - *On ostaje (uvijek) kratkih rukava.* – en[lit] He stays (always) with short sleeves.
- ostati,V+PHR+FXC+Type=3+SType=a+FLX=ZASTATI+SUFXA=bez +SUFXB=riječi+SUFXB=teksta
  - *Ostao je bez riječi.* – en[lit] He stayed withouth words. (*He was speechless.*)

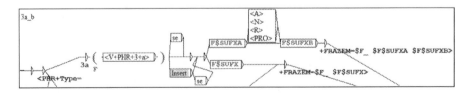

Fig. 2. Grammar for recognizing verbal idioms type 3a

SType=**b** is similar to the SType **a** but it uses SUFX and SUFXB attributes. The first one holds the obligatory part of expression that must always appear next to the verb, while the SUFXB holds an elective part of the expression that may or may not appear in order for the idiom to be valid.

– nestati,V+PHR+FXC+Type=3+SType=b+FLX=ZASTATI+SUFX=bez   traga
  +SUFXB=i glasa
  • *Nestao je bez traga (i glasa).* – en[lit] He disappeared without a trace (and voice).

SType=**m** has two verbs, one on the each side of the idiom, both of which may change in tense, gender, person and number all of which must match between the both verbs in order for the expression to be recognized.

– rezati,V+PHR+FXC+Type=3+SType=m+FLX=PODIZATI+SUFX=na   kojoj
  +SUFXV=sjediti
  • *rezati granu na kojoj sjediš* – en[lit] to cut the branch you are sitting on

SType=**n** uses verbs that exist in an idiom only if negated, thus the expression '*nije vidio ni prst pred nosom*' is marked an idiom, while the same construction without the negation 'nije' is not ('*vidio je prst pred nosom*'). Grammar recognizing this subtype is given in Fig. 3.

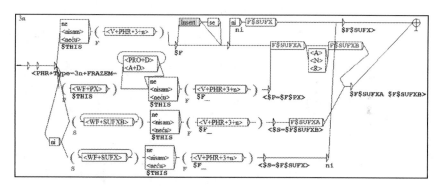

Fig. 3. Grammar for recognizing verbal idioms type 3n

– vidjeti,V+PHR+FXC+Type=3+SType=n+FLX=VIDJETI+SUFXA=pred
  +SUFXB=prst nosom
  • *nije vidio ni prst pred nosom* – en[lit] didn't see not even a finger in front of his nose

  SType=**p** has the verb that may only exist as an active (PDR) or passive (PDT) participle.

– premazati,V+PHR+FXC+Type=3+SType=p+FLX=KAZATI+SUFXA=svim
  +SUFXB=farbama

The grammar for idioms of type 4 recognizes both regular word order and inversion:

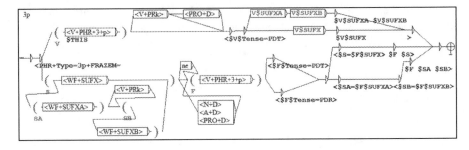

Fig. 4. Grammar for verbal idioms type 3p

- *premazan si svim mastima* – en[lit] you are painted with all different greases
- *svim si mastima premazan*

SType=**v** has two verbs (both verbs have to match in person, gender, number and tense) and have an expression 'nit | niti' before each verb. The grammar for subtypes v and w is given in Fig. 5 (lower path).

– smrdjeti,V+PHR+FXC+Type=3+SType=v+FLX=STIDJETI+SUFX=mirisati
  - *niti smrdi nit miriši* – en[lit] it neither stinks nor smells

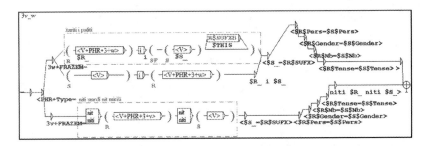

Fig. 5. Grammar for types 3v and 3w

SType=**w** is similar to the subcategory v as it also has two verbs that must match in person, gender, number and tense, but the two verbs are connected with a conjunction '*i*' (en. and) (see upper path in Fig. 5).

– žariti, NW+Type=3+SType=w+FLX=BILJEŽITI+SUFX=paliti
  - *on žari i pali* – en[lit] he anneals and burns.

3.2 Type 4 and Subtypes

As already noted, the main characteristic of type 4 verbal idioms is that the main verb requires noun phrase or prepositional phrase in particular case (Nominative, Genitive, Dative, Accusative, Locative or Instrumental) to be present in the sentence. Thus, this type allows for the insertion of an NP and/or a PP after the verb but also, although rarely, between the suffix sections. It is also possible that an NP or PP required by the verb is outside of the idiom borders, i.e. it occurs in the text before or after the verbal idiom. In such cases, the verbal idiom is recognized without the NP/PP section.

Another quite frequent insertion is that of an additional attribute(s) or pronoun either between a verb and a SUFX section or between SUFXA and SUFXB sections. In the later case, SUFXA is always a preposition. Examples for this would be *osvojio (njeno) srce* where an idiom 'to win a heart' has additional pronoun 'her' ('he won her hurt') while *ubacio je buhu u (njegovo malo) uho* has a pronoun (*njegovo*) and an adjective (*malo*) inserted between SUFXA=*u* and SUFXB=*uho* (en[lit] he inserted a bug into (his little) ear).

Verbal idioms of type 4 are further subcategorized into the following 8 subtypes:

SType=**a** has the verb that requires dative construction which may be inserted between a verb and the remaining part of the expression or it can appear between SUFXA and SUFXB.

– baciti,V+PHR+FXC+Type=4+SType=a+FLX=BACITI+SUFXA=rukavicu +SUFXB=u lice
   The grammar (Fig. X) recognizes both regular word order and inversion:
   - *bacio mu je rukavicu u lice* – en[lit] he throw him the glove into face
   - *u lice mu je bacio rukavicu*
   SType=**b** has the verb that requires accusative construction.

– poslati,V+PHR+FXC+Type=4+SType=b+FLX=POSLATI+SUFXA=k +SUFXB=vragu
   - *poslao svu birokraciju k vragu* – en[lit] send all the bureaucracy to the devil

   SType=**c** has the verb that requires genitive construction.

– izbiti,V+PHR+FXC+Type=4+SType=c+FLX=ZABITI+SUFXA=iz +SUFXB=glave
   - *izbio (ga) je iz glave* – en[lit] he beat (him) out of the head

   SType=**d** has the verb that requires instrumental construction.

– imati,V+PHR+FXC+Type=4+SType=d+FLX=SJATI+SUFXA=neraščišćene +SUFXB=račune
   - *imaju s nama neraščišćene račune* – en[lit] have with us unclear bills

   SType=**e** has the verb that requires possessive pronoun or possessive adjective.

– zakucati,V+PHR+FXC+Type=4+SType=e+FLX=SJATI+SUFXA=na +SUFXB=vrata
   - *zakucati na (njegova) vrata* – en[lit] to knock on (his) door

   SType=**f** has the verb that requires nominative construction.

– visjeti,V+PHR+FXC+Type=4+SType=f+FLX=SJATI+SUFXA=u +SUFXB=zraku
   - *visjelo je (to) u zraku* – en[lit]

SType=**p** has the verb that requires obligatory prefixal word (*čudom se čuditi, curkom curiti, daleko dogurati, bijelo gledati, lose\crno\slabo mu se piše*).

– dogurati,V+PHR+FXC+Type=4+SType=p+FLX=SJATI+SUFX=daleko
  • *oni će daleko dogurati* – en[lit] they will get far and away.

4   Evaluation

In this section, we will give the results (P = precision, R = recall and F = f measure) for each category (3 and 4) separately and in total to get a better understanding of graphs used for recognizing each category.

The problems we encountered may be divided into three different categories that we will exemplify in the following paragraphs. (Table 1)

Table 1. Results from the corpora

	words	Total in %			Type=3			Type=4		
		P	R	F	P	R	F	P	R	F
Training corpus	58 223 w	98,9	96,3	97,6	100	100	100	99,2	96,1	97,6
Testing corpus	2 247 Kw	100	96,2	98	100	96,9	98,4	100	95	97,4

The examples that were not recognized by our grammars are mostly due to the long distances between MWU sections or inserted comma sign. This is also, out of three, the most numerous category of unrecognized idioms.

• *Podršku jurišnicima počele su, i to obilno, __šakom i kapom__, __davati__ i banke.* (inversion with inserted comma sign)
• *Karijeristi su brzo napredovali, a on, sposobniji od njih, __OSTAO JE__ zbog svoje skromnosti cijeli život __U SJENI__.* (long distance between MWU sections)

Another category of unrecognized idioms belongs to the false positives like it was the case with the sentence:

• *__Stajao__ je pred učiteljem oborene __glave__.*

where the idiom *stajao glave* (meaning 'to cost someone his/her life') was falsely recognized. The similar situation is with the sentence:

• *Samo se htio poigrati s tvojim psićem i slučajno mu je __stao na rep__.*

where the expression *stao na rep* exists as an idiom meaning 'to stop someone', but in this case it is used in its literal meaning (he stepped on his tail).

The last group of unrecognized idioms belongs to colloquial usage of language, i.e. to colloquialized idioms. Since our dictionary has idioms written only in standard Croatian language, such colloquial examples remain unrecognized by our grammars.

5   Conclusion

In this paper, we have argued for a grammar driven approach to two types of verb-based idioms in Croatian. We collected the idioms from Croatian Dictionary of Idioms (Menac et al. 2003) and described them syntactically. For verbs, we found two distinct categories – one that cannot be interrupted with the insertion of an inflected word, and one that can. Since this work is a continuation of our comprehensive approach to idioms as MWE (Kocijan and Librenjak, 2016a), we refer to the verb-based idioms as types 3 and 4, as other types are described in other articles. After describing them, we constructed the NooJ grammars for both types and all of their subtypes. Although we have covered all of the examples found in Menac et al. (2003), the list of verb-based idioms is still not complete and can be extended with additional ones, for example (Arsovski et al. 2010). During the testing phase, we have also added some additional idioms found in web corpus.

Since this is the first attempt at grammar driven approach (compare with Ljubešić et al. 2014 for statistical approach) to identify such occurrences in the text, we expect some additional changes and adjustments to take place in any future projects that would include verbal idioms. The results for this work, being greater than 98 %, 96 % and 97 % for precision, recall and f-measure respectfully, show that grammars suggested in this paper prove quite capable in recognizing the Croatian verb-based idioms.

References

Agić, Ž., Ljubešić, N.: The SETimes. HR linguistically annotated corpus of croatian. In: Proceedings of the Ninth International Conference on Language Resources and Evaluation, pp. 1724–1727, Reykjavik (2014)

Arsovski, F.Ž., Kovačević, B., Hrnjak, A.: Bibliografija hrvatske frazeologije i popis frazema analiziranih u znanstvenim i stručnim radovima. Knjigra, Zagreb (2010)

Chatzitheodorou, K.: Paraphrasing of Italian support verb constructions based on lexical and grammatical resources. In: Proceedings of the Workshop on Lexical and Grammatical Resources for Language Processing, Coling 2014, Dublin, Ireland, pp.1–7 (2014)

Fink, Ž., Menac, A.: Hrvatska frazeologija – staro i novo. In: Mokienko, W., Walter, H. (eds). Frazeologia. Komparacja spółczesnych języków słowiańskich, 3. Opole: Universität Greifswald – Institut für Slawistik, Uniwersytet Opolski – Instytut Filologii Polskiej, pp. 88–100 (2008)

Gavriilidou Z., Papadopoulou E., Chadjipapa E.: Processing greek frozen expressions with NooJ. In: Formalising Natural Languages with NooJ: Selected Papers from the NooJ 2011 International Conference, Dubrovnik, Croatia, pp. 63–74. Cambridge Scholars Publishing, Newcastle (2012)

Granger, S., Paquot, M., Rayson, P.: Extraction of multiword units from EFL and native English corpora. the phraseology of the verb 'make'. In: Buhofer, A.H., Burger, H. (eds.) Phraseology in Motion I, pp. 57–68. Schneider, Baltmannsweiler (2006)

Kocijan, K., Librenjak, S.: The quest for croatian idioms as multi word units. In: Monti, J., Mitkov, R., Corpas Pastor, G., Seretan, V. (eds.) Multiword Units in Machine Translation and Translation Technology. John Benjamins Publishing, Amsterdam (2016a)

Kocijan, K., Librenjak, S.: Comparative idioms in croatian: MWU approach. In: Corpas Pastor, G. (ed.) Computerised and Corpus-based Approaches to Phraseology: Monolingual and Multilingual Perspectives, pp. 523–532. Editions Tradulex, Geneva (2016b)

Ljubešić, N., Dobrovoljc, K., Krek, S., Antonić, M.P., Fišer, D.: hrMWELex – a MWE lexicon of croatian extracted from a parsed gigacorpus. In: Language Technologies: Proceedings of the 17th International Multiconference Information Society, IS2014, Ljubljana, Slovenia (2014)

Machonis, P.A.: English phrasal verbs: from lexicon-grammar to natural language processing. South. J. Linguist. **34**(1), 21–48 (2010)

Machonis P.A.: Sorting NooJ out to take multiword expressions into account. In: Vučković, K., Bekavac, B., Silberztein, M. (eds.) Formalising Natural Languages with NooJ: Selected Papers from the NooJ 2011 International Conference, Dubrovnik, Croatia, pp. 152–165. Cambridge Scholars Publishing, Newcastle (2012)

Matešić, J.: Frazeološki rječnik hrvatskoga ili srpskog jezika. Školska knjiga, Zagreb (1982)

Menac, A., Arsovski, F.Ž., Venturin, R.: Hrvatski frazeološki rječnik. Naklada Ljevak, Zagreb (2003)

Menac, A.: Hrvatska frazeologija. Knjigra, Zagreb (2007)

Menac-Mihalić, M.: Hrvatski dijalektni frazemi s antroponimom kao sastavnicom. In: Folia Onomastica Croatica, no. 12/13, pp. 361-385 (2007)

Sag, I.A., Baldwin, T., Bond, F., Copestake, A., Flickinger, D.: Multiword expressions: a pain in the neck for NLP. In: Gelbukh, A. (ed.) CICLing 2002. LNCS, vol. 2276, pp. 1–15. Springer, Heidelberg (2002)

Sakaeva, L.R., Nurullina, A.G.: Comparative analysis of verbal, adjectival, adverbial and modal phraseological units with a lexeme "devil" in english and russian languages. Middle-East J. Sci. Res. **18**(1), 50–54 (2013). doi:10.5829/idosi.mejsr.2013.18.1.12354

Silberztein, M.: NooJ Manual (2003). www.nooj4nlp.net

Todorova M.: Morpho-syntactic properties of bulgarian verbal idiomatic expressions. In Blanco, X., Silberztein, M., (eds.) Proceedings of the 2007 International NooJ Conference, pp. 273–279. Cambridge Scholars Publishing, Newcastle (2008)

Wehrli, E.: Translating idioms. In: Proceedings of the 36th Annual Meeting of the ACL and 17th International Conference on Computational Linguistics: COLING/ACL-98, Montreal, Canada, pp. 1388–1392 (1998)

Generating Paraphrases of Human Intransitive Adjective Constructions with Port4NooJ

Cristina Mota[1][✉], Paula Carvalho[1,2], Francisco Raposo[1],
and Anabela Barreiro[1]

[1] INESC-ID Lisboa, Lisbon, Portugal
{cmota,francisco.afonso.raposo}@ist.utl.pt, {abarreiro,pcc}@inesc-id.pt
[2] Universidade Europeia – Laureate International Universites, Lisbon, Portugal

Abstract. This paper details the integration into Port4NooJ of 15 lexicon-grammar tables describing the distributional properties of 4,248 human intransitive adjectives. The properties described in these tables enable the recognition and generation of adjectival constructions where the adjective has a predicative function. These properties also establish semantic relationships between adjective, noun and verb predicates, allowing new paraphrasing capabilities that were described in NooJ grammars. The new dictionary of human intransitive adjectives created by merging the information on those tables with the Port4NooJ homograph adjectives is comprised of 5,177 entries. The enhanced Port4NooJ is being used in eSPERTo, a NooJ-based paraphrase generation platform.

1 Introduction

Port4NooJ (Barreiro 2010) is a set of resources that allows the generation of paraphrases for Portuguese, feeding the linguistic engine of the eSPERTo paraphrasing system[1] based on NooJ technology (Silberztein 2015). The term paraphrase is commonly used to refer the relation between two or more constructions that are morpho-syntactically and/or semantically related (e.g. *to make a presentation (of)* = *to present*). In most cases, this relation is established between constructions corresponding to the same syntactic unit. However, the transformations described in lexicon-grammar tables also allow establishing relations between different syntactic units (e.g. *These teachers are Portuguese* = *The Portuguese teachers* [...]). Hence, we extend the term paraphrase to the semantico-syntactic relation between two or more sentences and/or their constituents.

This paper presents an enhanced Port4NooJ that includes 15 lexicon-grammar tables describing the distributional properties of 4,248 human intransitive adjectives formalized by Carvalho (2007). Among other properties, these linguistic resources provide information on: (i) the syntactic and semantic nature of the subject modified by each adjective, which can correspond to a human noun, a complex noun phrase involving an appropriate noun, or to a finite or non-finite clause; (ii) the copulative verbs (and aspectual variants) selected by

---

[1] https://esperto.l2f.inesc-id.pt/.

© Springer International Publishing Switzerland 2016
T. Okrut et al. (Eds.): NooJ 2015, CCIS 607, pp. 107–122, 2016.
DOI: 10.1007/978-3-319-42471-2_10

each adjective; (iii) the constraints related to the quantification of adjectives by an adverb or a degree morpheme; (iv) the position of adjectives in adnominal context (pre- or post-nominal position); (v) the possibility of certain adjectives being optionally followed by an infinitive clause, with causal interpretation, or by a human noun phrase introduced by the preposition *para* (*for*). In addition to general properties, these resources also describe particular constructions in which human intransitive adjectives may occur, as in: (vi) generic and cross-constructions, where the adjective fills the head of a noun phrase; (vii) characterizing indefinite constructions, where the adjective occurs after an indefinite article; (viii) exclamative sentences expressing insult. Moreover, these lexicon-grammar tables specify the morpho-syntactically related predicative nouns and verbs, whenever they exist, as well as the appropriate nouns that can appear in specific adjective constructions.

The properties described in the lexicon-grammar tables add new paraphrasing capabilities to eSPERTo. Port4Nooj initial paraphrases involved transformations of support verb constructions (or their stylistic or aspectual variants) into single verbs. Later on, new paraphrasing capabilities were added to Port4NooJ, namely transformations of phrasal verbs into equivalent expressions, compound adverbs into single adverbs, relatives into participial adjectives, relatives into possessives, relatives into compound nouns, and agentive passives into actives. Section 4 presents examples of these paraphrases, but a more detailed description of Port4NooJ first paraphrasing capabilities can be found in Barreiro (2009) and Barreiro (2011).

The use of the linguistic knowledge described in the integrated tables allows mapping of several other types of paraphrasing constructions resulting in a semantic relationship between adjective, noun and verb predicates. The lexicon-grammar tables enable eSPERTo to paraphrase (i) adjective, noun and verb morphologically related constructions (*está zangado* (*is angry*) = *zangou-se* (*got (self) angry*) = *esteve envolvido numa zanga* (*was involved in anger*)); (ii) adjective constructions supported by different copulative verbs (*estar perdido* (*to be lost*) = *andar perdido* (*walk around lost*)); (iii) constructions involving nationality and other membership relations (*de origem portuguesa* (*of Portuguese origin/roots*) = *portugueses* (*Portuguese*) = *de Portugal* (*from Portugal*); *benfiquista* (*Benfica fan*) = *do Sport Lisboa e Benfica* (*a fan of Sport Lisboa e Benfica*)); (iv) cross-constructions (*o idiota do rapaz* (*the idiot of the boy*) = *o rapaz é um idiota* (*the boy is an idiot*)); appropriate noun constructions (*foi moderado nos seus comentários* (*he was moderated in his comments*) = *os seus comentários foram moderados* (*his comments were moderated*) = *foi moderado* (*he was moderated*), (v) generic noun phrases (*é um indivíduo estúpido* (*he is a fool*) = *é um estúpido* (*he is a fool*) = *é estúpido* (*he is fool*)), among others.

2 Related Work

Our work follows previous attempts to integrate lexicon-grammar tables in natural language processing systems.

Machonis (2010) presents experiments in NooJ with lexicon-grammar tables of transitive and neutral phrasal verbs in English to identify these types of constructions in texts with and without insertion. The author corroborates that, on the one hand, NooJ is a very powerful tool for parsing compound expressions that involve insertion, such as English phrasal verbs, and, on the other hand, a lexicon-grammar of phrasal verbs can help distinguish prepositional usage from true particles in natural language processing.

Vietri (2010) describes the integration, also into NooJ, of one of her 13 lexicon-grammar tables, table EpinC, which contains 900 Italian idioms with the structure N_0 *essere in C*, where *essere* (*to be*) is a support verb, and *in C* is a frozen or semi-frozen prepositional phrase starting with the preposition *in*. The author shows that this integration allowed to refine the linguistic analysis of this type of sequences.

Baptista et al. (2014) discuss lexical and parsing issues of integrating a lexicon-grammar of Portuguese verbal idioms into STRING, a hybrid statistical and rule-based pipeline for natural language processing of Portuguese. More than 2,000 rules were created semi-automatically for ten formal classes of verbal idioms. The system precision was estimated after processing a large Portuguese corpus of news texts.

3   The eSPERTo Project

This research work was developed in the scope of the eSPERTo[2] project. The main objective of this project is the development of a context-sensitive and linguistically enhanced paraphrase generator that recognizes semantico-syntactic, multiwords and other phrasal units, and transforms them into semantically equivalent phrases, expressions, or sentences. This semantically-driven paraphrasing system uses a new hybrid technique that combines statistics and local grammars to acquire linguistic knowledge applied in the identification and generation of new and increasingly more complex paraphrases. Currently, eSPERTo is integrated in an interactive application that helps Portuguese language learners in producing and revising their texts. The utility of eSPERTo's paraphrasing capabilities are now being explored in two other application scenarios: (i) in a question-answering system to increase the linguistic knowledge of an intelligent conversational virtual agent, and (ii) in a summarization tool to assist the paraphrasing task. Figure 1 shows eSPERTo's current interactive Web interface designed to help Portuguese language learners in producing and revising their texts. Among other functionalities, the platform includes text-editing mechanisms, which provide a variety of alternatives for each expression, allowing the user to choose among several suggestions that can be immediately applied to text. For the sentence illustrated in Fig. 1: *O homem americano apresentou o*

---

[2] In Portuguese, "esperto" means "smart", but here it is also an acronym for "System of Paraphrasing for Editing and Revision of Text" ("Sistema de Parafraseamento para Edição e Revisão de Texto"). eSPERTo is a "smart system" in the sense that it contains semantic "understanding" in its linguistic knowledge base.

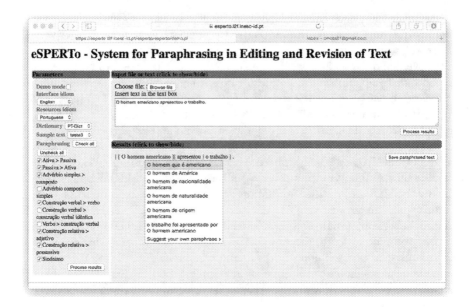

Fig. 1. Online use of eSPERTo in text editing and revision

trabalho (*The American man presented the work*), eSPERTo suggests its equivalent passive paraphrase: *O trabalho foi apresentado pelo homem americano* (*The work was presented by the American man*). For the noun phrase *o homem americano* (*the American man*), eSPERTo suggests paraphrases such as: *o homem que é americano* (*the man who is American*), *o homem de nacionalidade americana* (*the man with American nationality*), *o homem de naturalidade americana* (*the man with American origin*), *o homem de origem americana* (*the man with American origin*). The user can then select any of the paraphrases listed, or provide his/her own paraphrase.[3]

4   Port4NooJ and Its First Paraphrases

Port4NooJ is the Portuguese linguistic module of NooJ. The module can be downloaded from the NooJ website[4] or from the Linguateca's resources repository[5]. The initial Port4NooJ resources derive from OpenLogos. OpenLogos is an open source derivative of the commercial Logos system downloadable from the DFKI website[6] and available for testing at INESC-ID[7]. The Logos system

---

[3] For more information about the eSPERTo paraphrasing system and interface, see Mota et al. (2015 forthcoming).

[4] http://www.nooj-association.org.

[5] http://www.linguateca.pt/Repositorio/Port4Nooj/.

[6] http://logos-os.dfki.de/.

[7] http://www.l2f.inesc-id.pt/openlogos/demo.html.

was built on the Logos Model (Scott 2003), (Barreiro et al. 2011). In order to create Port4NooJ, the OpenLogos English-Portuguese bilingual dictionary was converted into NooJ format and its language pair order was inverted. Besides the large coverage electronic dictionary with English transfers, the Port4NooJ module contains two other important components: (i) the rules which formalize and document Portuguese inflectional and derivational descriptions, and (ii) different types of grammar, namely morphological[8], disambiguation, semantico-syntactic, multiword expressions, and translation and paraphrasing grammars. The different components of Port4NooJ interact among them and are used to process texts. Several processing functions can be performed with these resources, among others, part of speech annotation, pattern recognition, semantic unit analysis, concordances, information extraction, paraphrasing and translation.[9] Barreiro (2008) and Barreiro (2010) describe in detail the initial dictionary and its enhancement with new linguistic knowledge, namely inflectional, derivational and morpho-syntactic properties, and semantic relations that permitted the generation of paraphrases.

Initially, Port4NooJ contemplated paraphrases involving support verb constructions or their stylistic or aspectual variants and corresponding single verbs (*fazer/realizar/efetuar uma apresentação* (*make a presentation (of)*) = *apresentar* (*present*)), compound and single adverbs (*de uma forma interativa* (*in an interactive way*) = *interativamente* (*interactively*); *com entusiasmo* (*with enthusiasm*) = *entusiasticamente* (*enthusiastically*)), relatives and participial adjectives (*que foram escritos* (*that were written*) = *escritos* (*written*)), relatives and possessive constructions *o papel que a Europa tem/desempenha* (*the role that Europe plays*) = *o papel da Europa* (*the role of Europe*)), and active/passive constructions (*A solta B* (*A releases B*) = *B é solto por A* (*B is released by A*)), among others. In Sect. 5, we will describe the new Port4NooJ paraphrases resulting from the transformation of human intransitive adjective constructions described in the lexicon-grammar tables.

5   Lexicon-Grammar of Human Intransitive Adjectives

The lexicon-grammar tables explored in this study describe 4,248 human intransitive adjectives, i.e. adjectives that select a human noun as subject and do not require any complement. These adjectives were grouped into 15 subclasses, which present different lexico-syntactic properties, as illustrated in Table 1.

These properties relate specifically to: (i) the syntactic nature of the human subject: depending on the adjective class, this position can be headed by a human noun (Nhum), (ii) a complex noun phrase involving an appropriate noun (Nap de Nhum), and/or (iii) by a finite clause (QueF), (iv) the nature of the copular verb (Cop) selected by the adjective: there are adjectives that co-occur

---

[8] The morphological component includes a morphological grammar to process contracted forms.

[9] Due to its bilingual characteristics, Port4NooJ dictionary can be used in translation (with embedded paraphrasing).

Table 1. Classes and distributional properties of human intransitive adjectives

	N0		QueF	Cop		CCI	
	Nhum	Nap de Nhum		ser	estar	um Adj	
SAHP1	+	+	+	+	-	-	Ele é honesto – He is honest A atitude dele é honesta – His attitude is honest Que ele faça isso é honesto da sua parte – Doing that is honest on his part
SAHP2	+	+	-	+	-	-	Ele é atlético – He is athletic O seu porte é atlético – His look is athletic
SAHP3	+	-	-	+	-	-	Ele é comunicativo – He is communicative
SAHC1	+	+	+	+	-	+	Ele é arrogante – He is arrogant Ele é um arrogante – He is an arrogant O comportamento dele é arrogante – His behavior is arrogant Que ele se comporte assim é arrogante da sua parte – Behaving like that is arrogant on his part
SAHC2	+	+	-	+	-	+	Ele é introvertido – He is introvert Ele é um introvertido – He is an introvert A sua maneira de ser é introvertida – His way of being is introvert
SAHC3	+	-	-	+	-	+	Ele é aselha – He is a clumsy Ele é um aselha – He is a clumsy
EAHP2	+	+	-	-	+	-	Ele está bronzeado – He is tanned O rosto dele está bronzeado – His face is tanned
EAHP3	+	+	-	-	+	-	Ele está zangado – He is angry
SEAHP2	+	+	-	+	+	-	Ele (é + está) cadavérico – He is cadaverous O seu rosto (é + está) cadavérico – His face is cadaverous
SEAHP3	+	-	-	+	+	-	Ele (é + está) calvo – He is bald
SEAHC2	+	+	-	+	+	+	Ele (é + está) esquelético – He is cadaverous As pernas dele (são + estão) esqueléticas – His legs are cadaverous Ele é um esquelético – He is a cadaverous
SEAHC3	+	-	-	+	+	+	Ele (é + está) alucinado – He is alucinated Ele é alucinado – He is alucinated Ele é um alucinado – He is an alucinated
SAN	+	+	-	+	-	-	Ele é português – He is Portuguese A sua nacionalidade é portuguesa – His nationality is Portuguese
SAF	+	-	-	+	-	+/-	Ele é socialista – He is socialist Ele é fascista – He is a fascist
SEAD	+	+/-	-	+/-	+/-	+/-	Ele é autista – He is autistic Ele está constipado – He has a cold Ele (é + está) anorético – He is anoretic As suas pernas estão inchadas – His legs are swollen Ele é cleptomaníaco – He is Kleptomaniac Ele é um cleptomaníaco – He is a kleptomaniac

only with the verb *ser* or *estar*, while others co-occur with both copula verbs, (v) the possibility of the predicative adjective appearing in another indefinite construction (CCI).

In addition to these generic properties, the tables describe specific distributional and transformational attributes of the adjective, allowing recognition and generation of a variety of syntactic constructions where each adjective occurs. Some of these properties depend on the adjective subclass, while others depend on the adjective itself. Figure 2 presents some examples extracted from the lexicon-grammar table that describes the adjectives of nationality. As illustrated in the table, the adjectives of this semantico-syntactic class require a human noun (Nhum) to fill the subject position (N0). In predicative context, they are linked to its subject by the verb *ser*, and they cannot be quantified or intensified (Quant). Moreover, in adnominal context, the adjectives of nationality can only occur in post-adnominal position. However, there are some properties in the table that may vary depending on the adjective. For example, even though all the adjectives of this class are able to modify the generic predicative classifier *origem* (designation of origin), the presence of a more specific noun classifier, such as *nacionalidade* (nationality/country of origin), *naturalidade* (place of origin), *etnia* (ethnicity) or *raça* (race), depends on the semantics of the adjective (i.e., on the nature of the locative noun with which each adjective is associated). The information described in Table 2 allows generating the following constructions, among others:

```
Ele é açoriano - He is Azorean
Ele é um açoriano [simpático] - He is a [friendly] Azorean
Ele é um rapaz açoriano - He is an Azorean boy
Ele é de origem açoriana - He is of Azorean origin
Ele é de naturalidade açoriana - He is of Azorean origin
Ele é dos Açores - He is from Azores
```

Fig. 2. Lexicon-grammar table SAN describing adjectives of nationality

Figure 3 presents an excerpt of the table describing the predicative adjectives classified as SAHC1. The adjectives of this class select the verb *ser*, and some of their aspectual or stylistic variants, in particular *mostrar-se* (show self as),

SAHC1																																	
N0						Vcop											Class		Quant			P_Adn		Reest N.			(W+E)		CC		
Nhum	Nap de Nhum	Nap		Que F	N-Nhum	ser	estar	andar	ficar	permanecer	viver	encontrar-se	sentir-se	mostrar-se	revelar-se	tornar-se	UM Nclas	Um +Modif	Adv Quant	Superlativo	Adjective	N Adj	Adj N	Nhum Vop A Prep Nap	(de + em) (E+Det) Nap	em Dposs Nap	sei Vinf	para com Nhum	CC	(Seu + Mais Adj)	Nome
		Nabstr	Npc																												
+	+	+	-	+	-	+	-	-	-	-	-	-	-	+	+	+	+	+	+	-	adulador	+	-	+	-	+	+	+	+	+	adulação
+	+	+	-	+	-	+	-	-	-	-	-	-	-	+	+	+	+	+	+	-	agourento	+	-	+	-	+	+	-	+	+	mau agouro
+	+	+	-	+	-	+	-	-	-	-	-	-	-	+	+	+	+	+	+	-	alarmista	+	-	+	-	+	+	-	+	+	alarmismo
+	+	+	-	+	-	+	-	-	-	-	-	-	-	+	+	+	+	+	+	-	alentador	+	-	+	-	+	+	-	+	-	alento
+	+	+	-	+	-	+	-	-	-	-	-	-	-	+	+	+	+	+	+	-	altruista	+	-	+	-	+	+	-	+	-	altruísmo
+	+	+	-	+	-	+	-	-	-	-	-	-	-	+	+	+	+	+	+	+	ambicioso	+	-	+	-	+	+	-	+	+	ambição
+	+	-	-	-	+	-	-	-	-	-	-	-	-	-	+	+	+	+	+	+	anormal	+	-	+	-	+	-	+	-	+	anormalidade
+	+	+	-	+	-	+	-	-	-	-	-	-	-	+	+	+	+	+	+	-	antidesportista	+	-	+	-	+	+	-	+	+	antidesportivismo
+	+	+	-	+	-	+	-	-	-	-	-	-	-	+	+	+	+	+	+	+	antipático	+	+	+	-	+	+	+	+	+	antipatia
+	+	+	-	+	-	+	-	-	-	-	-	-	-	+	+	+	+	+	+	-	antipatriota	+	-	+	-	+	+	-	+	+	antipatriotismo

Fig. 3. Lexicon-grammar table SAHC1 describing a subclass of predicative adjectives

revelar-se (reveal self as), and/or *tornar-se* (become). Their subject position can be filled by a human noun (Nhum), an appropriate noun (Nap), or a finite clause. Most adjectives described in this table can be quantified by an adverb (Adv), and some can also receive a degree morpheme (Sup). In adnominal context, there are adjectives, like *antipático* (unfriendly), that can occur both in post- and pre-adnominal position. Among other properties, this table provides information on particular syntactic constructions derived from a set of transformations involving the subject (Reest N0). Below, we present some examples represented in this lexicon-grammar.

```
O rapaz antipático - The unfriendly boy
Um antipático rapaz - An unfriendly boy
Ele (é + mostrou-se + revelou-se) antipático
   - He (is + showed himself as + revealed himself as) unfriendly
Ele é um antipático - He is such an unfriendly person
Ele é uma pessoa antipática - He is an unfriendly person
A sua maneira de ser é antipática - His personality is unfriendly
Que ele faça isso é antipático da sua parte - What he is doing is unfriendly
Ele revela antipatia - He reveals unfriendliness
Ele é antipático na sua maneira de ser - He is unfriendly in his ways
Ele é antipático para com toda a gente - He is unfriendly with everybody
Seu antipático! - Unfriendly you!
```

6 Integration of the Lexicon-Grammar Tables in Port4NooJ

6.1 From Lexicon-Grammar Tables to NooJ Dictionaries

The conversion of the 15 lexicon-grammar tables into a NooJ dictionary of human intransitive adjectives was mostly done automatically with different scripts. The process is hence easily adaptable to integrate other lexicon-grammar tables. For each entry in a lexicon-grammar table, we applied the following main steps:

1. If adjective is already in Port4NooJ, merge the lexicon-grammar properties with every homograph adjectival entry in Port4NooJ dictionary, by adding the new properties to that entry, otherwise create a new entry;
2. Create inflectional (FLX) and derivational (DRV) codes and corresponding rules as needed;
3. Check for missing FLX and DRV codes, and create new ones as needed.

6.1.1   Representation of Lexicon-Grammar Table Properties

The properties +IH and +Table=<table_name> were added to all human intransitive adjectives. The first property indicates that the adjective is a human intransitive adjective, and the second one refers to the lexicon-grammar table where the adjective properties are formalized.

For each different column in a lexicon-grammar table, a property +<name_of_ prop> was created. If the adjective row is marked with the value +, then that property was added to the adjective entry. Properties that have a value other than +/- were added as +<name_of_prop>=value_of_prop. For properties Nome and Verbo, instead of creating +Nome=<value> and +Verbo=<value>, a script translates the pair(s) adjective/noun and adjective/verb, if they exist, into a derivation paradigm and creates attributes +DRV=A2N<drv_code1>:<flx_code1> and +DRV=A2V<drv_code2>:<flx_code2>, respectively.

The drv code is determined and formalized automatically by finding the radical between the adjective and the noun or verb. For example, the adjective *alegre* (*happy*) is associated with the corresponding noun *alegria* (*happiness*) and the corresponding verb *alegrar* (*become happy*) through derivation rules (cf. A2B143 and A2V6 below), which replace the adjectival ending *-e* with the noun and verb endings *-ia* and *-ar*, respectively.

```
alegr(e|ia) => A2N143 = <B1>ia/N
alegr(e|ar) => A2V6 = <B1>ar/V
```

The inflection of the derived word (flx_code1 or flx_code2) is determined by consulting Port4NooJ (cf. FLX=CASA for the noun and FLX=FALAR for the verb).

```
alegria,N+FLX=CASA+AB+state+EN=joy+SYNN=contentamento
alegrar,V+FLX=FALAR+Aux=1+PRECVagree-type+Subset=...
```

In cases where the derived forms did not exist, their codes were assigned automatically. The FLX code of the base form, the adjective, was determined in the same way: the inflection code is looked up in Port4NooJ or assigned automatically in cases where the word does not exist.

Additional properties were created to account for specific knowledge required in paraphrasing. For example, the property +TopDET={o|a|os|as|undef} indicates the determiner that co-occurs with a toponym:

```
o homem abissínio <-> o homem da Abissínia
the Abyssinian man <-> the man from Abyssinia

o homem açoriano <-> o homem dos Açores
the Azorean man <-> the man from the Azores

o homem português <-> o homem de Portugal
the Portuguese man <-> the man from Portugal
```

The value of +TopDET was determined automatically by consulting the AC/DC corpora (28 corpora covering different variants of Portuguese in a total of 1,279 million words) and counting the distribution of the determiner that occurs (or its absence) in the context of the prepositions *de* (*of*) and *em* (*in*). For each toponym in the lexicon-grammar tables, a CQP query, the language used to query the AC/DC corpora, with the following structure was used to consult each corpora:

```
de+em+d(o+a+os+as)+n(o+a+os+as) <toponym>
```

In cases where the toponym did not occur in the corpora, +TopDET=undef was used to distinguish those cases from toponyms that do not accept determiners (i.e., the property +TopDET was not added to the adjective entry).

6.1.2   Integration with eSPERTo Dictionary Entries

After the properties of each adjective in the lexicon-grammar tables were created, the script merged those properties with the information corresponding to that adjective in the Port4NooJ entries. When the adjective already existed in Port4NooJ, the lexicon-grammar properties were added to all the adjective homograph entries in Port4NooJ. This means that, for example, the following Port4NooJ entries:

```
velho,A+FLX=ALTO+AB+class+EN=vintage
velho,A+FLX=ALTO+AN+Hum+EN=elder
velho,A+FLX=ALTO+NAV+Apred+EN=old
```

became the following new entries:

```
velho,A+FLX=ALTO+AB+class+EN=vintage+IH+Table=SEAHP3+Nhum
+Vcopser+Vcopestar+Vcopencontrarse+Vcopsentirse+Vcoptornarse
+UMNclas+UmModif+AdvQuant+Superlativo+NAdj+DRV=A2N164:CASA
+DRV=A2V67:AGRADECER

velho,A+FLX=ALTO+AN+Hum+EN=elder+IH+Table=SEAHP3
+Nhum+Vcopser+Vcopestar+Vcopencontrarse+Vcopsentirse+Vcoptornarse
+UMNclas+UmModif+AdvQuant+Superlativo+NAdj+DRV=A2N164:CASA
+DRV=A2V67:AGRADECER

velho,A+FLX=ALTO+NAV+Apred+EN=old+IH+Table=SEAHP3+Nhum
+Vcopser+Vcopestar+Vcopencontrarse+Vcopsentirse+Vcoptornarse
+UMNclas+UmModif+AdvQuant+Superlativo
+NAdj+DRV=A2N164:CASA+DRV=A2V67:AGRADECER
```

Initially, this process was done blindly, i.e., the Port4NooJ entries were not checked for properties that excluded them from being human intransitive adjectives, and that, consequently, should not receive lexicon-grammar attributes. In a second round, entries with at least the attribute +AB, i.e., adjectives that are classified as "abstract", such as the first entry above, should be discarded to obtain a more accurate version of the dictionary of human intransitive adjectives.

When the adjective did not exist in Port4NooJ, new entries were created. This happened for different reasons: the adjective was missing from Port4NooJ (e.g., *abissínio*), it derived from other base form (e.g., *arranhado* is the past participle of *arranhar*) or had another part of speech tag in Port4NooJ (e.g., *solteiro* in Port4Nooj is a noun only). In any of those cases, the inflection code was assigned automatically given that the suffixes of the human intransitive adjectives were very regular. A few exceptional adjectives with less productive suffixes were missing FLX codes. Those entries were reviewed by linguists and their codes were assigned manually. New FLX codes and corresponding inflectional paradigms were created as needed. All other properties of new adjectival entries came from the lexicon-grammar tables:

```
abissínio,A+FLX=ALTO+IH+Table=SAN+Nhum+Vcopser+Vcoptornarse+UMNclas+UmModif+
NclassPserde+NclassPorigem+NclassPnacionalidade+NclassPnaturalidade+NAdj+
Top=Abissínia+TopDET=a
(no entry in Port4Nooj)


arranhado,A+FLX=ALTO+IH+Table=EAHP2+Nhum+NapdeNhum+Npc+Vcopestar+AdvQuant+
Superlativo+NAdj+NhumVopAPrepNap+deemEDefNap+DRV=A2N4:BALÃO+DRV=A2V2:FALAR+
Reflexivo
(In Port4Nooj: arranhar,V+FLX=FALAR...)


solteiro,A+FLX=ALTO+IH+Table=SEAHP3+Nhum+Vcopser+Vcopestar+Vcopficar+
Vcoppermanecer+Vcopencontrarse+UMNclas+UmModif+Superlativo+NAdj
(In Port4NooJ: solteiro,N+FLX=ANO+AN+des+EN=bachelor)
```

6.2   From Lexicon-Grammar Tables to NooJ Grammars

Syntactic grammars in NooJ can be described and used in two different ways: for syntactic parsing, and for transformational analysis. We explored both, as described in Sects. 6.2.1 and 6.2.2. However, for the time being, eSPERTo is generating paraphrases through syntactic parsing.

6.2.1   Option 1: Syntactic Parsing

NooJ syntactic grammars that are used to parse a text, need to describe for each input the corresponding paraphrases that will be generated in the output. For example, the possibility of having the indefinite article, a construction common to several tables, can be described by recognizing the sequence without the article, and generating the construction including the determiner, or the reverse. However, we are duplicating information by swapping the input with the output (cf. top path with bottom path in Fig. 4). In the case of just two equivalent constructions, this is not a big problem. In the case of a set with more than two paraphrases (e.g., *o homem americano | o homem dos EUA | o homem de origem americana | o homem de nacionalidade americana |* etc.), the recognition of all constructions in the set and the generation of the alternative constructions, would require at least $n \times (n-1)$ paths, where n is the number of paraphrases in the set. For example, the grammar in Fig. 5 recognizes only *o homem americano* and generates the corresponding paraphrases. Similar grammars would have to be constructed for each paraphrase to be also recognized in a text.

6.2.2   Option 2: Transformational Module

A better description than option 1 is to represent that the construction without the indefinite article (top path in Fig. 4) and the construction with the indefinite article (bottom path in Fig. 4) are equivalents, as described in Fig. 6. This equivalency is expressed through the use of the global variable @A. That grammar can then be used in the transformational module to generate all the equivalent constructions.

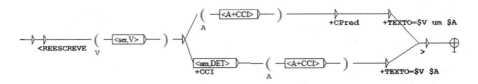

Fig. 4. Characterizing indefinite constructions: paraphrasing through parsing

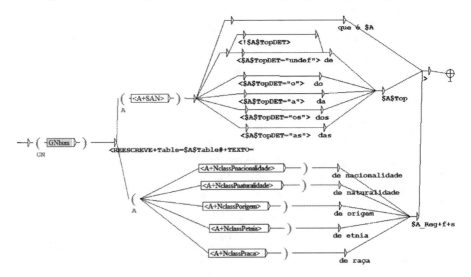

Fig. 5. Paraphrasing constructions involving patronymic adjectives

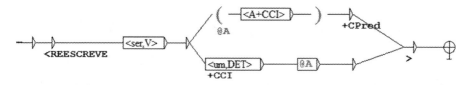

Fig. 6. Characterizing indefinite constructions: paraphrasing through transformational analysis

7   Preliminary Results

Port4NooJ dictionary formalizes 40,336 lemmas that recognize 1,006,424 word forms. There are 13,051 entries formalizing adjectives that correspond to 6,115 different adjectives.

The new standalone dictionary of human intransitive adjectives integrated in Port4NooJ includes 5,177 entries, that correspond to 4,138 different adjectives. Table 2 shows, for each lexicon-grammar table, how many adjectives existed already in Port4NooJ, and how many were added. Only 26 % of the adjectives for-

Table 2. Statistics on the merge between human intransitive adjectives and Port4NooJ adjectives

Table	In Port4NooJ	New	% In
EAHP2	18	86	17 %
EAHP3	54	212	20 %
SAF	70	233	23 %
SAHC1	115	228	34 %
SAHC2	41	176	19 %
SAHC3	54	464	10 %
SAHP1	303	246	55 %
SAHP2	142	225	39 %
SAHP3	97	262	27 %
SAN	108	543	17 %
SEAD	39	148	21 %
SEAHC2	14	40	26 %
SEAHC3	15	52	22 %
SEAHP2	53	86	38 %
SEAHP3	32	92	27 %
Total	1155	3093	26 %

malized in the lexicon-grammar tables were in Port4NooJ already[10]. This means that the number of different adjectives in Port4Nooj increased about 50 %.

A few grammars were constructed that explore the information in the new dictionary to extend eSPERTo paraphrase knowledge. We started by developing grammars to recognize and paraphrase (i) constructions involving patronymic adjectives, (ii) characterizing indefinite constructions, (iii) the possibility of alternating Vcop *ser* and *estar* with other aspectual variants, and (iv) cross constructions.

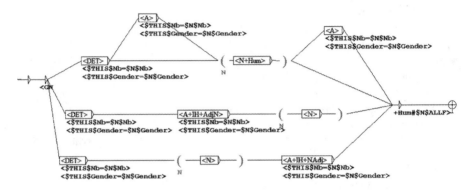

Fig. 7. Using properties of the human intransitive adjectives in noun phrase grammars

The information in the new dictionary of human intransitive adjectives was also used to improve the recognition of human noun phrases (see Fig. 7).

8   Conclusions and Future Work

We successfully integrated 15 lexicon-grammar tables describing the distributional properties of human intransitive adjectives into Port4NooJ by creating a standalone dictionary of human intransitive adjectives and by creating grammars that use information provided by the new dictionary to describe equivalent constructions involving those adjectives. In this way, we extended eSPERTo paraphrasing capabilities.

In the near future, we intend to: (i) create additional grammars to recognize the remaining constructions formalized in lexicon-grammar tables of human intransitive adjectives; (ii) revise and evaluate the new resources; (iii) integrate

---

[10] The difference between the number of different adjectives (4,138) and the number of adjectives in the lexicon-grammar tables (4,248) is due to a few adjectives belonging to more than one table as they have different meanings and distributional properties. One such adjective is *tonto*, which means either *dizzy* or *foolish/silly*. In the first case, *tonto* only occurs with Vcop *estar* as formalized in SEAD table of disease adjectives: *ele está tonto* (*he is dizzy*), whereas, in the second case, *tonto* only occurs with Vcop *ser* as formalized in table SAHC1: *ele é tonto* (*he is foolish/silly*).

and adapt additional lexicon-grammar tables, such as the ones formalizing constructions with Vsup *ser de* (Baptista 2000) and Vsup *fazer* (Chacoto 2005).

We will also use the Port4NooJ paraphrase knowledge to annotate a corpus with paraphrases. This corpus will be used to develop, train and test the eSPERTo's hybrid paraphrase acquisition engine. In turn, the new paraphrases will be merged with the existing paraphrases in Port4NooJ.

Acknowledgements. This research was supported by Fundação para a Ciência e Tecnologia (FCT), under exploratory project eSPERTo (Ref. EXPL/MHC-LIN/2260/2013). Anabela Barreiro was also funded by FCT through post-doctoral grant SFRH/BPD/91446/2012. The authors would like to thank Max Silberztein for his prompt support and guidance with all matters related to NooJ.

References

Baptista, J.: Sintaxe dos Predicados Nominais construídos com o verbo suporte SER DE. Ph.D. thesis. Universidade do Algarve, Faro, Portugal (2000)

Baptista, J., Mamede, N., Markov, I.: Integrating a lexicon grammar of verbal idioms in a Portuguese NLP system. PARSEME General Meeting, Athens, 10–11 March 2014, Poster Session (2014)

Barreiro, A.: Port4NooJ: Portuguese linguistic module and bilingual resources for machine translation. In: Blanco, X., Silberztein, M. (eds.) Proceedings of the 2007 International NooJ Conference, pp. 19–47. Cambridge Scholars Publishing, Newcastle upon Tyne (2008)

Barreiro, A.: Make it Simple with Paraphrases: Automated Paraphrasing for Authoring Aids and Machine Translation. Ph.D. thesis. Porto, Portugal: Universidade do Porto (2009)

Barreiro, A.: Linguistic resources and applications for Portuguese processing and machine translation. In: Kuti, J., Silberztein, M., Váradi, T. (eds.) Applications of Finite-State Language Processing: Selected Papers from the NooJ 2008 International Conference, pp. 41–51. Cambridge Scholars Publishing, Newcastle upon Tyne (2010)

Barreiro, A.: SPIDER: a system for paraphrasing in document editing and revision — applicability in machine translation pre-editing. In: Gelbukh, A. (ed.) CICLing 2011, Part II. LNCS, vol. 6609, pp. 365–376. Springer, Heidelberg (2011). ISBN: 978-3-642-19436-8

Barreiro, A., et al.: OpenLogos rule-based machine translation: philosophy, model, resources and customization. Mach. Transl. **25**(2), 107–126 (2011)

Carvalho, P.: Análise e Representação de Construções Adjectivais para Processamento Automático de Texto. Adjectivos Intransitivos Humanos. Ph.D. thesis. Universidade de Lisboa (2007)

Chacoto, L.: O Verbo Fazer em Construções Nominais Predicativas. Ph.D. thesis. Universidade do Algarve (2005)

Machonis, P.: English phrasal verbs: from lexicon-grammar to natural language processing. South. J. Linguist. **34**(1), 21–48 (2010)

Mota, C., et al.: The Logos legacy in the eSPERTo paraphrasing system. In: Turing's Footsteps. Logos Contribution to Machine Translation and Natural Language Processing (2015, forthcoming)

Scott, B.(Bud): The Logos model: an historical perspective. Mach. Transl. **18**(1), 1–72 (2003). ISSN: 0922-6567

Silberztein, M.: La formalisation des langues: l'approche de NooJ. ISTE, Londres, p. 426 (2015)

Vietri, S.: The formalization of Italian lexicon-grammar tables in a NooJ pair dictionary/grammar. In: Kuti, J., Silberztein, M., Váradi, T. (eds.) Applications of Finite-State Language Processing: Selected Papers from the NooJ 2008 International Conference, pp. 138–147. Cambridge Scholars Publishing, Newcastle-upon-Tyne (2010)

Study and Resolution of Arabic Lexical Ambiguity Through Transduction on Text Automaton

Nadia Ghezaiel[1(✉)] and Kais Haddar[2]

[1] Higher Institute of Computer and Communication Technologies
of Hammam Sousse, Miracl Laboratory, Sousse, Tunisia
ghezaielnadia.ing@gmail.com
[2] Faculty of Sciences of Sfax, Miracl Laboratory,
University of Sfax, Sfax, Tunisia
kais.haddar@yahoo.fr

Abstract. Lexical analysis can be a way to remove ambiguities in the Arabic language. So, their resolution is an important task in several domains of Natural Language Processing (NLP). In this context, this paper is inscribed. Our proposed resolution method is based essentially on the use of transducers on text automata. Indeed, these transducers specify the lexical rules of the Arabic language allowing corpus disambiguation. In order to achieve our resolution method, different types of lexical ambiguities are identified and studied. Then, an appropriate set of rules is proposed. After that, we represent all specified rules in NooJ. In addition, we present experimentation with NooJ platform conducted through various linguistic resources to obtain disambiguated syntactic structures suitable for the analysis. The results obtained are ambitious and can be improved by adding other rules and heuristics.

Keywords: Lexical ambiguity · Text annotation structure · Arabic lexical rule · NooJ transducer

1 Introduction

The need for disambiguation appears in several steps of analysis and applications such as syntactic analysis, recognition of named entities and morphological analysis. The disambiguation can be performed on different levels: morphological, syntactic and lexical levels. Indeed, disambiguating an Arabic corpus can widely facilitate several parsing processes which reduce largely the parsing time for researchers. For a successful resolution, we need a rigorous study of the Arabic language to facilitate the identification of rules which can be formalized through different frameworks. There are many theoretical platforms allowing formalization, such as grammars and finite state machines. In fact, finite automata and particularly transducers are increasingly used in NLP. Thanks to transducers, several local linguistic phenomena (e.g., recognition of named entities, morphological analysis) are treated appropriately. Transduction on text automata is so useful; it can remove paths representing morpho-syntactic ambiguities. Also, to formalize lexical rules, we need to find adequate criteria to classify lexical

© Springer International Publishing Switzerland 2016
T. Okrut et al. (Eds.): NooJ 2015, CCIS 607, pp. 123–133, 2016.
DOI: 10.1007/978-3-319-42471-2_11

rules in a specific order of application of rules and to define sufficient granularity levels of lexical categories allowing the identification of efficient rules. By these classifications, we aim to guarantee the optimization between rules, and to identify the disambiguation methods that can be exploitable by other steps of analysis.

In this context, our objectives are to study Arabic lexical ambiguities and to implement a lexical disambiguation tool for the Arabic language with NooJ platform through the transduction on text automaton. To do that, we need to identify and classify specific lexical rules for the Arabic language. Then, we implement these rules in NooJ platform and after that we call NooJ syntactic grammars in an adequate order to remove ambiguities existing in Text Annotation Structures (TAS).

In this paper, we begin by a state of the art presenting previous research interested in the resolution of ambiguities for the Arabic language. Next, we perform a study about lexical ambiguities. To resolve those lexical ambiguities, we establish transducers representing lexical rules. Then, we specify and test all these rules in NooJ linguistic platform.

2   State of the Art

Many studies aim to resolve Arabic lexical ambiguities at different levels: lexical, morphological, syntactic and semantic levels using different formalisms. In [12], the authors proposed a method for lexical disambiguation based on the cooperation between the morphological analyzer and the syntactic analyzer. In fact, all possible interpretations produced by the morphological analyzer will be the input of the syntactic one which consists in the application of constraints that are defined with the grammar rules. All grammar rules were specified in the Unification Based Grammar (UBG) formalism.

In [1], the author has developed a morphological syntactic analyzer for the Arabic language within LFG (Lexical Functional Grammar) formalism. The developed parser is based also on a cascade of finite state transducers for the sentence preprocessing and a set of syntactic rules specified in XLE (Xerox Linguistics Environment) for morphological analysis.

In [3], the proposed disambiguation method dealt with the 'alif-nûn' sequence in a given sentence. This method is based on the context-sensitive linguistic analysis to select the correct sense for a word in a given sentence without resorting to deep morpho-syntactic analysis.

Besides, in the last decades, we have witnessed a great increase in the number of systems which aim to disambiguate Modern Standard Arabic. Among those systems we mention MADA and TOKAN systems [7]. They are two complementary systems for Arabic morphological analysis and disambiguation process. Their applications include high-accuracy part-of-speech tagging, diacritization, lemmatization, disambiguation, stemming and glossing.

In [4], the system AMIRA is a set of tools built as a successor to the ASVMTools developed at Stanford University. The toolkit includes a tokenizer, a part of speech tagger (POS) and a Base Phrase Chucker (BPC). The technology AMIRA is based on supervised learning with no explicit dependence on knowledge of deep morphology. This system treats partially the disambiguation process in Arabic.

Concerning the finite state tools, we find the linguistic environment Xerox [2] which is based on finite state technology tools (e.g. xfst, twolc, lexc,) for NLP. These tools are used in several linguistic applications such as morphological analysis, tokenization, and shallow parsing of a wide variety of natural languages. The finite state tools here are built on top of a software library that provides algorithms to create automata from regular expressions and equivalent formalisms and contains both classical operations, such as union and composition, and new algorithms such as replacement and local sequentialization.

Moreover, there are several works in NooJ platform that address the disambiguation process in Arabic. We cite the work presented in [6]. This work presents an approach of recognition and translation based on a representation model of Arabic Named Entities and a set of transducers resolving morphological and syntactic phenomena. We can also cite the work [13]. This work is based on HPSG formalism to identify all possible syntactic representations of the Arabic relative sentences. The authors explain the different forms of relative clauses and the interaction of relatives with other linguistic phenomena such as ellipsis and coordination. Besides, there are many works specialized in a particular phenomenon without taking into account other phenomena. We can cite the work described in [5] to analyze the Arabic broken plural. This work is based on a set of morphological grammars used for the detection of the broken plural in Arabic texts. In fact, those transducers are the basis for a tool generated by the linguistic platform.

As we can see, the Arabic disambiguation process is not yet performed because of some difficulties linked to the Arabic natural structure. Also, difficulties are linked to the lack of a perfect disambiguation tool for rule formalization. Moreover, previous NooJ works are limited to just one level or one linguistic phenomenon that reduces the rate of perfect disambiguation and decreases the reuse of some applications on account of their incompatibility and the absence of consistency between works and applications.

3   Arabic Lexical Ambiguity

In the following, we focus especially on three ambiguity generating areas in Arabic, which have the greatest impact in our work.

3.1   Unvocalization

Unvocalization can cause lexical ambiguities. Sentences of example (1) illustrate more this phenomenon.

(1) ذهب أحمد إلى المنزل كي يأخذ ذهب أمه إلى التاجر

Ahmad went to the house to take his mother's gold to the merchant

In example (1), the word ذهب can refer to the noun the gold in English, or the verb to go. Also, the word كتب can belong to several grammatical categories: verb or noun.

The meaning of this word will be very different depending on its class: if it is a plural noun, كتب means books, and if it is a verb, كتب means writing. Also, the word درب can refer to the name of a type of yellow fish or an existing road in the mountains or a verb to lead.

3.2   The Emphasis Sign (Shadda ّ)

In Arabic, the emphasis sign Shadda is equivalent to writing the same letter twice. The first letter would have 'Skoon' (ْ) and the second letter would have 'Fatha' (َ), 'Dhamma' (ُ) or 'Kasra' (ِ). For example, the word فَضَّلَ is actually فَضْضَلَ but, instead of writing 'ض' twice, we replace it with one 'ض' with Shadda on it. The insertion of Shadda changes the meaning of the word. For example, there is confusion between word دَرَسَ and word دَرَّسَ, because they have different meanings. دَرَسَ darasa means 'he studied' while دَرَّسَ darrasa means 'he taught'. Note that Shadda can be in the middle or at the end of the word.

The presence of Shaddah in the middle of the word can reduce some ambiguities linked to unvocalization. In fact, trough Shaddah we can identify the grammatical category of the word and easily attribute the right category. As an example, the word "قبل" is doubly ambiguous (Noun or verb) but, after the insertion of Shaddah at the middle of the word, the ambiguity decreases to one category (verb "قَبّل").

3.3   Hamza

Hamza (همزة, hamzah) (ء) is a letter in the Arabic alphabet. It is not one of the 28 "full" letters, and the existence of this letter is due to historical inconsistencies in the standard writing system. Hamza is always written with its supports. They are three in number: the Alif ا Waw و and Nabira ئ. The Hamza is written in different ways depending on its place in the word: at the begging, the middle or the end of the word.

The presence of Hamzas in all their types reduces the number of ambiguities and reduces the lexical category of the word. As an example, the word "اذن" can be doubly ambiguous (verb and noun) but, if we add the Hamza to this word, we decrease the number of ambiguities to just one lexical category.

3.4   Agglutination

In the Arabic language, particles, prepositions and pronouns can be attached to the adjectives, nouns, verbs and particles to which they relate. Compared to French, an Arabic word can sometimes match an English phrase. This characteristic generates a lexical ambiguity during the analysis. Indeed, it is not always easy to distinguish a proclitic or enclitic of an original character of the word. For example, the character "ف" in the word "فصل" (season) is an original character while in the word "فصل" (then he prayed), it is rather a proclitic.

3.5 Compound Words

Another common type of lexical ambiguity involves compound words in which we find two types of ambiguity. The first is linked to the meaning of words as shown in (2) and (3), respectively, and the second is linked to adjunction between words and interpretation of reading as shown in (4), (5) respectively.

(2) جلس الولد أمام الشّاشة الصّغيرة

The boy sat in front of television

(3) إنّ الشّاشة الصّغيرة في الحواسيب المحمولة ذات جودة عالية

Laptops have small screens with a high quality

In (2), "الشّاشة الصّغيرة" is a compound noun and, as such, a minimal unit for linguistic processing; therefore, the tag for الشّاشة الصّغيرة will have to contain relevant syntactic information, e.g. the form and type of complements of this unit. In (3), الشّاشة and الصّغيرة are distinct units that make up a free noun phrase.

(4) استعمل الحاسوب المحمول في العربة

I use a laptop in the vehicle

(5) استعمل الحاسوب المحمول في العربة

I use the computer which is portable in the vehicle

In examples (4) and (5), the compound word is related to the flexibility of reading and the comprehension of the sentence. In fact, we find in sentence (4) a strict reading in which the compound noun is "الحاسوب المحمول" (laptop) although in sentence (5) we find a flexible reading by taking the compound noun "المحمول في العربة" (which is portable in the vehicle).

4 Identification of Lexical Rules and Constraints

We carried out a linguistic study which allows us to identify 30 lexical rules resolving several forms of ambiguities. The identified rules were classified trough the mechanism of sub-categorization for verbs, nouns and particles.

4.1 Rules for Particles

Particles can be subdivided into three categories: particles acting on nouns, particles acting on verbs and particles acting on both nouns and verbs.

4.1.1 Particles Acting on Nouns

There are Arabic particles which must be followed by a noun like prepositions, particles of call, and particles of restriction. As an example, if we find prepositions like {مِنْ، إلى، عنْ، على، في، بِ، كَ، لِ، حتّى، رُبَّ، واو القسم، تِ، حاشا، خلا،عدا}, then, they should be followed by a noun.

4.1.2   Particles Acting on Verbs

Particles can also be followed by a verb like subjunctive particles, apocopate particles, prohibition particles. As an example, if we find a subjunctive particle like {لن/ كي/ حتى/ لام التعليل/ إذن/ فاء السببية/ وأو المعية/ لام الجحود أن/ }, then, it should be followed by a verb.

4.1.3   Particles Acting on Both Nouns and Verbs

There are some particles that can be followed by a noun or a verb like particles of coordination or particles of explanation. To solve this ambiguity, we studied the context of the sentence, as an example of rules: if we find the particle of explanation "أن" then, it should be followed and preceded by a verb. Also, if we find a succession of two verbs, they should be separated by a particle like in the sentence "صلّى ثمّ نام" (he prayed then slept). The verb "صلى" (prayed) is succeeded by the particle "ثمّ" (then) then the verb "نام" (sleep). So, to solve an ambiguity linked to unvocalization, we can use the right and left context.

4.2   Rules for Verbs

We can apply the principle of sub-categorization to resolve the ambiguity linked to verbs. We are based essentially on the transitivity feature of verbs. In Arabic, a verb can be intransitive, transitive, double transitive and triple transitive. Either transitive or intransitive verbs can be transformed to transitive verbs with prepositions. Sentences of examples (6), (7) and (8) illustrate the Arabic transitivity mechanism.

(6) أكلت أختي وجبة لذيذة بسرعة (في مطبخنا) قبل ساعة

My sister ate a delicious meal quickly (in our kitchen) an hour ago

In example (6), the verb is "أكلت" (she ate) which is a transitive verb followed by a subject (noun) "أختي" (my sister), then an object (noun) "وجبة" (meal), and the remaining parts must be introduced through a particle like "في" which is a particle of preposition followed by a noun "مطبخنا" (our kitchen). Sentence (6) is composed of the verb (أكلت), the nominal phrase (أختي) (my sister), the nominal phrase (وجبة لذيذة), the prepositional phrase (بسرعة), the prepositional phrase (في مطبخنا), and the prepositional phrase (قبل ساعة).

(7) جلس أخي وحيدا في غرفته طوال اليوم

My brother sat alone in his room all day

In example (7), the verb "جلس" (he sat) is intransitive followed by a subject أخي (noun) (my brother), by an adverb (وحيدا) (alone) and two prepositional phrases. So, the sentence (7) is composed of the verb (جلس) (he sat), the nominal phrase (أخي) (my brother), by the adverb (وحيدا) (alone), by the prepositional phrase (في غرفته) (in his room) and by the prepositional phrase (طوال اليوم) (all day).

(8) خرج أخي من المكتبة منذ ساعتين

My brother came out from the library two hours ago

In example (8), the verb "خرج" (came out) is intransitive followed by a subject أخي (noun) (my brother), and two prepositional phrases. So, the sentence (8) is composed of the verb (خرج) (came out), the nominal phrase (أخي) (my brother), by the prepositional phrase (من المكتبة) (from the library) and by the prepositional phrase (منذ ساعتين) (two hours ago).

The mechanism of transitivity that is illustrated by the above sentences is summarized in the following table. Note that these examples respect the VSO order (Table 1).

Table 1. Transitivity summary table

Verb valency	Followed structures
Intransitive	NP (adverb) (PP)*
Transitive	NP NP (adverb) (PP)*
Double transitive	NP NP NP (adverb) (PP)*
Triple transitive	NP NP NP NP (adverb) (PP)*

4.3   Rules for Nouns

Concerning the sub-categorization of nouns, we are based on the contextual and lexical indices. In fact, the most reliable indicators for the detection and categorization are the right and the left contexts of a word. These indices are either internal or external contexts.

The internal indices are located inside the named entity. These are words that easily identify named entities. Example (9) illustrates the internal index.

(9) البنك العربي التّونسي

Arab Tunisian Bank

The word (البنك) (the bank) is an example of internal index.

The external index or right context refers to the context of an entity's occurrence in a sentence. In a speech, especially journalism, the author provides readers with additional information like people, places and organizations. This information can help to determine the type of an entity in an automatic process.

(10) مهدي جمعة الوزير الاول

Mehdi Jomaa, the Premier

The word (الوزير الأول) (the Premier) mentioned in example (10) shows an external index.

5   Proposed Approach

Now the formalization of extracted rules is finished and it is possible to apply our method of disambiguation. Our proposed approach consists of two main phases, the preprocessing phase and the application of the disambiguation process. The first phase consists in the segmentation, the agglutination of our corpus through morphological grammars and the annotation of the corpus through dictionaries. As an output of this phase, we get a TAS1 containing all possible annotations for the corpus. This TAS1 will be the input of the second phase. It contains all possible interpretations for an existing word in dictionaries. Note that the text annotation Structure of NooJ (TAS) is a representation type of text automaton.

The application of the disambiguation process consists in the suppression of wrong paths existing on the TAS1. This modification of TAS1 is the result of syntactic analyses which consist of the application of transducers representing lexical and contextual rules. These rules should respect a certain priority in their application from the most evident and intuitive rules until arriving at the least one (Fig. 1). The output of the disambiguation process will be a new TAS disambiguated containing the right paths and the right annotations.

The granularity is related to the existing lexical information in electronic dictionaries which may be more or less detailed, according to its nature and extension. The information in tags can be extended to 15 elements which make the information more detailed. This information has an important imprint in the disambiguation process. In fact, each level of lexical information can reduce the rate of ambiguous outputs. So, if the lexical information is detailed, the rate of granularity increases and the rate of ambiguous outputs decrease.

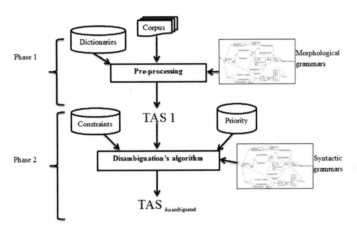

Fig. 1. Proposed approach

6   Implementation

The extracted rules have been formalized in the NooJ platform [11]. The process of disambiguation of text automaton is based on the set of the developed NooJ transducers. This set contains 17 grammars representing lexical and contextual rules. Figures 2 and 3 illustrate the implementation in NooJ of two lexical rules for Arabic particles.

Fig. 2. Exception particle rules

The represented transducer of Fig. 2 indicates that if we recognize one of the specified exception particles, it must be followed by a noun phrase. The second transducer of Fig. 3 indicates that if we recognize one of the particles acting on verbs, then it must be followed by a verb.

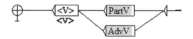

Fig. 3. Rule for particle acting on verbs

As we know, the Arabic sentence can be either verbal or nominal. So, we construct transducers to recognize these two specific forms. For a nominal sentence, it is generally formed by a topic and an attribute. Figure 4 indicates a transducer for recognition of a nominal sentence.

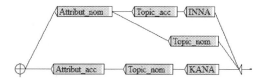

Fig. 4. Transducer representing a lexical rule for a nominal sentence

Figure 4 represents a transducer recognizing the nominal sentence; we distinguish different forms of topics and attributes. A nominal sentence can be formed by a nominative topic followed by a nominative attribute. Also, we can find the modal verb "KANA" followed by a nominative topic and an accusative attribute.

7 Experimentation and Evaluation

To experiment with our proposed method, we used a test corpus that contained 20000 meaningful sentences mainly from Tunisian newspapers and children's stories. Also, we used dictionaries containing 24732 nouns, 10375 verbs and 1234 particles. Besides, we used in our experimentation a list of morphological grammars containing 113 inflected verb form patterns, 10 broken plural patterns and 3 agglutination grammars. So, we used 17 graphs representing lexical rules, and a set of 10 constraints describing the execution of rules application. The obtained result is illustrated in Table 2.

Table 2 shows that 12000 sentences from the 20000 sentences existing in the corpus were totally disambiguated, which represents 60 %. Also, there are 6000 sentences partially disambiguated, which represents 30 %, and only 2000 sentences erroneously disambiguated, which represents 10 %. The partial disambiguation is due

Table 2. Table summarizing the obtained result

Corpus	Number	Percentage
Sentences	20000	100 %
Totally disambiguated	12000	60 %
Partial disambiguated	6000	30 %
Failed disambiguation	2000	10 %

to the lack of semantic rules. Also, sometimes, some rules were not correctly recognized. The erroneous disambiguation is linked to the lack of some information in our dictionaries which led to the wrong detection of left or right contexts.

During the disambiguation process, we got partially disambiguated sentences. This type of disambiguation is linked to different problems. These problems are due to the limited coverage of dictionaries as they did not contain all possible Arabic words. So, the produced TAS1 would be missing as well as the disambiguation process. Also, the lack of rules can be a source for partial disambiguating of sentences. In fact, the specificities of Arabic syntax may be the source of some additional processing difficulties. Besides, we need to elaborate other rules at different levels. There is another reason for the partial disambiguation which is linked to the granularity of lexical categories. Our evaluation is performed by the precision and recall measures (Table 3).

Table 3. Table summarizing the values of measures

Corpus	Precision	Recall	F-mesure
20000	0,6	0,9	0,72

In conclusion, the obtained results are ambitious and can be improved by adding other rules and heuristics. Thus, the creation of a tool allowing the transducer cascade generation that can be applied on the text automata is very useful. Such a tool can improve the obtained results.

8   Conclusion and Future Works

In this paper, we conducted a study on the different types of Arabic lexical ambiguities. This study allowed us to establish a set of lexical rules and constraints for lexical disambiguation. Established rules are specified with NooJ transducers. This disambiguation process will help us to reduce later parsing. Thus, an experiment is performed and satisfactory results are obtained. Also, we have shown the need to use the cascades on the text automata to simplify the ambiguity resolution process and make it more effective.

To perfectly annotate corpora, we need to enrich our resources by creating new dictionaries and new grammars representing the maximum of lexical rules. We need also to enrich our set of rules by adding new syntactic, morphological and semantic levels and extend this methodology to other phenomena (i.e., coordination). As perspectives, we hope to continue our study of lexical disambiguation by writing new local grammars and also implementing a management module to build an automatic annotation tool for corpora. This module can be integrated later in the NooJ linguistic platform.

References

1. Attia, M.: Handlinh Arabic morphological and syntactic ambiguity within the LFG framework with a view to machine translation. Ph.D. thesis in the University of Manchester (2008)
2. Beesley, K.: Finite-state morphological analysis and generation of arabic at xerox research: status and plans. In: ACL/EACL, Toulouse, France, 6 July 2001
3. Dichy, J., Alrahabi, M.: Levée d'ambiguité par la methode d'exploration contextuelle: la sequence 'alif-nûn' en arabic. In: SIIE, Hammamet, Tunisia (2009)
4. Diab, M.: Second generation tools (AMIRA 2.0): fast and robust tokenization, POS tagging, and base phrase chunking. In: MEDAR 2nd International Conference on Arabic Language Resources and Tools, April, Cairo, Egypt (2009)
5. Ellouze, S., Haddar, K., Abdelhamid, A.: Etude et analyse du pluriel brisé arabe avec la plateforme NooJ. In: NooJ Conference and Workshop. Tozeur, Tunisia (2009)
6. Fehri, H., Haddar, K., Abdelhamid, A.: Recognition and translation of Arabic named entities with NooJ using a new representation model. In: FSMNLP, pp. 134–142 (2011)
7. Habash, N., Rambow, O., Roth, R.: MADA + TOKAN: a toolkit for Arabic tokenization, diacritization, morphological disambiguation, POS tagging, stemming ald lemmatization. In: Proceedings of the 2nd International Conference on Arabic Language Resources and Tools (MEDAR), Cairo, Egypt (2009)
8. Othman, E., Shaalan, K., Rafea, A.: Towards resolving ambiguity in understanding Arabic sentence. In: International Conference on Arabic Language Resources and Tools (2006)
9. Mesfar, S.: Morphological grammars for standard Arabic tokenization. In: Proceedings of the International NooJ Conference, pp. 114–127. Cambridge Scholars Publishing, Newcastle (2010)
10. Mesfar, S.: Analyse morpho-syntaxique automatique et reconnaissance des entités nommées en arabe strandard. Ph.D. thesis in the University of Franche Comté, 235 (2008)
11. Silberztein, M.: Disambiguation tools for NooJ. In: Proceedings of the 2008 International NooJ Conference, pp. 158–171. Cambridge Scholars Publishing, Newcastle (2010)
12. Shaalan, K., Othman, E., Rafea, A.: Towards resolving ambiguity in understanding Arabic sentence. In: The Proceedings of the International Conference on Arabic Language Resources and Tools, NEMLAR, Cairo, Egypt, 22–23 September 2004, pp. 118–122 (2004)
13. Zalila, I, Haddar, K.: Construction of an HPSG grammar for the Arabic relative sentences. In: The Proceedings of RANLP, Hissar, Bulgaria (2011)

Application

Grapheme-to-Phoneme and Phoneme-to-Grapheme Conversion in Belarusian with NooJ for TTS and STT Systems

Vadim Zahariev[1]([✉]), Stanislau Lysy[2], Alena Hiuntar[2], and Yury Hetsevich[2]

[1] The Belarusian State University of Informatics and Radioelectronics, Minsk, Belarus
zahariev@bsuir.by
[2] The United Institute of Informatics Problems of National Academy of Sciences of Belarus, Minsk, Belarus
stanislau.lysy@gmail.com, lena205593@gmail.com, yury.hetsevich@gmail.com

Abstract. To process texts in any language, a full and thorough description of the given language is required. The authors of this article have noted that, while much has been done in the development of language processing with NooJ, so far little attention has been paid to issues related to phonetic language features.

Keywords: Text-to-speech · Speech-to-text · Grapheme-to-phoneme conversion · Phoneme-to-grapheme conversion · The Belarusian language · Phonetics · Transcription

1 Introduction

Natural language processing (NLP) is a field of computer science closely related to linguistics, and plays a significant role in advancing communication between human and computer. It is needed to transform relevant information locked in text into structured data that can be used by computer processes aimed at improving various aspects of life.

There are two main problems in the transition step between morphological and phonetic levels of texts. The first one is a transformation of orthographic text into its phonetic representation for further processing in the phonetic encoding/decoding step. The task of this transformation is very common in text-to-speech (TTS) systems (Fig. 1, solid lines). The second one is an inverse problem: the building of written orthographic text from transcribed spoken language. This issue is an important aspect within the framework of speech-to-text (STT) systems (Fig. 1, dashed lines). In both cases of grapheme-to-phoneme (G2P) and phoneme-to-grapheme (P2G) conversion, it is difficult to develop separate statistical models for all phonemes and words in TTS and STT systems with a rather large vocabulary. This is especially true for relatively localized languages, like Belarusian, when it is hard to collect a great amount of speech data for statistical models in training procedures.

© Springer International Publishing Switzerland 2016
T. Okrut et al. (Eds.): NooJ 2015, CCIS 607, pp. 137–150, 2016.
DOI: 10.1007/978-3-319-42471-2_12

We consider NooJ [1] to be an effective tool in solving these problems, as it can be used for creating dictionaries of correspondences between orthographic words and their phonetic transcriptions, as well as for development of rule-based grammars for G2P and P2G conversions.

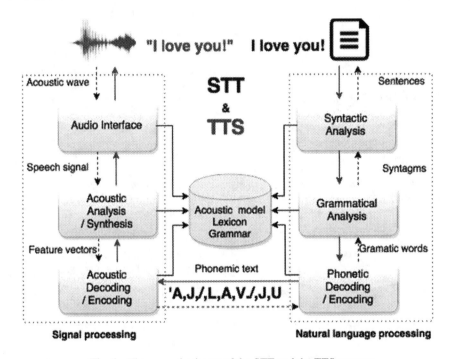

Fig. 1. The general scheme of the STT and the TTS systems

2 Specific Features of Belarusian in the Context of G2P and P2G Conversion

For both G2P and P2G conversion processes, a fundamental aspect is the choice of approach to the problem. There are two common approaches to the problem of G2P and P2G conversions: the first is related to statistical methods and uses phonetically transcribed corpuses or pronunciation dictionaries; the second is a rule-based method. The choice of approach greatly depends on the type of orthography of the processed language. An orthography in which the correspondences between spelling and pronunciation are highly complex or inconsistent is called a deep orthography. In such a case, statistical methods, or special databases, are used. Another type of orthography is called shallow orthography, and it is determined by relatively simple and consistent correspondences between spelling and pronunciation. In this case, the rule-based methods are more preferable.

Regarding the Belarusian language, we should take into account the fact that its orthography is based on a simple phonemic principle—words are pronounced as they are spelled. This is particularly true for Belarusian Classical Orthography, or *Tараš-kievica,* where the written and the phonetic forms are almost identical. In modern Belarusian, this is not so evident, but it is true to a greater degree than, for instance, in Russian. In Table 1, a short comparison of correspondences between some orthographic words and their transcriptions for Belarusian and Russian is presented [2].

Table 1. A comparison of correspondences between orthographic words and their phonetic transcriptions in Belarusian and Russian

English word	Belarusian/ Russian	Orthographic word	Cyrillic transcription	IPA transcription
River	Belarusian	рэчка	[рэ́чка]	['rɛʧka]
	Russian	речка	[p'эч'ка]	['rɛʧʲka]
Sun	Belarusian	сонца	[со́нца]	['sɔntsa]
	Russian	солнце	[со́нцэ]	['sɔntsɛ]
Laugh	Belarusian	смяяцца	[c'м'айа́цца]	[sʲmʲa'jatstsa]
	Russian	смеяться	[cм'ийа́цца]	[smʲi'jatstsa]

Due to the relative proximity of phonetic forms and spelling of the words in the Belarusian language, the G2P and the P2G conversion algorithms based on the rules are more preferable. Nevertheless, there are a number of Belarusian language features that create difficulties in performing these two kinds of transformations. Let us take a brief look at some examples.

The Belarusian language has ten letters representing vowel sounds. They can be divided into two categories: non-iotified (*a, o, y, э, i, ы*) and iotified (*я, ё, ю, е*) vowels. Letters in the second sequence represent four sounds of the first sequence, but with an initial [j] sound. When a consonant precedes an iotified vowel, it becomes palatized. Taking into account this fact, we have to define a rule that makes a consonant preceding an iotified vowel palatized for the G2P conversion, and in P2G conversion a rule that converts a non-iotified vowel into an iotified analogue after palatized consonant is needed.

The correspondences between orthography and phonetics in Belarusian also depend on accent position. For instance, vowel *ё* is almost always stressed, and when unstressed, *ё* changes to *e* or *я* depending on the accent position, and this is not always transmitted in writing [3].

It is also necessary to mention some of the most common sound changes in Belarusian: assimilation, dissimilation, and accommodation. These features are significant both for G2P and P2G conversations. For example, in the word *стужка* (Eng. 'ribbon'), the letter *ж* that usually designates the sound [z̪] changes into the sound [ş] as a result of assimilation.

The great value in the P2G conversion plays phenomenon of interaction between sounds existing in the flow of speech, and influence of sounds on each other, causing specific phonetic changes. The Belarusian language is characterized by changing of phonemes under the influence of neighboring elements (combinational), as well as changes resulting from the ratio of phonemes to verbal blows and their absolute location relative to the beginning or the end of the word (positional) [4].

Also almost every rule of Belarusian have its own set of exceptions. Most of them are connected with loanword. This fact should be taken in account while developing algorithms of grapheme-to-phoneme and phoneme-to-grapheme conversion.

3   Grapheme-to-Phoneme Conversion for the Belarusian NooJ Module

Grapheme-to-phoneme (G2P) conversion, or phonetization, is a process of defining the sequence of phonemes required to pronounce a word, phrase, or even a text. The G2P algorithms are used to generate the most probable phoneme list for a word not contained in the pronunciation dictionary. These algorithms are widely used in automated text-to-speech systems.

We developed two ways of obtaining phonetic transcriptions for each word in a Belarusian text. The first way involves creating a Belarusian dictionary in NooJ format, containing information on the pronunciation for each word. The second way involves developing morphological NooJ grammars for generating phonetic transcriptions for orthographic words. As such, we obtain two kinds of phonetic level representation, thus allowing us to perform G2P conversion.

To create the dictionary, a software tool which allows to quickly convert both single words and whole texts into phonetic transcription was developed. This tool is called "Transcription Generator" and is now available as web-service at [5].

The transcription generation system converts a Belarusian text into its phonetic transcription. It takes as an input any orthographic text in Belarusian, with labels of main and side accents. The character '+' (plus sign) after a vowel can be used to mark the main accent and the character '=' (equals sign) – to mark the side accent. As well as these characters, standard accent characters can be used. The system currently supports four types of transcription:

- Cyrillic transcription (based on [6]);
- transcription based on the work by U.A. Koshchanka [7];
- International Phonetic Alphabet (or IPA) [8];
- Extended Speech Assessment Methods Phonetic Alphabet (or X–SAMPA) [9].

The "Transcription Generator" algorithm was developed on the base of the multi-voice TTS system for the Belarusian and Russian languages [10]. The phonetic processor of this system uses two sets of rules. These rules represent almost a full set of grapheme-to-phoneme transformations for Belarusian. The first set of rules is a set of general rules that shows direct correlations between the letter and the phoneme, and the second set shows more complex rules, or exceptions to general rules, depending on letter context. An excerpt of these rules list is given in the Table 2.

Algorithms of transcription generation system convert orthographic texts into the phonemic form developed for the Belarusian TTS system. This phonemic notation could be converted into any common transcription notation. To do this, we created a base of "phoneme – transcription" correlations. An excerpt of this base is presented in Table 3.

Table 2. An excerpt of the list of general rules and their exceptions

General rules	Exceptions to general rules
А-А	(З)[ДГ]V-S
Б-В	(З)ДЖ-ZH
В-V	(З)[КПСТФХЦЧШ]-S
Г-GH	(З)[ЬЪ_V][КПСТФШ]-S
Д-D	(С)[БГДЗЖ]-Z
Е-E	(С)[ЬЪ_V][БВГДЗЖ]-Z
Ё-O	(Ж)[КПСТФХЦЧШ]-SH
…	…

Table 3. An excerpt of list of "phoneme – transcription" correspondences

TTS	Cyrillic	Latin	IPA	X-SAMPA
V0	в	v	v	v
V1	в:	v:	vv	vv
V'1	в':	v':	v^jv^j	v'v'
V'0	в'	v'	v^j	v'
GH0	γ	ɣ	ɣ	G
GH1	γ:	ɣ:	ɣɣ	GG
GH'1	γ':	ɣ':	$ɣ^jɣ^j$	G'G'
GH'0	γ'	ɣ'	$ɣ^j$	G'
G0	г	g	g	g
G'0	г'	g'	g^j	g'
…	…	…	…	…

With the help of the transcription generation system, a phonetic dictionary of arbitrary format can be generated, including a format supported by NooJ. To create a NooJ dictionary with phonetic transcriptions, the following format was developed:

word, PART–OF–SPEECH
+TranscriptionCyr = [*transcription*]
+TranscriptionLat = [*transcription*]
+TranscriptionIPA = [*transcription*]
+TranscriptionXSAMPA = [*transcription*].

For instance, the word **сакаляня** would have the following view:

сакаляня, NOUN
+TranscriptionCyr = [сакал'ан'á]
+TranscriptionLat = [sakal'an'á]
+TranscriptionIPA = [sakal^{j}a'n^{j}a]
+TranscriptionXSAMPA = [sakal'a"n'a].

To generate a dictionary in NooJ format for all Belarusian words, a special algorithm was developed and implemented. It takes as an input an orthographic dictionary of the

Belarusian language, allocates all dictionary entries, obtains the required information on every entry (word with accent, part-of-speech), uses the transcription generation system to produce phonetic transcriptions of every word in four forms, and compiles all this information into NooJ dictionary format. In the Fig. 2 a NooJ dictionary excerpt is presented.

Entry	Category	TranscriptionCyr	TranscriptionLat
сакол	NOUN	[сакол]	[sakól]
саколік	NOUN	[сакол'ік]	[sakól'ik]
саколка	NOUN	[саколка]	[sakólka]
сакол-каршачок	NOUN	[саколкаршачок]	[sakòlkarşat⌢şók]
сакольнік	NOUN	[сакол'н'ік]	[sakól'n'ik]
сакольнічы	NOUN	[сакол'н'ічы]	[sakól'n'it⌢şy]
сакраментальнасць	NOUN	[сакрам'энтал'нас'ц']	[sakram'entál'nas't⌢s']
сакратар	NOUN	[сакратар]	[sakratár]
сакратарка	NOUN	[сакратарка]	[sakratárka]
сакратарства	NOUN	[сакратарства]	[sakratárstva]
сакратарыят	NOUN	[сакратарыйат]	[sakrataryját]
сакрацін	NOUN	[сакрац'ін]	[sakrat⌢s'ín]
сакрэт	NOUN	[сакрэт]	[sakrét]
сакрэтка	NOUN	[сакрэтка]	[sakrétka]
сакрэтнасць	NOUN	[сакрэтнас'ц']	[sakrétnas't⌢s']
сакрэтнік	NOUN	[сакрэтн'ік]	[sakrétn'ik]
сакрэтнічанне	NOUN	[сакрэтн'ічан':э]	[sakrétn'it⌢şan':e]
сакрэцыя	NOUN	[сакрэцыйа]	[sakrét⌢syja]
сакс	NOUN	[сакс]	[sáks]

Fig. 2. An excerpt of the phonetic dictionary in the NooJ format

Since every dictionary is a finite set of words and their descriptions, for phonetization of words not contained in the dictionary, morphological NooJ grammars were developed. These grammars represent rules for the multivoice TTS system phonetic processor in the form of a finite automaton (Fig. 3).

In Belarusian, one letter may be represented by different phonemes, depending on their surrounding letters or position in the word. The most common sound changes in Belarusian are assimilation, elision and positional fortition. For instance, in the word дуб 'dub – Eng. oak', the last letter В changes into the sound [p] as a result of end-word fortition. These sound changes are presented in the grammar as follows: all the graphemes, which are surrounded by other particular graphemes, are given as an output allophone match, for instance, grapheme В from the example above will be marked by P as a corresponding allophone.

4   Phoneme-to-Grapheme Conversion for the Belarusian NooJ Module

Speech recognition systems are complex technical systems in which information passes through a large number of processing steps and transformations. A typical system consists of two main parts: signal processing and natural language processing. Most of the recent publications are focused on questions related to signal processing, including such techniques as dynamic time warping, hidden Markovs models and neural networks [11, 12].

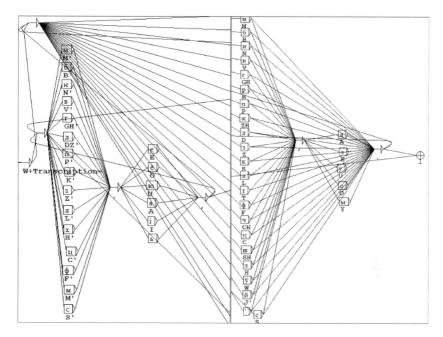

Fig. 3. An excerpt of the morphological NooJ grammar illustrating consonant softening (left) and hard consonants (right)

However, in the latest research, NLP is almost never mentioned. This observation is especially true for lesser known languages such as Belarusian. However, this part of the system contains many compelling challenges for researchers, which will provide ample opportunity for further research.

One of the basic tasks for developing the NLP part of a SST system is to transform phonetic elements into their graphemic representation (P2G). After acoustical decoding of separate phonetic units from feature vectors of a speech signal, phonemic text is obtained. This text is a source for the next language processing steps on morphological, syntactic and semantic levels. Therefore, effective implementation of phoneme-to-grapheme transformation is the first important task in the construction of the NLP part of a STT system. We would like to show how this problem could be effectively solved with the help of NooJ instruments for the Belarusian language.

During the process of conversion P2G, all of the abovementioned language phenomena should be taken into account. Considering the peculiarities of the Belarusian language we made the following assumption: it is possible to build a compact system of rules, which would constitute the core of the conversion algorithm according to these rules, then extend it according to accounting-specific conversion rules and a dictionary for words not included in the basic set, as well as phonetic contexts.

Therefore, the above situations require further description of certain rules. We propose to use NooJ to develop grammars because they are extremely simple objects to build, and there is no complex formalism to learn. NooJ includes tools to check, debug, adapt, maintain, and share language resources. NooJ can effectively solve the problem with the development of rules (linguists' responsibility) and then by conversion into a useful form for further formalization in terms of algorithm and implementation in the code (programmers' responsibility). This is especially important for non-engineering staff (linguists, phoneticians), as NooJ provides a user-friendly graphical interface which is easy to learn and use, in contrast, for example, with a regular-expression language.

We offer a solution to the problem of converting P2G using NooJ in two stages. The first stage is based on the rules for conversion using a NooJ grammar. The grammar contains the set of rules for the phoneme-to-grapheme conversion of the following classes:

- Rules for the base cases of phoneme-to-grapheme mapping. They use the principle of a return to the basic rule based on the phonetic spelling principle. These G2P rules can be relatively easily transformed into the rules designed to reverse conversion. For example:
  - $[\widehat{dz}]$ – дж;
  - $[\gamma]$ – г.
- The rules for considering cases of combinatorial changes (assimilation, accommodation, dissimilation sounds) the interaction between the phonemes of the language and their rules. For example:
  - $['s^jv^jata]$ – свята (holiday);
  - $[\widehat{dz}^j\varepsilon\widehat{ts}^ji]$ – дзеці (children).
- Rules take into account positional changes as well as the effects (diarezis, epintezis, konraktasis) and phenomena occurring at the junction of phonetic words. For example:
  - $['va'wla\widehat{dz}^j\varepsilon]$ – ва ўладзе (in power);
  - $[\gamma ara'tsk^ji]$ – гарадскі (city *adv.*).

The second stage of the conversion is carried out using a dictionary approach to define exception words and resolve conflicts on the morphological and syntactic levels. We should also use an exception lexicon and even go beyond words to consider the context. The exception lexicon contains the pronunciations for irregular words. If we find such a word in the exception lexicon, we get the correct spelling at once and the two previous steps can be skipped. One more and very important task involves homonyms (words that share the same pronunciation but have different meanings). Consider the following case:

- $[pra'\gamma ramni]$ $['k\!\!\jmath t]$ – праграмны код (programming code);
- $[pu'\!\!\;sisti]$ $['k\!\!\jmath t]$ – пушысты кот (fluffy cat).

In this example, the words **код** (*code*) and **кот** (*cat*) are phonetically identical. In this case, the G2P conversion of words is only possible by analyzing beyond the boundaries of the phonetic elements of speech. Namely, this can be done by semantic analysis of these fragments.

Currently, we are developing the first rule-based stage of the proposed approach. We assume that a real STT system P2G conversion process, executed by phonetic-decoding block (Fig. 1), will include the following basic steps (Fig. 4):

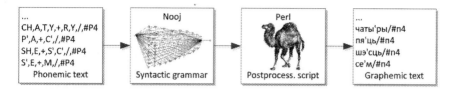

Fig. 4. Scheme of the phonetic decoding process in the context of STT

From the acoustic decoding block of STT, we obtain preliminary information in the form of an allophone sequence. Allophones are positional and combinatorial variants of phonemes and can also be used for P2G conversion. However, the sequence of allophones is not suitable for conversion into orthographic words directly, because of the large number of possible combinations. Thus, it is necessary to reduce the spatial dimension of this sequence. To do this instead of handling the direct allophonic sequence, we convert it into phonemic text. This problem can also be solved with the help of NooJ. However, implementation of this task is not within the scope of this publication, so the details are not presented here. This raw allophonic sequence from the acoustic decoding block is preprocessed to get a phonemic text. This text is converted into one of the text formats supported by NooJ and is then loaded into the system for the further processing.

Firstly, the algorithm detects phrases and sentences, replaces pauses, collapses sentences to phonetic words and finally generates the list of phonetic elements. Then the system processes each element in this list to get grammatical annotations using NooJ syntactic grammars. The main graph of one of the core grammars is presented in Fig. 5.

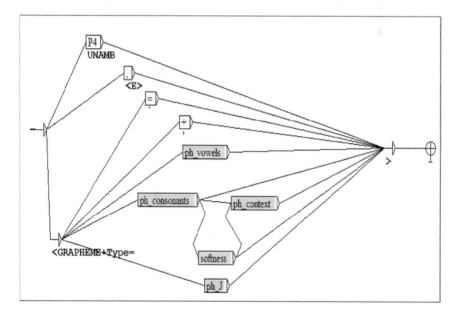

Fig. 5. Grammar of the upper level

One of the features of our work is that we used a grammar of a syntactic not a morphological level for the processing of phonetic units. This is due to the fact that the acoustic decoding block can generate the phonetic sequence in different formats (different types of separators, etc.). A syntactic level grammar allows us to consider phonemes as stand-alone words in a given environment and also allows for more flexibility. The grammar on the top level includes a set of sub-graphs for the left and right context for the given symbol and allows us to consider the cases described above, which can be executed recursively. One of the sub-graphs is presented in Fig. 6.

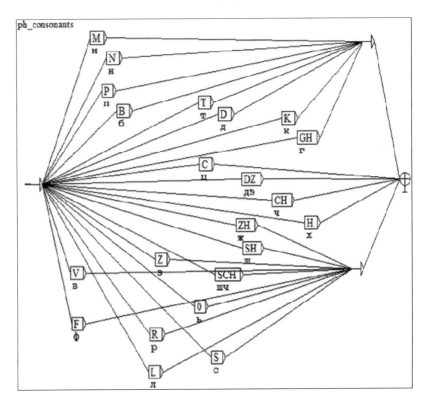

Fig. 6. One of the sub-graphs representing consonant conversion rules

The result of the conversion is exported to an XML file. Then it is processed with a special Perl script, which transforms NooJ annotations into general orthographic text, makes a plain text and saves it as an HTML file.

An example of grammatical annotation to be converted into graphemic form:

```
<GRAPHEME Type="л">L</GRAPHEME><GRAPHEME Type="">,</GRAPH
EME><GRAPHEME Type="i">I</GRAPHEME><GRAPHEME Type="">,</G
RAPHEME><GRAPHEME Type="'">+</GRAPHEME><GRAPHEME Type="">
,</GRAPHEME><GRAPHEME Type="к">K</GRAPHEME><GRAPHEME Type
="">,</GRAPHEME><GRAPHEME Type="i">I</GRAPHEME><GRAPHEME
Type="">,</GRAPHEME><GRAPHEME Type="">,</GRAPHEME><GRAPHE
ME Type="п">P</GRAPHEME><GRAPHEME Type="п">P</GRAPHEME>…
```

The suggested grammars are quite simple in form, but they allow us to quickly and easily perform the P2G conversion. Even if all the words are not fully recognized, this could be done later using a dictionary of exclusion words, which we plan to develop in the future.

5   Experimental Results

To determine the effectiveness of the linguistic resources developed for the Belarusian module of NooJ—one vocabulary and two grammars—a series of tests was performed. One test method involved the comparison of converted words with words from the reference source. If the resulting form did not coincide with the sample and had at least one error, it was marked as incorrect but converted. The errors committed by the algorithm were calculated for each test word separately and for the entire sample as a whole. In order to evaluate the effectiveness of the algorithms and the proposed grammars, we used the metrics of precision and recall described in [13]. *Precision* (P) is equal to the number of cases where conversion was correct (M) divided by the total number of phonetic cases retrieved by grammars (L). It can be determined according to the expression:

$$P = M/L.$$

Recall (R) is equal to the number of cases where conversion was correct (M) divided by the number of valid cases predetermined by expert assessment (N):

$$R = M/N.$$

It should be noted that these two quantities are trade off one against another. Recall is a non-decreasing function of the number of cases retrieved. On the other hand, in a good system, precision usually decreases as the number of cases retrieved is increased. In general, we want to get some amount of recall while tolerating only a certain percentage of false positives. To provide unbiased evaluation, it is desirable to use a certain metric that balances the previous two. *Weighted harmonic mean* (F) is a single measure of precision versus recall compromise degree:

$$F = 2 * P * R/(P + R),$$

where P and R are *precision* and *recall*, respectively. Recall, precision and F measure have a values between 0 and 1, but they are also very commonly written as percentages, on a scale between 0 and 100 %. The experimental results are presented in Table 4.

Table 4. Error rates of G2P and P2G conversion process experiments

Conversion type	Metric type	Part of speech					
		Noun		Verb		Adjective	
		I	II	I	II	I	II
G2P	P	0,90	0,88	0,91	0,90	0,92	0,89
	R	0,91	0,82	0,93	0,87	0,85	0,83
	F, %	90	86	92	88	87	85
	Avg. F, %	88		91		86	
P2G	P	0,87	0,86	0,84	0,82	0,90	0,86
	R	0,81	0,85	0,84	0,86	0,79	0,79
	F, %	84	83	84	84	84	82
	Avg. F, %	85		84		83	

To carry out a sample test, information from three sources was used, among them the Belarusian phonetic dictionary, the English-Belarusian phrasebook," Orthoepic Dictionary Generator", and linguistic resources from "corpus.by" project [7, 14–16]. The size of the test corpus is 2400 words. It was formed in a special way for testing G2P and P2G conversion algorithms for Belarusian. It is representative in terms of lexical content and also phonetically balanced. The corpus includes both individual words and phrases, as well as whole sentences. Since the character is the basic unit of transformation and the average length of the corpus element is about 9,5 symbols, the total size of the test sample is about 22800 characters. The corpus was divided into three subsets of different size, depending on the part of speech: nouns (1000 words), verbs (800 words) and adjectives (600 words). Each subset in turn was divided into type I and type II groups, depending on the frequency of occurrence of words in the texts. The average F-measures for G2P and P2G conversion were grouped by part of speech as presented in the following histograms (Fig. 7).

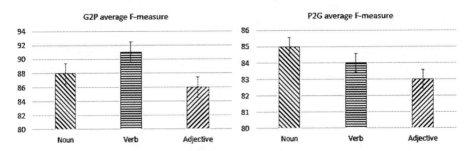

Fig. 7. Average error of G2P (left side) and P2G (right side) conversion

Analysis of the results leads to some compelling conclusions. Firstly, the F-measures of G2P conversion are on average 5 % higher than the measures for P2G conversion. This can be explained by the presence of well-defined rules for Belarusian for conversions of the first kind; however, the rules are not always suitable for conversion in the opposite direction. Secondly, there is some sort of correlation between error rates and part of speech. The average length of adjectives in the Belarusian language is more than for other parts of speech, so it is natural that more errors were observed, which means that more attention and highly complex transformation rules are needed for the handling of exceptions. The third largest component of the total conversion error is determined by the part not yet covered by the rules and not covered by the dictionary of exceptions. As such, it is the aim of our future research to reduce errors and improve the quality of conversion. On the other hand, the number of direct conversion mistakes is not so high, so we can conclude that the grammar we developed showed good results.

6   Conclusion

As part of this ongoing research, procedures and algorithms for the conversion of G2P and P2G processes using a linguistic development environment NooJ have been developed. A dictionary containing words and their transcriptions was made. A morphological transformation grammar and rules for processing written words in phonetic form and for the reverse transformation were built.

The results of this research could be used to solve various computer-linguistic problems: forward and reverse phonetization, adding phonetic level to information processing in the Belarusian NooJ module, and developing a SST system. In addition, we are planning to use the G2P dictionary and grammar in the multivoice TTS system for the Belarusian language [17].

It should be noted that one of the main objectives of this work was also the author's desire to show the capability of NooJ tools to work on various linguistic levels including the phonetic representation of written language. NooJ tools can be fully utilized for processing all kinds of texts, including phonetic representation.

Future work will involve adding to and expanding the existing system of rules for G2P conversion as well as the addition of exceptions and special cases for the P2G conversion process and further integration of these results into the Belarusian module of NooJ.

References

1. Silberztein, M.: NooJ Manual (2003). www.nooj4nlp.net
2. Marchant, C.C.: Fundamentals of Modern Belarusian (2004). http://www.vitba.org/fofmb/introduction.html
3. Сцяцко, П.: Уводзіны у мовазнаўства. Вышэйшая школа, Мінск (2001)
4. Андарала, Г.: Сучасная беларуская мова: фанетыка. БГУ, Мінск (2013)
5. Transcription Generator. http://corpus.by/transcriptionGenerator/. Accessed 6 Oct 2015
6. Падлужны, А.I.: Фанетыка беларускай літаратурнай мовы. Навука і тэхніка, Мінск (1989)
7. Кошчанка, У.А.: Беларуска-англійскі размоўнік. Артыя Груп, Мінск (2010)
8. The International Phonetic Alphabet and the IPA Chart. https://www.internationalphonetic association.org/content/ipa-chart. Accessed 6 Oct 2015
9. Computer-coding the IPA: a proposed extension of SAMPA. http://www.phon.ucl.ac.uk/home/sampa/x-sampa.htm. Accessed 6 Oct 2015

10. Text-to-Speech PHP-Based Synthesizer. http://corpus.by/tts3. Accessed 6 Oct 2015
11. Dutoit, T., Marques, F.: Applied Signal Processing: A Matlab-based Proof of Concept. Springer Science, Buisness Media, LLC, New York (2009)
12. Mitkov, R.: The Oxford Handbook of Computational Linguistics. Oxford University Press, Oxford (2005)
13. Manning, D., Raghavan, P., Shutze, H.: An Introduction to Information Retrieval. Cambridge University Press, Cambridge (2009)
14. Слоўнік граматычна-лінгвістычнае тэрмінолёгіі (проект). Менск: Інбелкульт (1927)
15. Пашкевіч, В.: Ангельска-беларускі слоўнік/English-Belarusian Dictionary. Менск (2006)
16. Orthoepic Dictionary Generator. http://corpus.by/transcriptionGenerator/. Accessed 6 Oct 2015
17. Zahariev, V., Petrovsky, A., Lobanov, B.: Multivoice text to speech synthesis system. In: 12th International Conference on Pattern Recognition and Information Processing (PRIP 2014), Conference Proceedings, 28–30 May 2014. UIIP NASB, Minsk, pp. 320–324 (2014)

Semi-automatic Indexing and Parsing
Information on the Web with NooJ

Maria Pia di Buono[(✉)]

Department of Political, Social and Communication Sciences,
University of Salerno, Fisciano (SA), Italy
mdibuono@unisa.it

Abstract. Due to the large amount of data available on the Web, indexing information represents a crucial step to guarantee fast and accurate Information Retrieval (IR). Indexing content allows to find relevant documents on the basis of a user's query. Numerous researches discuss the use of automated indexing, considered faster and cheaper than manual systems. However, in order to produce the index, using algorithms, entails low precision, low recall, and generic results [1]. This is the reason why in this paper we propose a NooJ-based system, by means of which we will develop a search engine able to process online documents, starting from a natural language query, and to return information to users. To do this, and in order to analyze user's request, we will employ software automations to apply NooJ and its Linguistic Resources (LRs).

Keywords: Semantic indexing · Archaeological Italian electronic dictionaries · CIDOC CRM · NooJ linguistic resources

1   Introduction

Indexing information represents a crucial step in order to guarantee fast and accurate Information Retrieval (IR). Actually, according to the definition of [2], IR is composed of different steps which are clearly summarized by [3]:

> "finding material (usually documents) of an unstructured nature (usually text) that satisfies an information need from within large collections (usually stored on computers)".

Such definition allows us to focus on the main characteristic of IR process, namely the need of dealing with three elements: Web pages, queries, sets of relevant Web pages. Thus, indexing content allows extracting relevant documents from Knowledge Bases (KBs) starting from user's queries.

This process presents some problems related to information fragmentation and the growing complexity of KBs. Most approaches employ a shallow linguistic analysis[1], based on the use of statistical parsers, in order to analyze users' queries and convert them into a machine-readable format.

---

[1] "The shallow semantic analysis measures only word overlap between text and hypothesis" [6]. This means that starting from tokenization and lemmatization of text and hypothesis, this analysis uses Web documents as corpus and assigns inverse document frequency as weight to each entry in the hypothesis.

© Springer International Publishing Switzerland 2016
T. Okrut et al. (Eds.): NooJ 2015, CCIS 607, pp. 151–161, 2016.
DOI: 10.1007/978-3-319-42471-2_13

In our opinion, applying a deep linguistic analysis to free-texts and queries represents the possibility to overcome boundaries in IR systems, guaranteeing an improvement of results.

2 State of Art

Generally speaking automated indexing is considered faster and cheaper than manual systems, even if results do not seem have a high level of accuracy.

Actually, also according to [1], using stochastic algorithms entails:

- Low precision due to the indexing of common Atomic Linguistic Units (ALUs) or sentences.
- Low recall caused by the presence of synonyms.
- Generic results arising from the use of too board or too narrow terms.

Usually IR systems are based on invert text index, namely an index data structure storing a mapping from content to its locations in a database file, or in a document or a set of documents[2].

Most traditional IR systems process each document separately to retrieve terms in free-text query, which means that they do not compare results provided from different sources.

Such lack of integration in results causes overlapping and decreasing in the positive predictive value, due to the fact that shared content are indexed several times. Various approaches have been proposed to overcome this boundary, increasing recall and precision in results.

[4] propose a mixed approach in order to process queries, involving both tree-based navigation and pattern matching similar to that structured information retrieval domains.

In his presentation [5] from Yahoo! Labs deals with query evaluation strategies, based on Term-at-a-Time (TAAT) and Document-at-a-Time Evaluation (DAAT) processing. TAAT scan postings list one at a time, maintain a set of potential matching documents along with their partial scores. On the other hand, DAAT scan postings lists in parallel, identifying at each point the next potential candidate document and scoring it.

In recent times, various semantic approaches have been proposed in order to outline concept identification methods, able to assign document ALUs to the correct ontological entries [7–9].

Furthermore, different researches employ concept-based in order to process both documents and queries through semantic entities and concepts.

[10] propose an approach for semantic indexing based on concepts identified from a linguistic resource. In their work, authors use WordNet and WordNetDomains lexical databases with the aim to identify concepts and they also apply a concept-based indexing evaluation.

---

[2] Source: https://en.wikipedia.org/wiki/Inverted_index.

2.1   Framework

Our research activities are based on Lexicon-Grammar (LG) theoretical and practical framework, which is one of the most consistent methods for natural language formalization, automatic textual analysis and parsing. LG, set up by the French linguist Maurice Gross during the '60s [11, 12], was applied to Italian by [13]. The Italian Linguistic Resources have been built by the Computational Linguistic group of University of Salerno, which started its study of language formalization from 1981. Our analysis is based on the Italian module for NooJ [14], which is enriched with specific-domain LRs, namely Archaeological domain LRs.

3   System Overview

We propose a system workflow [Fig. 1] which aims at integrating a semantic annotation process for both query analysis and document retrieval.

Also, we propose an architecture, which takes advantage from semantic information stored both in electronic dictionaries and Finite State Automata and Transducers (FSA/FSTs). Furthermore, this architecture may also map linguistic tags (i.e. POS) and structures (i.e. sentences, ALUs) to domain concepts employing metadata from conceptual schemata.

Therefore, the system workflow is based on a representation model applied to both users' queries and to documents, and on a match between these two elements.

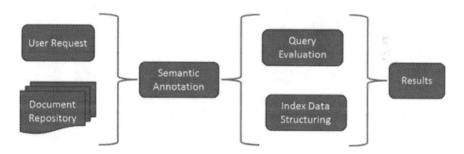

Fig. 1. System workflow.

The representation model proposed is developed on a semantic annotation process to guarantee the interoperability between metadata. In fact, queries may include some restrictions on metadata, such as URL, domain, etc., which are typically different for each document. In order to support these queries, the representation model uses ontological schema to map ALUs with concepts for avoiding overlapping and indexing shared content just once. Semantic association is also used to infer Boolean relationship between elements in a free-text queries and relative meta-data.

In other words, starting from the analysis of users' queries and structured documents, we employ a semantic annotation process in order to create a match among concepts.

In the following paragraphs, we will introduce our methodology based on the use of NooJ and its LRs.

4   Linguistic Resources

In our experiment, we use DBpedia database as knowledge source of structured data in RDF/XML and we test our system outputs using its SPARQL (Protocol and RDF Query Language) Endpoint.[3]

The proposed hybrid approach applies the Lexicon-Grammar framework and its language formalization approach. Thus, firstly we develop Linguistic Resources (LRs), then we model data semantically using two kinds of ontologies: an upper level ontology, namely a cross-domain ontology, and a specific-domain ontology.

The main components of our system are LRs, namely electronic dictionaries, FSA/FSTs [15, 16]. Actually, we develop Italian LRs for the Archaeological Domain, starting from NooJ module for Italian. Such resources have been created and maintained by the research group of University of Salerno, under the LG framework.

As presented in [17, 18], we developed the ARCHAEOLOGICAL ITALIAN Electronic Dictionary (AIED) starting from Thesauri and Guidelines of the Italian Central Institute for the Catalogue and Documentation (ICCD)[4]. Such resources are useful to provide information about the use of terminology and controlled vocabularies for cataloguers and other professionals. It means that they include terms, descriptions and other information needful to objects cataloguing.

In our dictionary, for each entry we indicate:

- Its POS (Category), internal structure and inflectional code (FLX). These information represent a formal and morphological description. In fact, the category and the internal structure indicate that the given ALU is formally a Noun and is formed by different single elements. In Table 1, the tag "NPREPNPREPN" describes how the given ALU, *dinos con anse ad anello*, is formed (i.e. N stands for Noun and PREP for Preposition). At the same time, the tag "FLX = C610" refers to the ALU number and gender recalling a local grammar in order to generate and recognize correspondent forms (e.g. singular/plural, masculine/feminine).
- Its variants (VAR) and synonyms (SYN), if any;
- The type of link (LINK) (RDF and/or HTML), associated to the linguistic resource;
- With reference to a taxonomy, the pertaining knowledge domain (DOM); for our dictionary we have developed a taxonomy, based on ICCD prescriptions, therefore all entries have a terminological and domain label usable for ontology population.
- The use of domain label subset tags is also previewed for those domain sectors which include specific sub-sectors. This is the case with Archaeological Remains,

---

[3] A SPARQL Endpoint is a service which accept a SPARQL query against a knowledge base and return results. Several tools, able to connect and semi-automatically construct a SPARQL query for a SPARQL endpoint, are available, e.g., ViziQuer.
DBpedia SPARQL Endpoint is available at http://dbpedia.org/isparql/.

[4] http://www.iccd.beniculturali.it/index.php?it/240/vocabolari. Last visit: February 2014.

for which a generic tag «RA1» is used, while more explicit tags are used for Object Type, Subject, Primary Material, Method of Manufacture, Object Description.

- The ICOM International Committee for Documentation (CIDOC) Conceptual Reference Model (CRM) Class (CCL). In AIED we associate the ontology schema, provided by CIDOC[5] and compatible with the Resource Description Framework (RDF), to lexical entries. Actually, the tag CCL allows us to derive definitions and a formal structure for describing the implicit and explicit concepts and relationships used in Cultural Heritage documentation.

Table 1. Sample of AIED entries.

Entry	Category	Internal structure	FLX	VAR	SYN	LINK	DOM	CCL
dinos con anse ad anello	N	NPNPN	C610	dynos/déinos		RDF	RA1SUOCR	E22
kylix a labbro risparmiato	N	NPNA	C611		lip cup	RDF	RA1SUOCR	E22

CCL label and grammatical information with which dictionary entries are tagged, are the basis on which we develop role set matrixes. Such matrixes are useful to identify predicate-argument structures related to sentence contexts and consequently to achieve the semantic annotation process. Context information inserted inside the matrix tables together with NooJ concordances are employed as weighting preferences.

These matrix tables are developed analyzing semantic role sets established on the basis of CIDOC CRM constraints (properties) matched with grammatical and syntactic rules. Also, they indicate if a verb allows active/passive constructions, in order to recognize entities also when analyzing transformed active declarative sentences.

5   Semantic Annotation

In our system, we present a semantic annotation process which works simultaneously on two sides. Actually, it analyses (I) the user's query, and (II) documents in KBs.

Such annotation process is based on a deep Natural Language Analysis, which means that we perform a linguistic analysis of user's queries and documents in order to annotate them.

Semantic annotation represents a key step in our procedure, due to the fact that annotating text requires the capability of matching correctly a natural language formalism and a data model formalism. Actually, as stated in [19], "annotation is the

---

[5] The CIDOC Conceptual Reference Model (CRM) aims at providing semantic definitions to describe implicit and explicit concepts and relations between Cultural Heritage objects and museum documentations. It is a formal ontology, which allows integration, mediation and interchange of heterogeneous information. CIDOC CRM only defines basic semantics for database schemes and document structures.

inverse of normalization. Just as different strings of characters may have the same meaning, it also happens that identical strings of characters may have different meanings, depending on the context".

Thus, we may divide semantic annotation task into two subtasks: natural language analysis and data representation.

Therefore, during such process we employ two conceptual schemata:

- DBpedia (upper level) ontology which is composed of:
    Classes: 734
    Properties: 2975
- CIDOC CRM (domain) ontology which is composed of:
    Classes: 90
    Properties: 148.

5.1   Natural Language Analysis

The first task concerns the processing of user's queries in order to annotate them, domain-independent semantic data modeling (DBpedia cross-domain ontology) and inferring Boolean relationship among elements in a free-text query and relative meta-data. In our work, we develop NooJ FSA/FSTs in order to process a given query.

Starting from the entries retrieved and from their specific tags, stored in electronic dictionaries and in FSA/FSTs, we use NooJ to write and fill all fields directly using RDF schema and OWL, automatically generating the strings while correctly coupling ontologies and compound words.

In fact, in our FSA-based system we recognize RDF triples in sentence structures.

According to our approach, electronic dictionaries entries (simple words and ALUs) are the subject and the object of the RDF triple.

Also, as regards declarative sentences, RDF gives the possibility to recognize sentences conveying information of the type "X is an element of Y", which also have recursive structures.

All this means that a single FSA/FST can be used to:

- account for all the items of an open list;
- account for all declarative sentences of the type "X is a part of Y", in which X and Y are pre-defined classes;
- allow the matching of POS to RDF triples.

In the following images Figs. 2 and 3[6], we will show a sample of FSA/FST which may be used to analyze users' queries. Such automaton allows us to recognize entities involved in RDF relationships, namely *Person* and *date*. In such RDF triple, the subject, *Person*, and the object, *date,* are trigged by a predicate, namely a Verb Phrase (VP). This VP is represented by a class verb which may co-occur together with the given entities in sentence contexts. Therefore, the VP may hold verbs such as *live* or *born* followed by a

---

[6] We had to split FSA image in order to improve reading, thus, Figs. 2 and 3 represent respectively the left side and the right side of the automaton. The node *Person*, which stands for the variable "activity2", is repeated twice in order to link the two split figures.

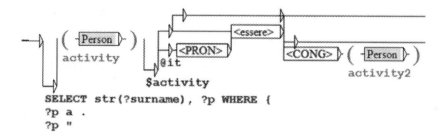

Fig. 2. FSA for annotating users' queries (left side).

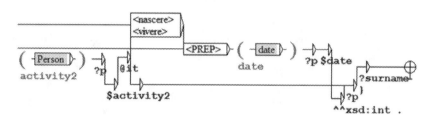

Fig. 3. FSA for annotating users' queries (right side).

preposition. It is worth noticing that in our sample we insert two nodes containing the same entity (*Person*), which stands for two different variables, namely *activity* and *activity2*. Such variables refer to a specific CCL tag, which is used to identify a specific attribute, namely profession, for elements belonging to the generic class *Person*.

Values, produced by variables (*activity, activity2* and *date*), are employed to generate a SPARQL query, able to retrieve surname of such persons which perform a specific activity/job/profession in a determinate interval.

The following sample shows the result of FSA applied to the previous query.

```
SELECT str(?surname), ?p WHERE {
    ?p a .
    ?p "scrittore"@it .
    ?p "archeologo"@it .
    ?p "1900"^^xsd:int .
    ?p ?surname
}
```

[Example of pseudo-code query in SPARQL which may be used into an Endpoint]

Thus, the output of FSA may be used in order to generate a query which may be run against any SPARQL endpoint or repository in which documents are formalized using RDF.

5.2   Data Representation

The second subtask, namely data representation, involves appropriate operations on the RDF-based data layer, mapping OWL concepts to object-oriented classes with methods for interrelations and domain-specific rules used to generate and consolidate processes (e.g. CIDOC CRM ontology).

Such process of data representation aims at analyzing information stored in RDF documents, which means that we may retrieve information from any repository directly. Actually, we use RDF data representation in order to process documents and create a match between users' requests and concepts stored in KBs.

We develop NooJ FSA in order to process information stored in DBpedia KB, matching values of semantic attributes with the ones retrieved from users' queries analysis.

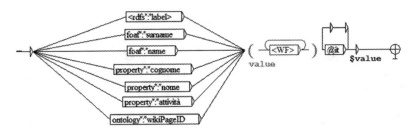

Fig. 4. Sample of FSA for analyzing DBpedia documents.

In the previous FSA (Fig. 4) we use the nodes on the left in order to recognize labels used inside RDF documents, which are stored, for example, in DBpedia KB. It means that first we process tags which describe elements semantically and subsequently we analyze which values are assumed for such descriptions. Actually, in the following node, we insert a generic *WF* class, in order to recognize each word form

rdfs:label	Peter Levi @it
ontology:wikiPageID	2168662
foaf:name	Peter Chad Tigar @it
ontology:wikiPageLength	11646
ontology:birthYear	1931-01-01T00:00:00+01:00
ontology:deathYear	2000-01-01T00:00:00+01:00
foaf:surname	Levi @it
property:nome	Peter Chad Tigar @it
property:cognome	Levi @it
property:sesso	M @it
property:attività	scrittore @it
	poeta @it
	archeologo @it

Fig. 5. Sample of RDF-structured document from Italian DBpedia resources.

which is present inside documents. These word forms represent values stored for each specific semantic descriptive tag, i.e. for *foaf:surname* Levi value (see Fig. 4).

On the other hand, the final node *@it* indicates language tag in resource description schemata (i.e., Italian).

Thus, we may retrieve information structured as the previous sample of RDF-structured document (Fig. 5).

6   Tests and Conclusions

We decide to test our system against DBpedia Knowledge Base (KB)[7], which is structured in RDF. There also is a public SPARQL endpoint over the DBpedia data set[8] and, as reported in the site, users can ask queries against DBpedia using:

- the Leipzig query builder[9];
- the OpenLink Interactive SPARQL Query Builder (iSPARQL)[10];
- the SNORQL query explorer[11]; or
- any other SPARQL-aware client(s).

Therefore, DBpedia endpoints may be accessed just using a query encoded in SPARQL. We test our system outputs, i.e. SPARQL queries and data representations, using Italian DBpedia KB[12].

For example, if we run the following query against a KB:

Tutti gli archeologi che sono stati anche scrittori nati nel '900 (Archaeologists that have been also a writer lived in 19th century)[13].

Actually our system displays the results as they are showed in DBpedia Endpoint, after processing the query (Table 2); namely as a table which contains surname value, i.e. Levi, and the specific resource URL.

Thus, for the given query we obtain a list of RDF pages which match with user's information need.

We also test our data representation, obtained through NooJ FSA, on a corpus dumped from the Italian Wikipedia Database.

After being tested and debugged, the LRs described so far are actually under final development and completion and they will be proposed as part of the NooJ Italian module.

---

[7] DBpedia is a crowd-sourced community effort to extract structured information from Wikipedia and make this information available on the Web. http://wiki.dbpedia.org/.

[8] http://dbpedia.org/OnlineAccess.

[9] http://querybuilder.dbpedia.org.

[10] http://dbpedia.org/isparql.

[11] http://dbpedia.org/snorql (does not work with Internet Explorer).

[12] DBpedia Italian is an open and collaborative project for the extraction and reuse of semantically structured information of the Italian version of Wikipedia. For more information see: http://it.dbpedia.org.

[13] Sample adapted from the one presented in the Italian DBpedia project. http://it.dbpedia.org/esempi/.

Table 2. Results from SPARQL query.

Surname value	Resource
Levi	http://it.dbpedia.org/resource/Peter_Levi
Matthiae	http://it.dbpedia.org/resource/Paolo_Mattiae
Hansen	http://it.dbpedia.org/resource/Thorkild_Hansen
Cooper	http://it.dbpedia.org/resource/Glenn_Cooper
Duggan	http://it.dbpedia.org/resource/Alfred_Duggan
Mallowan	http://it.dbpedia.org/resource/Max_Mallowan
Meomartini	http://it.dbpedia.org/resource/Almerico_Meomartini
Coe	http://it.dbpedia.org/resource/Michael_D._Coe
Kondylis	http://it.dbpedia.org/resource/Thanos_Kondylis
Zecca	http://it.dbpedia.org/resource/Vincenzo_Zecca
Bellis	http://it.dbpedia.org/resource/En_Bellis
Consoli	http://it.dbpedia.org/resource/Sebastaino_Consoli

Subsequently, we will integrate such LRs in our environment, considering that our final aim is to propose the development of a SPARQL endpoint based on NooJ. Furthermore, we will focus on an improvement of result displaying.

Future work also aims at improving both index data structuring and a query evaluation process. It also necessary testing the system in a consistent way on other KBs, in order to propose an independent-domain approach.

References

1. Hjorland, B.: Semantics and knowledge organization. Ann. Rev. Inf. Sci. Technol. **41**, 367–405 (2007)
2. Manning, C.D., Raghavan, P., Schütze, H.: An Introduction to Information Retrieval. Cambridge University Press, Cambridge (2008)
3. Teufel S.: Lecture 1: Introduction and Overview. Information Retrieval Computer Science Tripos Part II. http://www.cl.cam.ac.uk/teaching/1314/InfoRtrv/lecture1.pdf
4. Halverson, A., Burger, J., Galanis, L., Kini, A., et al.: Mixed mode XML query processing. In: Proceedings of the 29th VLDB Conference, Berlin, German (2003)
5. Lempel, R.: http://webcourse.cs.technion.ac.il/236621/Winter2010-2011/ho/WCFiles/lec4-evaluation.pdf
6. Bos, J., Markert, K.: Marketer combining shallow and deep NLP methods for recognizing textual entailment. In: Proceedings of the First Challenge Workshop, Recognizing Textual Entailment. PASCAL (2005)
7. Baziz, M., Boughanem, M., Aussenac-Gilles, N.: Conceptual indexing based on document content representation. In: Crestani, F., Ruthven, I. (eds.) CoLIS 2005. LNCS, vol. 3507, pp. 171–186. Springer, Heidelberg (2005)
8. Boubekeur, F., Boughanem, M., Tamine, L., Daoud, M.: Using WordNet for concept-based document indexing in information retrieval. In: Fourth International Conference on Semantic Processing (SEMAPRO), Florence, Italy, October 2010

9. Sussna, M.: Word sense disambiguation for free-text indexing using a massive semantic network. In: 2nd International Conference on Information and Knowledge Management (CIKM-1993), pp. 67–74 (1993)
10. Boubekeur, F., Azzoug, W.: Concept-based indexing in text information retrieval. Int. J. Comput. Sci. Inf. Technol. (IJCSIT) **5**(1), 119–136 (2013)
11. Gross, M.: Grammaire transformationnelle du français. Cantilène (1968)
12. Gross, M.: Méthodes en syntaxe. Hermann (1975)
13. Elia, A., Martinelli, M., D'Agostino, E.: Lessico e strutture sintattiche: introduzione alla sintassi del verbo italiano. Liguori (1981)
14. Vietri, S.: The Italian module for NooJ. In: Proceedings of the First Italian Conference on Computational Linguistics, CLiC-it 2014. Pisa University Press (2014)
15. Silberztein, M.: La Formalisation des Langues. L'Approche de NooJ. ISTE Edition (2015)
16. Silberztein, M.: NooJ computational devices. In: Donabédian, A., Khurshudian, V., Silberztein, M. (eds.) Formalising Natural Languages with NooJ: Selected Papers from the NooJ 2012 International Conference. Cambridge Scholars Publishing, Newcastle (2013)
17. di Buono, M.P.: Information extraction for ontology population tasks. An application to the Italian archaeological domain. Int. J. Comput. Sci. Theor. Appl. **3**(2), 40–50 (2015). ORB Academic Publisher
18. di Buono, M.P., Monteleone, M., Elia, A.: Terminology and knowledge representation Italian linguistic resources for the archaeological domain. In: Proceedings of 25th International Conference on Computational Linguistics (COLING 2014) - Workshop on Lexical and Grammatical Resources for Language Processing (LG-LP 2014) (2014)
19. Turney, P.D.: From frequency to meaning: vector space models of semantics. J. Artif. Intell. Res. **37**, 141–188 (2010)

Language Modeling for Robots-Human Interaction

Lesia Kaigorodova[1($\boxtimes$)], K. Rusetski[2], Kiryl Nikalaenka[1],
Yuras Hetsevich[1], S. Gerasuto[1], R. Prakapovich[1], U. Sychou[1],
and S. Lysy[1]

[1] United Institute of Informatics Problems, Minsk, Belarus
lesia.piatrouskaya@gmail.com, anak247@gmail.com,
yury.hetsevich@gmail.com, stanislau.lysy@gmail.com,
{contacts, rprakapovich, vsychyov}@robotics.by
[2] Belarusian State University of Informatics and Radioelectronics,
Minsk, Belarus
rusetski.k@gmail.com

Abstract. Building systems for speech communication between robots and humans is considered to be a difficult task since nowadays speech recognition systems still have poor performance and at the same time the ambiguity of recognized commands is unacceptable for safety reasons. We introduce the SAOF concepts for language models to define standards for communication.

The article covers the approach for language modeling for robots-human interaction, i.e. a standard for robots' behavior in order to make them perform commands. We consider two tools that allow us to go through this process. The first one is the NooJ tool and the second one is the Open Semantic Technology for Intelligent Systems (OSTIS) tool. The NooJ tool is easy to apply and solve many NLP problems while the OSTIS claims to be a universal solution for the tasks dealing with semantics though quite tricky to use.

Keywords: Human-robot interaction · OSTIS · Language model · Syntactic grammar · SAO format · SAOF format

1 Introduction

Building the architecture of systems for controlling a robot or a group of robots through speech is a tricky and special task. It is much different from the architectures of the systems with manual control of robots. There are some substantial reasons for this statement. The two main issues are: poor speech recognition performance of speech recognition systems nowadays and the problem of safety while dealing with robots.

Today speech recognition software in general is still producing poor quality results. Especially this concerns languages that are not world-widely used. For instance, Slavic speech is still hard to recognize. All the problems that are connected with speech recognition systems are usually narrowed down to some simpler problems or problems with a set of restrictions in order to achieve more accurate results.

© Springer International Publishing Switzerland 2016
T. Okrut et al. (Eds.): NooJ 2015, CCIS 607, pp. 162–171, 2016.
DOI: 10.1007/978-3-319-42471-2_14

The problem of safety while dealing with robots can be resolved by obtaining higher accuracy and disambiguation of recognized commands. If we want to control and interact with a robot or a group of robots easily and safely, the communication problem should be solved by designing the language that is common to everyday use of humans and that is 'understood' by robots as easily and quickly as possible. It is easy for humans to understand speech, but it is not so easy to make machines do this.

Given that, we should define the appropriate standard for robot's behavior in order to make them perform commands. If we use speech as a means of communication, we can say that a language model in some way defines this standard, it defines robots behavior, i.e. what they can perform and what they cannot perform, what they can 'understand' and what they cannot 'understand'.

For language modeling we will use both NooJ and OSTIS tools. NooJ tool is easy to use and it allows solving many NLP problems. And as for OSTIS, it is claimed to be a universal solution for the tasks dealing with semantics but it is quite difficult to operate.

2 Concepts of the Language Model

We have already stated that we should define an appropriate language model to define the standard for communication between humans and robots. Now we will introduce some concepts for this model.

At the first stage of the design of the Language Model we use *deep syntactic analysis* to obtain the model that is as simple as possible and yet far from underfitting the real model. We will use such concepts as *'Subject'*, *'Action'*, *'Object'* and *'Features'* (SAOF format).

'Subject' refers to a robot's name. *'Action'* refers to an action to be performed by robots that is usually represented by a verb. *'Object'* represents a target of the action. And *'Features'* is an add-on to specify *'Object'* or *'Action'*.

3 Introduction to NooJ Tool

In our work we use *NooJ* tool for designing the Language Model for robots-human interaction. NooJ is a development environment mainly used to construct large-coverage formalized descriptions of natural languages, and apply them to a large corpora, in real time. It also can be used not only for pattern recognition in texts but also for the generation of some patterns.

Finite State Transducer is a great solution for generating languages or dictionaries for languages, especially when they are not too complex. This type of language representation is simple to implement, understand and modify. And we will use *Finite State Automata* for pattern location while performing speech recognition.

Here are some definitions of the concepts in NooJ terms.

A *finite-state transducer* (FST) is a graph that represents a set of text sequences and then associates each recognized sequence with some analysis result. The text sequences are described in the *input* part of the FST; the corresponding results are described in the *output* part of the FST.

In NooJ, *Finite-State Automata* (FSA) are a special case of finite-state transducers that do not produce any result (i.e. they have no output).

Typically, a syntactic FST represents word sequences, and then produces linguistic information (such as phrasal structure). A morphological FST represents sequences of letters that spell a word form, and then produces lexical information (such as a part of speech, a set of morphological, syntactic and semantic codes).

NooJ contains a graphical editor (as well as a dozen tools) to facilitate the construction of FSTs and their variants (FSA, *Recursive Transition Networks* and *Enhanced Recursive Transition Networks*).

NooJ users typically use FSA to locate morpho-syntactic patterns in corpora, and extract the matching sequences to build indices, concordances, etc.

4 Language Modeling Using NooJ Syntactic Grammar

In NooJ, *Syntactic Grammars* are the grammars that process sequences of tokens (as opposed to the morphological grammars that process sequences of letters in tokens). Syntactic grammars are organized sets of graphs, and are called local grammars. For instance, NooJ can be used for building grammars that are used to recognize and annotate multi-word units and semi-frozen expressions, Context-Free parsers that can compute sentence structure, Enhanced Grammars that can perform semantic analysis transformations on texts and translations, etc.

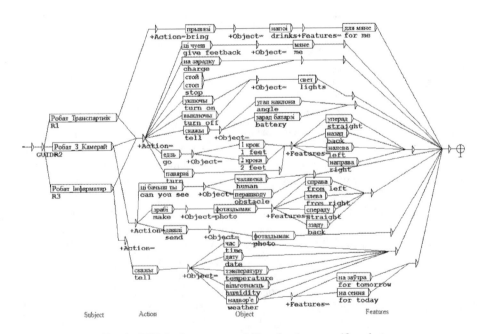

Fig. 1. FST for language modelling for three specific robots

We use NooJ Syntactic Grammar to design the transducer for combining all the concepts of our Language Model mentioned above ('Subject', 'Action', 'Object' and 'Features') and linguistic units that will refer to them.

Here is a simple example of the Language Model for the communication of a human that speaks Belarusian with a group of robots (Fig. 1). In this example each of robots can perform primitive commands, but, in group, all the robots may perform something more complex and reasonable.

Once the Language Model has been designed, we can either keep it further strictly untouched as it is predefined or we can add the possibility of developing the language. We can develop it, for example, by adding a reduced set of commands (which is natural for everyday human speech, military men, etc.) or synonyms, etc.

5   Language Generation Using NooJ Dictionary

In NooJ, *Dictionaries* usually associate words or phrases with a set of information, such as category, one or more inflectional and/or derivational paradigms, one or more syntactic or semantic properties, domain classes, etc.

NooJ dictionaries can store syntactic and semantic information (just like a lexicon-grammar) as well as multilingual information and thus can be used in machine translation systems.

We use a play-out approach to generate a dictionary of the language for robots using our FST and *NooJ Dictionary tool*. Here are some units that comprise the generated dictionary. Each unit in the dictionary below is the result of one of the paths started with 'start/in node' and ended with 'end/out node'.

An example of the generated language:

…

…

Робат _ Інфарматар скажы дату, GUID = R3 + Action = tell + Object = date

Робат _ Інфарматар скажы тэмпературу, GUID = R3 + Action = tell + Object = temperature

Робат _ Інфарматар скажы час, GUID = R3 + Action = tell + Object = time

Робат _ 3 _ Камерай дашлі фотаздымак, GUID = R2 + Action = send + Object = photo

Робат _ 3 _ Камерай зрабі фотаздымак злева, GUID = R2 + Action = make + Object = photo + Features = from right

Робат _ 3 _ Камерай зрабі фотаздымак справа, GUID = R2 + Action = make + Object = photo + Features = from left

Робат _ Транспартнік едзь 2 крока направа, GUID = R1 + Action = go + Object = 2 feet + Features = right

Робат _ Транспартнік едзь 2 крока налева, GUID = R1 + Action = go + Object = 2 feet + Features = left

Робат _ Транспартнік едзь 2 крока назад, GUID = R1 + Action = go + Object = 2 feet + Features = back

Робат _ Транспартнік едзь 2 крока уперад, GUID = R1 + Action = go + Object = 2 feet + Features = straight

Робат _ 3 _ Камерай скажы угал наклона, GUID = R2 + Action = tell + Object = angle

Робат _ 3 _ Камерай выключы свет, GUID = R2 + Action = turn off + Object = lights

Робат _ 3 _ Камерай ці чуеш мяне, GUID = R2 + Action = give_feetback + Object = me

Робат _ 3 _ Камерай на зарадку, GUID = R2 + Action = charge

Робат _ 3 _ Камерай уключы свет, GUID = R2 + Action = turn on + Object = lights

Робат _ 3 _ Камерай стой, GUID = R2 + Action = stop

...

...

6   Language Modeling Using OSTIS & NooJ Grammars

Open Semantic Technology for Intelligent Systems [4] (OSTIS) is a tool that facilitates semantic analysis by providing a unified semantic network [2] (USN) approach to knowledge representation. USNs allow knowledge engineers to represent a multitude of knowledge types within a single, unified framework using specially constructed graphs.

In this section we illustrate how to generate the same Language Model for human interaction with a mobile robot using OSTIS. We will consider the mapping of the NooJ Graph for syntactic grammar to the graph that is specific to OSTIS technology. High-level mapping model and OSTIS-based system is shown as a data flow diagram in Fig. 2.

The data flow process is as follows:

1. The user puts in a query to the system using either voice (through a speech recognition system) or keyboard. It might as well be any other input device that his system is equipped with, the only requirement being the ability to output a text in some way.
2. The query is then analyzed using the NooJ grammar, which had been converted to USN beforehand with a specialized conversion agent and stored in a shared semantic memory. Shared semantic memory is a part of a software implementation of dynamical graph models [2] provided by OSTIS technology.
3. The user input analyzer outputs up to four request components as a result, depending on the request complexity and grammar structure.
4. Request generator then builds a request instance and stores it in a shared memory as well.
5. Semantic memory notifies all the subscribed robots about a newly formed request. Notification is triggered by creating an arc from a certain request class to a certain request instance
6. Each robot decides if that request is referred to it and if so, performs the requested action with a requested object, and then leaves an execution report for other parts of the system to process.

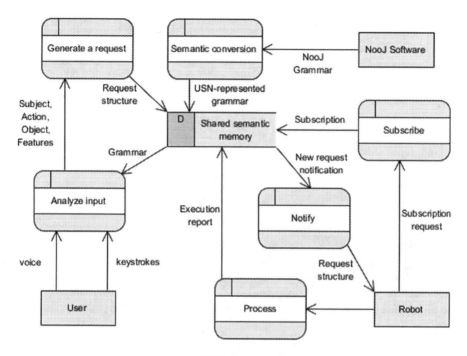

Fig. 2. OSTIS data flow diagram

The diagram above shows that the shared semantic memory plays a crucial role in the interaction, serving as an integration medium between the user and the mobile service robot.

7   OSTIS Representation of NooJ Concepts

To map NooJ graphs into OSTIS-based graphs successfully it is necessary to represent both NooJ concepts and target system's concepts and entities using USNs.

Firstly, the target system's entities and concepts need to be defined. In terms of NooJ grammars, they can be represented by the values of the +Object attribute. To define and appropriately group them, subject domains are used in OSTIS. If we consider the human-robot interaction, we have a sample subject domain called "Service Robot subject domain" which consists of entity classes, such as "human", "obstacle" and "photograph", their particular instances and relationships between them. USN representation of this subject domain's entity classes is shown in Fig. 3.

Secondly, we have to define a system of commands for our robots to understand. In OSTIS user-interface subsystem terms, they can be atomic and non-atomic. Non-atomic commands decompose into atomics and narrower non-atomics. Non-atomic commands can be thought of as the top-level menu items or items with submenus in GUI programs. Atomic commands can be thought of as the items without submenus. Even though menu metaphor is used here, this doesn't mean that actual

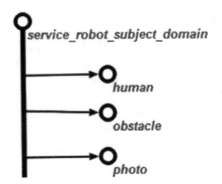

Fig. 3. Sample subject domain entities

on-screen menus must be used, since the user interface is applied here in general sense (as the means of user interaction with a technical system, not necessary graphical). Figure 4 below depicts a number of atomic commands a robot can understand (walk, turn, stop, tell, send and so forth) along with some non-atomic ones (move, report, do action, etc.). Atomic commands correspond to +Action attribute values in NooJ grammar. When a command is triggered, it initiates a request by putting a special construction in memory, which will be shown next.

When +Subject, +Object, +Action and +Features attributes are retrieved, a request structure can be built. +Action attribute becomes a request type. +Subject, +Object and +Features become its arguments. Then those are annotated accordingly. Empty node with no label denotes a specific instance of the request. Robot can subscribe to a specific event in a semantic network (node creation or deletion, arc creation or deletion from or to a specific node) via a wireless connection over a specialized network protocol. Once a structure, such as one depicted in Fig. 5, has been constructed in memory, the notification is sent to a participating robot. Then this robot determines if it can perform the request and if it does, then it leaves a report in memory for other software or hardware agents to possibly process it.

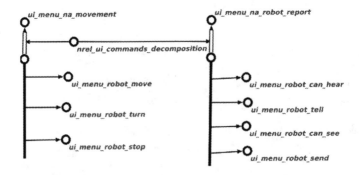

Fig. 4. USN representation of the commands

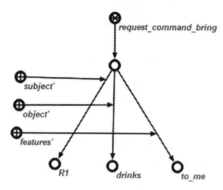

Fig. 5. USN representation of the sample request

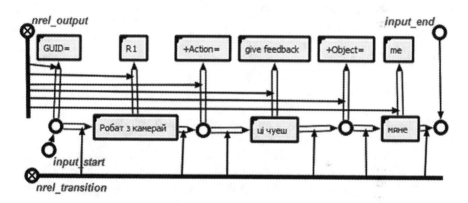

Fig. 6. USN representation of the NooJ grammar fragment

Since both technologies are graph-based, the USN representation of NooJ grammar is pretty straightforward (Fig. 6). Empty nodes with no labels denote epsilon-transitions. Wide arrows denote arbitrary connections that must be further specified. In our case we use two relations – transition and output. Narrower arrows denote an "is-a" relation (set membership or class-to-entity, to be exact) – the only relation that doesn't need to be specified. Thick dark lines denote so-called "buses" used to extend node's contact area. Text boxes denote specific input or output strings.

8   Example of OSTIS-Specific Grammar Processing

Now we can use the graph in Fig. 6 to generate a dictionary. In particular, we traverse the graph and retrieve all the inputs using a specialized language. And we only need 13 low-level (abstract graph processing machine) operators to do this. An excerpt of traversal results can be seen below in Fig. 7. Furthermore, those graphs can be programmatically transformed. And the transformation/traversal programs can transform

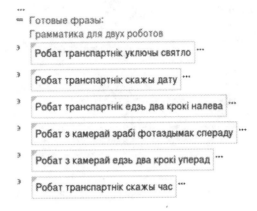

Fig. 7. Partial traversal results

itself since they are graphs as well and reside in the same memory as anything else mentioned above.

9   Conclusion

Language modeling for robots-human interaction through speech is a tricky task. On the one hand it should be simple enough to meet recognition performance requirements and on the other hand it should be close to human speech. These requirements lead us to design a language model without ambiguity. When recognizing commands, any possible uncertainty should be resolved by communication between robots and a human.

In this paper we presented the way of language modeling using SAOF concepts. We showed two different tools that could be used for this. The first one is NooJ — the development environment mainly used to construct large-coverage formalized descriptions of natural languages, and apply them to some large corpora, in real time. The second one is OSTIS – a tool that facilitates semantic analysis by providing a unified semantic network approach to knowledge representation. As we see, any of these tools can be helpful for the language modeling and dictionary generation. NooJ has simpler notation and thus is simpler to use. OSTIS claims to have universality and robustness that could be helpful when dealing with semantics though it lacks clarity in usability. The developer of the systems should decide for himself which tool to use since it is more likely to be a matter of convenience.

References

1. Silberztein, M.: Nooj Manual [Electronic resource]. Mode of access (2014). http://www. nooj4nlp.net. Accessed 31 Dec 2014

2. Golenkov, V.V.: Graphodynamical models of parallel knowledge processing. In: Golenkov, V.V., Guliakina, N.A. (eds.) Open Semantic Technologies for Intelligent Systems (OSTIS-2012). BSUIR, Minsk, pp. 23–52 (2012)
3. Yeliseyeva, O.E.: Component design of intelligent tutoring system to prepare students for centralized testing in a foreign language. In: Yeliseyeva, O.E., Rusetski, K.V. (eds.) Open Semantic Technologies for Intelligent Systems (OSTIS-2013). BSUIR, Minsk, pp. 511–516 (2013)
4. OSTIS [Electronic resource]. Mode of access (2015). http://ims.ostis.net. Accessed 30 Sep 2015

Morpheme-Based Recognition and Translation of Medical Terms

Alessandro Maisto[(✉)] and Raffaele Guarasci

Dipartimento di Scienze Politiche, Sociali e della Comunicazione,
Università degli Studi di Salerno,
Via Giovanni Paolo II, 84084 Fisciano (SA), Italy
{amaisto,rguarasci}@unisa.it

Abstract. In this paper we use Nooj to solve a recognition and translation task on medical terms with a morphosemantic approach. The Medical domain is characterized by a huge number of different terms that appear in corpora with very low frequencies. For this reason, machine learning or statistical approaches do not achieve good results on this domain. In our work we apply a morpho-semantic approach that take advantage from a number of Italian and English word-formation strategies for the automatic analysis of Italian words and for the generation of Italian/English bilingual lexicons in the medical sub-code. Using Nooj we built a series of Italian and bilingual dictionaries of morphemes, a set of morphological grammars that specify how morphemes combine with each other, a syntactic grammar for the recognition of compound terms and a Finite State Transducer (FST) for the translation of medical terms based on morphemes. This approach produces as output: a categorized Italian electronic dictionary of medical simple words, provided with labels specifying the meaning of each term; a Thesaurus of simples and compounds medical terms, organized in 22 medical subcategories; A an Italian/English translation of medical terms.

Keywords: Morpho-semantic · Medical domain · Translation · Recognition · NooJ · Finite state automatas

1 Introduction

The technical-scientific language of the medicine, provided with a number of technical lemmas that is larger than any other sub-code, is a part of the set of sub-codes that are organized in taxonomies and strong notional fields. Each term of this huge sub-dictionary, besides, occurs in texts with a very low frequency. For this reason, the majority of medical sub-domain terms could be defined as "rare events" (Möbius 2003). This phenomenon could has a negative impact on the performances of the statistical and the machine learning methods. In general, free lexical resources for the medical domain, are often few and incomplete for every kind of language. Multilingual resources, in addition, are very rare and have a crucial role in every NLP systems. The idea of the paper is to approach this large number of medical terms starting from a restricted dictionary (about 1000) of morphemes that, combined one another, allow the recognition of a huge number of terms, at least in two languages: Italian, English. This kind of approach, called Morpho-semantics, can be used to describe, in an analytical

© Springer International Publishing Switzerland 2016
T. Okrut et al. (Eds.): NooJ 2015, CCIS 607, pp. 172–181, 2016.
DOI: 10.1007/978-3-319-42471-2_15

way, the meaning of the words that belong to the same subdomain or to the same "morphological family" (e.g. words: *iper-acusia, ipo-acusia*; subdomain: *-acusia* "otolaryngology"; description: *ipo-* "lack", *iper-* "excess", etc.). We grounded the automatic creation of medical lexical databases on specific formative elements that are able to define a meaning in a univocal way, thanks to the regular combination of modules defined independently. Such elements do not represent mere terminations, but possess their own semantic self-sufficiency (Iacobini 2004). In order to build a multi-lingual medical thesaurus in which every lemma is automatically associated with its own terminological and semantic properties and with the respective English translations we created a small *NooJ* (Silberztein 2003) dictionaries of morphemes. Morphemes may belong to three morphological categories, *Prefixes, Confixes,* and *Suffixes,* which are provided with semantic annotations (explaining the meaning of the morpheme), terminological annotations (that refers to the medical class to which the morpheme belongs to) and with the translation of the morpheme in the other language (e.g. *iper*, "hyper"). A Morphological Grammar finds every possible combination of Prefixes, Confixes and Suffixes and annotates the recognized medical term separating it in different units, according with the morphemes that compose the words. Two corpora of Italian Medical Records have been analyzed with this resources configuration and, later, a syntactic translation grammar has been applied: for every combination of morphemes, the grammar transcribes as output the English transduction of the morpheme.

2   Related Work

Morpho-semantic approaches have been already applied to the medical domain in many languages. Works that deserve to be mentioned are Pratt (Pratt and Pacak 1969) on the identification and on the transformation of terminal morphemes in the English medical dictionary; Wolff (Wolff 1984) on the classification of the medical lexicon based on formative elements of Latin and Greek origin; Pacak et al. (Pacak et al. 1980) on the diseases words ending in *-itis*; Norton e Pacak (Norton and Pacak 1983) on the surgical operation words ending in *-ectomy* or *-stomy*; (Dujols et al. 1991) on the suffix *-osis*.

Between the nineties and the 2000, many studies have been published on the automatic population of thesauri, we recollect among others (Lovis et al. 1995), that derived the meaning of the words from the morphemes that compose them; (Lovis et al. 1998) that identified ICD codes in diagnoses written in different languages; (Hahn et al. 2001) that segmented the subwords in order to recognize and extract medical documents; and (Grabar e Zweigenbaum 2000) that used machine learning methods on the morphological data of the thesaurus SNOWMED (French, Russian, English). An advantage of the morphosemantic method is that complex linguistic analyses designed for a language can be often transferred to other languages. (Deléger et al. 2007), as an example, adapted the morphosemantic analyzer DériF (Namer 2009), designed for the French language, for the automatic analysis of English medical neoclassical compounds. (Amato et al. 2014) present a system for morpho-semantic classification of medical simple and compound terms that use Nooj dictionaries and Grammars in order to create a medical thesaurus.

As regards morphological approaches in machine translation tasks, we mention a lexical morphology based Italian-French MT tool (Cartoni 2009), that implemented lexical morphology principles into an Italian-French machine translation tool, to manage computational treatment of neologisms. We than consider (Toutanova 2008) and (Minkov et al. 2007), that proposed models for the prediction of inflected word forms for the generation of morphologically rich languages (e.g. Russian and Arabic) into a machine translation context. Furthermore, (Virpioja et al. 2007) exploited the *Morfessor* algorithm, a method for the unsupervised morph-tokens analysis, with the purpose of reducing the size of the lexicon and improving the ability to generalize in machine translation tasks. Their approach, which basically treated morphemes as word-tokens, has been tested on the Danish, Finnish, and Swedish languages.

(Daumake et al. 1999) exploited a set of subwords (morphologically meaningful units) to automatically translate biomedical terms from German to English, with the purpose to morphologically reduce the number of lexical entries to sufficiently cover a specific domain. (Lee 2004) explored a novel morphological analysis technique that involved languages with highly asymmetrical morphological structures (e.g. Arabic and English) in order to improve the results of statistical machine translations. In the end, (Amtrup 2003) proposed a method that involved finite state technologies for the morphological analysis and generation tasks compatible with Machine Translation systems.

3   Methodology

The morpho-semantic approach allows the analytical description of the meaning of the words that belong to the same subdomain or to the same "morphological family" (Jacquemin 1999).

Because of its frequency distribution (very large number of different terms that appear in texts with a very low frequency), medical terms could be considered as "rare event". This feature of the medical domain has a strong impact on the performances of the statistical and the machine learning methods, and, for this reason, the technical-scientific language of the medicine, rich of technical lemmas, in great part derived from neoclassical terms, is especially adapt to a morpho-semantic approach.

Our approach allow to manage a very large number of medical terms, starting from a restricted dictionary (about 1000) of morphemes pertaining to the domain. Combining these morphemes it is possible to recognize a huge number of terms and translate it into English.

In addition, finding *(almost-)synonym sets* (Namer 2005) on the base of the words that share morphemes endowed with a particular meaning (e.g. *-acusia*, hearing disorders), we can infer the domain of the medical knowledge to which the synonym set belongs (e.g. "otolaryngology") and, in the end, we can differentiate any item of the set by exploiting the meaning of the other morphemes involved in the words.

- synset: *iper-acusia, ipo-acusia, presbi-acusia, dipl-acusia*;
- subdomain: *-acusia* "otolaryngology'";
- description: *ipo-* "lack", *iper-* "excess", *presbi-* "old age", *diplo-* "double".

3.1   Lexical Resources

Thanks to the electronic version of the GRADIT (De Mauro 2003) it has been possible to collect three kind of morphemes related to the medical domain:

- Prefixes
  - quantitative description of the terms (*hyper-, hypo-, normo-, extra-...*)
  - qualitative description (*emo-, per-, peri-, pre-, pro-, trans-...*)
- Confixes
  - meaning of the single term (acusia, cancero, pulmono...)
- Suffixes
  - meaning of the term (*-oma, -asis, -itis...*)
  - grammatical category (*-able, -aceous, -atory...*)

The domain of medicine has been divided into 22 subcategories (cardiology, neurology, gastroenterology, oncology, etc.), and the majority of morphemes has been attributed to one of them.

A class "*undefined*" has been used as residual category, in order to collect the words particularly difficult to classify.

The morpheme dictionary, built with Nooj, has been enriched with other semantic information, concerning the meaning they express.

Each morpheme has been compared with the morphemes presented into the Open Dictionary of English by the *LearnThat Foundation* (https://www.learnthat.org/) and the respective English translation has been added to the NooJ Dictionary.

Furthermore, also other morphemes, that had not been treated by the GRADIT as medical ones, have been added to our list. Table 1 presents a list of morphemes types used in our dictionary.

Table 1. Number and types of morphemes of the Morphenita.nod dictionary

Manner of use	Category	Number	Translated
Medicine	Confixes	451	349
Medicine	Suffixes	14	13
Medicine	Prefixes	7	7
Anatomy	Confixes	45	27
General	Suffixes	19	18

The Nooj Medical Morpheme Dictionary specifies the category of the morpheme (PFX, SFX, etc.), and provides semantic descriptions about the meaning they confer to the words composed with them. Such semantic information regard the three following aspects:

- Meaning: introduced by the code "+Sens", this semantic label describes the specific meaning of the morpheme (e.g. *-oma* corresponds to the descriptions *tumori*, "tumors" and *-ite* to *infiammazioni*, "inflammations");
- Medical Class: introduced by the code "+Med", this terminological label gives information regarding the medical subdomain to which the morpheme belongs

(e.g. *cardio-* let the machine know that every word formed with it pertains to the subdomain of cardiology);

- Translation: introduced by the code "+EN", presents the corresponding translation of the morpheme in English.

The dictionary, compiled into the file *Morphenita.nod*, contains the three categories presented before (CFX for the confixes, SFX for the Suffixes and PFX for the Prefixes) and two new categories (as shown in Fig. 1):

```
#CONFIXES
cardio,CFX+SensCP=cuore+Med=CARDIO+EN=cardio
cerebro,CFX+SensCP=cervello+Med=NEUROEN=cerebro
epitelio,CFX+SensCP=tessutoInterno+Med=INTERN+EN=epithelio
patia,CFX+SensCP=malattia+EN=pathy
toraco,CFX+SensCP=torace+EN=thoraco

#CONFIXES BEFORE THE END
biosi,CFXE+SensCP=vita+EN=biosis
cardio,CFXE+SensCP=cuore+Med=CARDIO+EN=cardium
cerebro,CFXE+SensCP=cervello+Med=NEUROEN=cerebral
epitelio,CFXE+SensCP=tessutoInterno+Med=INTERN+EN=epithelium
toraco,CFXE+SensCP=torace+EN=thorax

#CONFIXES BEFORE SUFFIXES
bronco,CFXS+SensCP=bronchi+Med=PNEUMO+EN=bronch
carcino,CFXS+SensCP=cancro+Med=ONCOL+EN=carcin
cardio,CFXS+SensCP=cuore+Med=CARDIO+EN=cardi
toraco,CFXS+SensCP=torace+EN=thorac

#PREFIXES
emo,PFX+SensP=sangue+EN=hemo
iper,PFX+SensP=eccesso+EN=hyper
ipo,PFX+SensP=poco+EN=hypo

#SUFFIXES
ite,SFX+SensS=infiammazione+EN=itis
oma,SFX+SensS=tumoriInfiammazioniTumefazioni+Med=ONCOL+EN=oma
osi,SFX+SensS=lesione+EN=osis
```

Fig. 1. Extract of the dictionary

- CFXS, that includes all the Confixes that can appear before a suffix, with its correspondent English morpheme deprived of the final part, in order to avoid vocal repetition in case of suffixation. The word *Ateroscelrosi*, "Atherosclerosis", for example, that is composed by three morphemes, *atero*, *sclero* and *osi*, with the respective translation of morphemes, "athero", "sclera" and "osis"; when translated, produces the sequence "atherosclerosis". Since is not possible to operate directly on English morphemes, to prevent these kind of errors, the system contemplates the new category CFXS for Confixes that are followed by a Suffix. While the sequence of morphemes CFX-CFX-SFX produce "Atheroscleroosis", a sequence CFX-CFXS-SFX translate correctly the medical term.
- CFXE, that includes all the Confixes that can appear at the end of a world, with the correspondent English morpheme modified ad it appear when close the world. For example, *Emotorace*, in English "Hemotorax", with a normal sequence of CFX-CFX, produce "Hemotoraco". With the sequence CFX-CFXE produce the correct translation.

3.2 Grammars

The creation of the Morphenita.nod dictionary represents the first step of the method: in order to automatically recognize and translate medical words in real text occurrences, needs the support of morphological and syntactic local grammars.

Morphological Grammars. For the recognition of medical terms we use seven parallel morphological grammars, called *Medita#.nom*, that automatically assign semantic tags to the simple words found in free texts, according to the meaning of the formative elements that compose the same words.

The seven grammars built with Nooj include the following combination of morphemes:

1. confixes-confixes or prefixes-confixes or prefixes-confixes-confixes;
2. confixes-suffixes or prefixes-confixes-suffixes;
3. confixes-confixes-suffixes or prefixes-confixes-confixes-suffixes;
4. nouns-confixes;
5. prefixes-nouns-confixes;
6. confixes-nouns-confixes;
7. nouns-suffixes;

In Fig. 2 is presented a sample of the morphological grammar: The code <+MEDICINA$1S$2S$ > allows the grammar to assign to the words the information inherited by the morphemes that compose them.

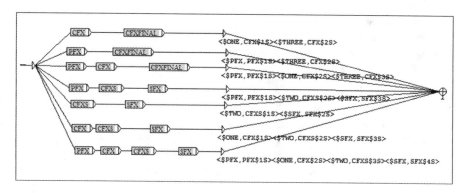

Fig. 2. Sample of morphological grammar *Medita1.nom*

To allows the automatic translation of medical terms, we built another morphological grammar with seven paths (corresponding to the seven grammars used for the classification task), called *MedItEn.nom*, that recognize each morphemes of the word as separate entities, and tag it independently as show in Fig. 3:

Syntactical Grams. In order to extract and classify multiword expressions, we exploited a Nooj syntactic grammar. The one designed for this work, called *MedClass. nog*, includes seven main paths based on different combinations of Nouns (N), Adjectives (A) and Prepositions (PREP) (Fig. 4).

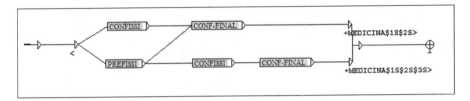

Fig. 3. The morphological Grammar *MedItEn.nom*

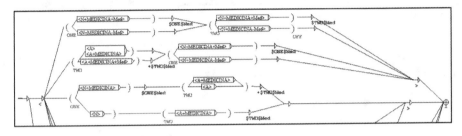

Fig. 4. Extract of the syntactic grammar *MedClass.nog*

1. Noun;
2. Noun + Noun;
3. Adjective + Noun;
4. Noun + Adjective;
5. Noun + Noun + Adjective;
6. Noun + Adjective + Adjective;
7. Noun + Preposition + Noun;

Every path attributes to the matched sequence the label that belongs to the head of the compound. In the case in which the head is not endowed with a semantic label, the compound receives the residual tag "undefined".

For the Translation task, we construct a different syntactic transducer called *Transiten.nog*, that simply consider the recognized morphemes and translate them into the respective English translation specified by the dictionary (Fig. 5).

4   Experimentation

In order to evaluate the precision of our morpho-semantic method, so for the classification task as for the translation task, we experiment them on two different corpora:

- a first corpus of about 5.000 simplified medical records, spliced into 20 subsections with a total of 64.360 tokens and 41.468 annotated word forms
- a second corpus of 330 complete Medical records. 38.696 tokens and 20.261 word forms.

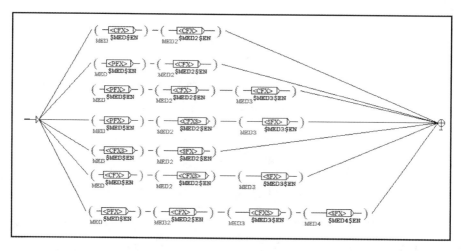

Fig. 5. The Finite State Transducer *Transiten.nog*

The classification task produce as output an Electronic Dictionary of simple medical words and a Thesaurus of simple and compound medical words.

Into the dictionary, the lemmas extracted from the diagnoses are systematically associated with their terminological ("\Med") and semantic ("\Sens") descriptions as in the example:

```
gastrite,N+SensCP=apparatoGastrico+Med=GASTRO+SensS=infiammazione
cardiopatia,N+SensCP=cuore+Med=CARDIO+SensCS=malattia
ipertensiva,A+SensP=eccesso+SensCP=tensione+Med=CARDIO
aortica,A+SensCP=aorta+Med=CARDIO
```

Into the thesaurus, medical terms recognized are grouped together on the base of their medical classes

The precision for the classification task is calculated by subdomain in order to underline strengths and weaknesses of the method in relation with a specific class or group of worlds.

As the Table 2 shows, best results has been obtained with Traumatology, Surgery, Pneumology and Gastroenterology classes. The Endocrinology class is the worst class due to problems with the recognition of the morpheme *Tiroido*, "Thyroid", that could be corrected in future works.

For what concern the translation task, the output is represented by a list of English Medical Terms preceded by the respective Italian words.

The evaluation of translation task has been carried out by comparing our method with google translate for 214 words presented in the corpus. Google obtain a 84,11 % of precision but our method achieve the 74,77 %, but with good performances with neologisms and scientific diseases terms (such as Hemorrhage, «bleeding» for Google Translate). Furthermore, our morpho-semantic method, in combination with Google Translate, reach the 93 % of precision, that is a very good results for a translation task.

Table 2. Precision values

Detected classes	Precision %
Traumatology	100
Surgery	97,82
Pneumology	95,83
Gastroenterology	89,18
Orthopedic	80,95
Urology	76,19
Intern Medicine	69,04
Cardiology	66,96
Endocrinology	23,80
Undefined	50,80
Tot	69,50

5   Conclusions

We presented a morpho-semantic approach for automatic recognition and translation of medical domain terms. For what concern the recognition task, we classify a great number of simple and compound terms with a good total precision value. Furthermore, it will be possible to improve this value working on a few number of morphemes pertaining at the Endocrinology sub-domain and increasing the number of medical morphemes presents into the dictionary. We automatically generate a Thesaurus of medical terms and a dictionary provided with description of the meaning of each term. In addition, this kind of approach do not suffer for the presence of neologisms into the medical corpora.

As seen in the evaluation phase, although the system do not reach the precision of Google in a translation task, it achieve good results in translation of neologisms or scientific disease terms. In future works it could be possible to extend the method to other languages such as Spanish by simply add the Spanish translation of the morphemes present into the dictionary. Moreover, improving the Finite State Translator and the morphological grammar, the precision of the translation task will grow.

References

Amato, F., Elia, A., Maisto, A., Mazzeo, A., Pelosi, S.: Automatic population of italian medical thesauri: a morphosemantic approach. In: 9th International Conference on P2P, Parallel, Grid, Cloud and Internet Computing, pp. 432–436. IEEE, Guangzhou (2014)

Amtrup, J.W.: Morphology in machine translation systems: efficient integration of finite state transducers and feature structure descriptions. Mach. Transl. **18**(3), 217–238 (2003)

Cartoni, B.: Lexical morphology in machine translation: a feasibility study. In: Proceedings of the 12th Conference of the European Chapter of the Association for Computational Linguistics, pp. 130–138. Association for Computational Linguistics (2009)

Daumke, P., Schulz, S., Markó, K.: Subword Approach for Acquiring and Crosslinking Multilingual Specialized Lexicons. Programme Committee (2006)

De Mauro, T.: Nuove Parole Italiane dell'uso, GRADIT, vol. 7 (2003)

Deléger, L., Naner, F., Zweigenbaum, P., et al.: Defining medical words: transposing morphosemantic analysis from French to English (2007)

Dujols, P., Aubas, P., Baylon, C., Grémy, F.: Morpho-semantic analysis and translation of medical compound terms. Methods Inf. Med. **30**(1), 30 (1991)

Hahn, U., Honeck, M., Piotrowski, M., Schulz, S.: Subword segmentation-leveling out morphological variations for medical document retrieval. In: Proceedings of the AMIA Symposium, p. 229. American Medical Informatics Association (2001)

Iacobini, C.: Composizione con elementi neoclassici, in La formazione delle parole in italiano, a cura di Grossmann, M., Rainer, F., pp. 69–95 (2004)

Jacquemin, C.: Syntagmatic and paradigmatic representations of term variation. In: Proceedings of the 37th Annual Meeting of the Association for Computational Linguistics on Computational Linguistics, pp. 341–348. Association for Computational Linguistics (1999)

Lee, Y.S.: Morphological analysis for statistical machine translation. In: Proceedings of HLT-NAACL 2004: Short Papers, pp. 57–60. Association for Computational Linguistics (2004)

Lovis, C., Baud, R., Rassinoux, A.M., Michel, P.A., Scherrer, J.R.: Medical dictionaries for patient encoding systems: a methodology. Artif. Intell. Med. **14**(1), 201–214 (1998)

Lovis, C., Michel, P.A., Baud, R., Scherrer, J.R.: Word segmentation processing: a way to exponentially extend medical dictionaries. Medinfo **8**(pt 1), 28–32 (1995)

Minkov, E., Toutanova, K., Suzuki, H.: Generating complex morphology for machine translation. ACL **7**, 128–135 (2007)

Möbius, B.: Rare events and closed domains: two delicate concepts in speech synthesis. Int. J. Speech Technol. **6**(1), 57–71 (2003)

Namer, F.: Acquisizione automatica di semantica lessicale in francese: il sistema di trattamento computazionale della formazione delle parole dérif. In: Thornton, A.M, Grossmann, M. (eds.) Atti del XXVII Congresso internazionale di studi Società di Linguistica Italiana: La Formazione delle parole, pp. 369–388 (2005)

Namer, F.: Morphologie, lexique et traitement automatique des langues (2009)

Norton, L., Pacak, M.G.: Morphosemantic analysis of compound word forms denoting surgical procedures. Methods Inf. Med. **22**(1), 29–36 (1983)

Pacak, M.G., Norton, L., Dunham, G.S.: Morphosemantic analysis of-ITIS forms in medical language. Methods Inf. Med. **19**(2), 99–105 (1980)

Pratt, A.W., Pacak, M.: Identification and transformation of terminal morphemes in medical english. Methods Inf. Med. **8**(2), 84–90 (1969)

Silberztein, M.: NooJ manual (2003). www.nooj4nlp.net

Toutanova, K., Suzuki, H., Ruopp, A.: Applying morphology generation models to machine translation. In: ACL, pp. 514–522 (2008)

Virpioja, S., Väyrynen, J.J., Creutz, M., Sadeniemi, M.: Morphology-aware statistical machine translation based on morphs induced in an unsupervised manner. Mach. Transl. Summit XI **2007**, 491–498 (2007)

Wolff, S.: The use of morphosemantic regularities in the medical vocabulary for automatic lexical coding. Methods Inf. Med. **23**(4), 195–203 (1984)

Using NooJ to Process Satellite Data

Julia Borodina$^{(\boxtimes)}$ and Yuras Hetsevich

United Institute of Informatics Problems, Minsk, Belarus
julia.baradzina@gmail.com, yury.hetsevich@gmail.com

Abstract. This paper describes the processing of satellite telemetry data and its conversion from reduced form into full, orthographically correct word sequences for further use in text-to-speech synthesis or other applications.

The purpose of a telemetry system is to reliably and transparently convey measurement information from a remotely located data-generating source to users located in space or on Earth. For the purpose of this paper, by satellite telemetry data, we are also referring to the results of measurements made by nanosatellites in space and received with antennas.

In this study, we used a text corpus which was created with the data from satellite telemetry converter software. The data is provided in the form of abbreviations, numbers, and measurement units, along with orthographical words (e.g. Voltage of 5 V system is 4.904 [V]; Temperature of the 145 MHz TX: 16 °C). Telemetry data is mostly collected in English as an international language for science, yet Belarusian national space tradition requires this information to be available in one of the national languages of Belarus, Belarusian or Russian.

As input, the grammar takes as text sequences like 0.9708 A and transforms first the numerical part, then measurement units, into a Belarusian phrase: *нуль цэлых дзевяць тысяч семсот восем дзесяцітысячных ампера* 'zero point nine thousand seven hundred and eight ten-thousandths of an ampere'. Due to the fact that Belarusian and Russian are both synthetic languages, the declension paradigm of such numerals can be very complex.

Keywords: Nooj · Nanosatellite · Telemetry · Quantitative expressions with measurement units · QEMU · Russian · Belarusian · Syntactic grammar

1 Introduction

Remote transmission of data is commonly used nowadays in many fields, including meteorology, space science, transportation, agriculture, water management, health care, energy monitoring. Wireless data transfer mechanisms allow monitoring in real time by sending measurements to a receiver. This process of automated communication by which measurements are made and data is collected at remote or inaccessible points and transmitted to receiving equipment for monitoring is called telemetry [1].

Telemetry (from the Greek *tele* = remote, and *metron* = measure) is the wireless transmission and reception of measured quantities for the purpose of remotely monitoring environmental conditions or equipment parameters. Data obtained in this way is also called telemetry.

© Springer International Publishing Switzerland 2016
T. Okrut et al. (Eds.): NooJ 2015, CCIS 607, pp. 182–190, 2016.
DOI: 10.1007/978-3-319-42471-2_16

There are many kinds of satellites flying in the outer space, and all of them collect and transmit telemetry, but the most interesting for the purposes of this study are miniaturized satellites — specifically, nanosatellites. Their small size (about 10 × 10 × 10 cm) and weight (approx. 1.3 kg) makes them more cost-effective and therefore allows them to be used for university-related research. Nanosatellites are used primarily by universities for research purposes, typically in low Earth orbits.

In Fig. 1 you may see what a typical nanosatellite looks like. Despite its tiny size, this satellite receives and sends to Earth information about its own condition (whether battery is full, what is a temperature on each panel etc.) and information about outside "environment".

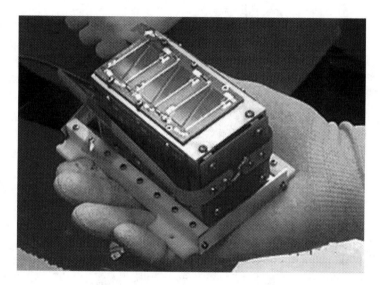

Fig. 1. A nanosatellite $50SAT - Eagle2

At the moment, there are about 100 active satellites, and each of them may have a different: measurements of ionospheric space weather, space communication research, infrared camera imaging, earthquake detection, and so on. Depending on the mission, the set of measured parameters and telemetry formats can vary. However, every spacecraft has a minimum of essential measurements, like the temperature of its side panels, battery voltage, battery current etc.

After the series of transformations described below, satellite data takes the form of a quantitative expression with measurement units (QEMU) such as *126 mA; 10.66 V; 6.34 C* etc. Our goal is to transform those expressions into full orthographic form in the Belarusian and Russian languages: *сто дваццаць шэсць міліампер (Belarusian)* and *сто двадцать шесть миллиампер (Russian)* 'one hundred twenty-six milliamperes'; *дзесяць цэлых шэсцьдзясят шэсць сотых вольта* (Belarusian) and *десять целых шестьдесят шесть сотых Вольта* 'ten and sixty-six one-hundredths volts'; *шэсць цэлых трыццаць чатыры сотых градуса Цэльсія* (Belarusian) and *шесть целых тридцать четыре сотых градуса Цельсия* (Russian) 'six point thirty-four degrees Celsius'.

2   Algorithm of Telemetry Processing

The algorithm of telemetry processing from the moment it is transmitted via Teletype to a grammatically correct, non-abbreviated text in Belarusian or Russian includes a few steps.

The first step is the actual reception of telemetry. It is received in hexadecimal notation, and the date and time of reception is also indicated. The portion of telemetry sent by satellite at one time is called a packet.

A data packet from a UWE-2 satellite:

```
2015-01-01T01:29:37.060Z  JA6PL  (130.718611E;  33.862056 N)
frame: 88 88 60 AA AE 8A 60 88 A0 60 AA AE 8E E1 03 F0 80 48 20 64 64
89 B5 21 02 03 1F 02 23 06 00 88 21 4F D8 42 5D 64 50 10 16 00 0E A4 10
09 00 0E 20 01 F3 F7 E3 1D DF F1 E5
```

In the second step, this packet gets converted by a decoder from hexadecimal code into a sequence of numbers. These numbers are called comma-separated values and they are a tabular data presented in plain text. The line below is a data record. Each record consists of many fields, separated by commas.

```
2015-01-0101:29:37,:fcs:1444,8,18,98,:eps:8.04,8.05,8.10,
8.09,3,3,4,3,248,8,  100001110000000001011000,8.3,22.2,9.7,
21.9,-34,23,-19,12,-24,166,-29,
```

Third, CSV files are transferred into a telemetry decoding program, which is individualized for every satellite. One such program you can see in Fig. 2. Every value is assigned to the table cell, where it gets captions and measurement units. The mission of this satellite, UWE-2, is to test methods and algorithms for attitude determination and to optimize internet protocol parameters, in order to adapt to the particular space environment. Hence it collects data on battery voltage, battery temperature, and current on every side of the satellite.

Time	02/20/201508:02:52		Spacecraft	FM2	
Switch states	100001110000000001011000				
Hard Resets	248	2A Batt0 Volt	8.04 V	BCR Z- Volt	8.3 V
Soft Resets	8	2A Batt1 Volt	8.05 V	BCR Y+ Volt	22.2 V
FCS Reset	1444	2E Batt0 Volt	8.10 V	BCR X Volt	9.7 V
		2E Batt1 Volt	8.09 V	BCR Y Volt	21.9 V
CPU Temp	8 C	2A Batt0 Temp	3 C	BCR Z- Curr	-34 mA
UHF Radio Temp	18 C	2A Batt1 Temp	3 C	BCR Y+2 Curr	23 mA
UHF RSSI	98	2E Batt0 Temp	4 C	BCR Y-2 Curr	-19 mA
		2E Batt1 Temp	3 C	BCR X+ Curr	12 mA
				BCR X- Curr	-24 mA
				BCR Y+3 Curr	166 mA
				BCR Y-3 Curr	-29 mA

Fig. 2. An example of decoded telemetry from the satellite UWE-2

All the procedures described above can be considered engineering tasks. However, since our objective is to get non-abbreviated, grammatically correct text, there is a linguistic task that needs to be completed, too.

3   Formulation of a Linguistic Task

In the past, we have developed prototype grammars in NooJ [2] to process a wide range of QEMU in various contexts. We analysed the texts and all the QEMUs the grammar is likely to encounter. Structural and linguistic features of QEMU were collected and incorporated into our prototype grammars in order to maximize performance on precision and recall. The Belarusian syntactic grammar applied to a text corpus of over 100,000 tokens has achieved 86 % precision and 82 % recall. The set of features for this grammar is listed in Table 1.

Table 1. Features of prototype NooJ grammars and those customized for telemetry processing

	Prototype grammars	Customized grammars
1. Number of grammatical cases	3 cases: Nominative, Genitive, Accusative;	1 case: Nominative;
2. Quantity of measurement units	About 120 measurement units;	25 measurement units;
3. Format of the number	Whole and decimal numbers, intervals, exponents;	Whole and decimal numbers;
4. Formal models of QEMU structure	11 models;	3 models;
5. Input and output language	Belarusian > Belarusian	English > Belarusian English > Russian

Firstly, the prototype grammar had covered three grammatical cases: we have chosen the most frequently used, which are Nominative, Genitive and Accusative.

Secondly, our first grammar had included 120 units to cover measurement units of mass, length, volume, speed, time, electric current, temperature, luminous intensity, etc.; units with different status with respect to the SI (SI, derived from SI and non-SI); units used with different prefixes (millimetres, centimetres, meters, kilometres, etc.).

Next, the grammar can process whole and decimal numbers with up to nine digits on either side of the decimal, plus intervals and exponents, as well as different structural types of numerals, which in Russian and Belarusian affects cases of numerals themselves and measurement units.

The prototype version is able to work with 11 formal models of QEMU structure, such as "X Y", "X and X Y", "X...X Y" etc., where X is a numeral part, and Y is a unit of measurement.

Finally, the prototype grammar has been designed as language-dependent, since the task itself requires a certain input language and a certain output language. In our case, this was Belarusian on both input and output. Also this grammar doesn't use any dictionaries.

Let us take a closer look at telemetry material (Figs. 2 and 3), as such data includes some peculiarities.

Firstly, the decoding program has predetermined form with the fields for exact numbers, and this limits the number of contexts and allows syntactical structure of the sentence we build to be simple, hence, the number of grammatical cases we need is also decreasing. Basically, in both Belarusian and Russian we only need one case, which is Nominative (e.g. *CPU Temp 3.50 C* gets to be converted to *Тэмпература ЦПУ – тры цэлых пяць дзесятых градуса Цэльсія* (Belarusian) or Температура ЦПУ – три целых пять десятых градуса Цельсия (Russian) 'CPU temperature **is** three point five Celsius degrees').

Secondly, we see that relatively few units of measurement are needed in telemetry. For instance, satellite UWE-2 (Fig. 2) measures temperature (C), voltage (V) and electric current (mA); another satellite, TigriSat, adds to the list measurements of magnetic induction (G, mG), angles (deg) and angular speed (d/s). All in all we analysed telemetry from 15 active satellites and collected 25 different measurement units, so we can see that the number of measurement units is limited due to the specific tasks of the nanosatellites.

Thirdly, the need for telemetry data in numeral formats is much less than in initial corpora: our research has shown that the whole part of numerals includes a maximum

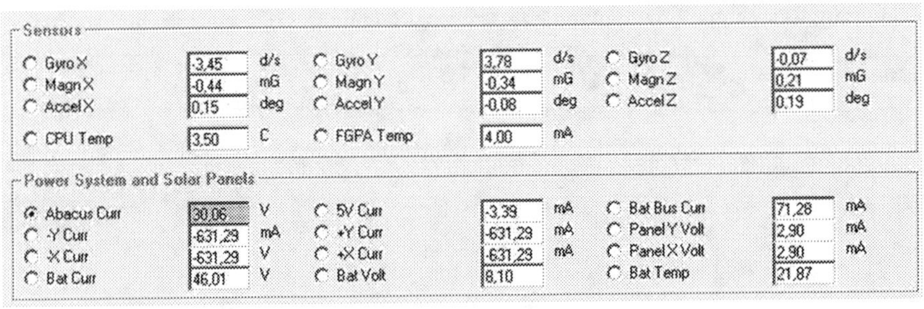

Fig. 3. An example of decoded telemetry from satellite TigriSat

of six digits, while the number of digits after the decimal point is restricted to a maximum of three digits. Also, in telemetry there are neither intervals nor exponents.

As for the telemetry format, there are only three models: X Y (*4 mA*), -X Y (*- 0.44 mG*) and X Y/Y (*-0.07 d/s*).

Another important difference between initial material and telemetry is that the input and output are in different languages, since telemetry from one satellite can be received all over the world. Therefore, decoding programs by default are dealing with English. However, according to tradition, research carried out in Belarus is required to be available in one of the national languages of the country — Belarusian or Russian.

With all this in mind, we can conclude that more specific task of processing not the entire set of possible QEMU, but nanosatellite telemetry requires certain adjustments to grammars. From the one hand the algorithm should be simpler, but from the other hand it is to be complicated by more languages involved.

4   Description of NooJ Grammars

In order to process QEMU, we use language processing software called NooJ. All the processing algorithms were developed with NooJ syntactic grammars and then tested in NooJ corpora.

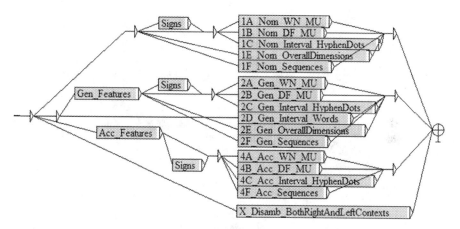

Fig. 4. The prototype QEMU grammar for Belarusian

Built first was a syntactic grammar, which helps to detect quantitative expressions and measurement units, and transform them into fully written form. The grammar is language-dependent, self-containable and has 351 graphs (Fig. 4). A detailed description of this grammar can be found in [3].

Fig. 5. The telemetry adjusted grammar for Belarusian

With all this in mind, we created new grammars for QEMU transformation, which are adapted for use in telemetry. You can see the Belarusian grammar in Fig. 5. It includes only one case, but there are still branches for signs, whole numbers, and decimals.

In Fig. 6 you can see a graph for processing QEMU with decimal numbers in the nominative case. The left side describes numeral part of the QEMU, which may take different grammatical forms, depending on the form of the measurement unit. The common rule is that the numeral 1 and all complex numerals ending in 1 (i.e. 21, 31, 101, etc.) get grammatical gender form based on the gender form of its measurement unit, while the measurement unit remains unchanged in nominative singular (Bel.: *адзін ампер, адна секунда*, Rus.: *один ампер, одна секунда* 'one ampere -

1A_Nom_WN_MU

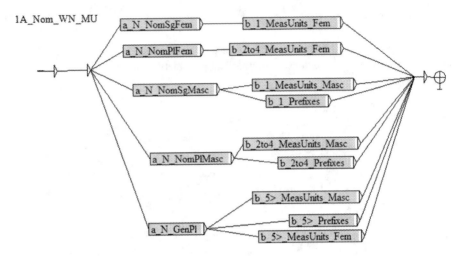

Fig. 6. Graph 1A_Nom_WN_MU of the Russian grammar for telemetry processing

masculine, one second - feminine'); 2, 3 and 4 require measurement units in nominative plural for feminine, and an archaic form of dual grammatical number for masculine (Bel.: *два амперы, дзве секунды*, Rus.: *два ампера, две секунды*, 'two amperes, two seconds'); 5 and all the numerals above it put measurement units in genitive plural

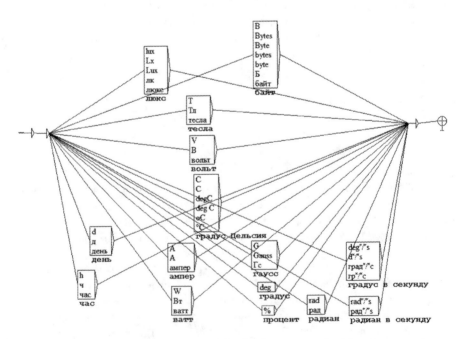

Fig. 7. Graph b_1_MeasUnits_Masc of the Russian grammar for telemetry processing

(Bel.: *дзесяць ампер, дзесяць секунд*, Rus.: *десять ампер, десять секунд* 'ten amperes, ten seconds').

Figure 7 contains a graph from the syntactic grammar for Russian with measurement units processed therein. The measurement units are those that follow after 1, so they are in the nominative singular form. Each graph in NooJ consists of rectangles, which are called nodes, and arcs. In nodes there are options for the English abbreviation or the full word, as well as the Russian, but they all have Russian output. Belarusian grammar works the same way; namely, all the measurement units both in English and in Belarusian get replaced by the output in Belarusian.

Belarusian and Russian are close enough to share some grammatical peculiarities in relation to numerals. However, the differences can be observed in our new grammars. This difference lies in the declension of decimal fractions. In Russian, all measurement units after decimal fractions take the nominative plural form, which is homonymic to the form we use after 2, 3, and 4. This homonymy allows us to use the same graph twice. In Belarusian, the form of units required after a decimal fraction is different (Bel.: *два амперы* and *нуль цэлых дзве дзясятыя ампера*, Rus.: *два ампера* and *ноль целых две десятых ампера* 'two amperes, zero point two amperes'). As a result, the Russian grammar has 37 embedded graphs, and the Belarusian grammar has 39.

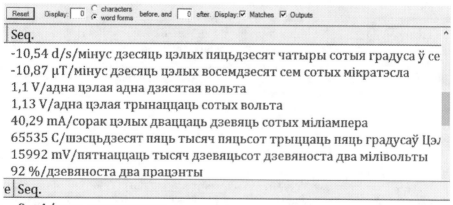

Fig. 8. Concordances with QEMU transformed into full orthographic form in Belarusian (top) and Russian (bottom)

5   Evaluation of Results

To test the grammars, we collected 100 telemetry examples from 15 active satellites. Both Belarusian and Russian grammars were tested on the same set of telemetry, since in application there should be two language interfaces, Belarusian and Russian. The resulting concordances are presented in Fig. 8.

On the one hand, the grammars are broad enough to cover various kinds of nanosatellite telemetry, and on the other hand, they are to be shortened and simplified in structure. Both grammars performed really well, displaying 100 % precision and 99 % recall, which are expected for such a specific task, where units are mostly predefined. Thus, all possible errors occur in identifying a measurement unit, since its spelling and abbreviation may vary from one telemetry example to another.

6   Conclusion and Future Work

The satellite data transmitted to a receiver is called telemetry. Telemetry is mainly a set of measured values of certain sensors. From a linguistic point of view, the satellite data is a collocation of number and an abbreviation. Processed as one, they are to be presented as a numeral and measurement unit coordinated in grammatical categories of case, gender, and number. This normalisation is made in order to voice the telemetry correctly, since numbers and abbreviations have always been a problem for various natural language processing tasks.

Firstly, future work with the processing of satellite data will involve in-depth testing of all the stages of the algorithm and grammar. Future research will also include applying the grammars as linguistic resources to a text-to-speech synthesizer, created in the Speech Synthesis and Recognition lab of UIIP NAN of Belarus.

References

1. TC Synchronization: Channel Coding—Summary of Concept and Rationale. Report Concerning Space Data System Standard. Informational Report CCSDS (2006)
2. Silberztein, M.: NooJ manual (2003). www.nooj4nlp.net
3. Skopinava, A., Hetsevich, Y., Borodina, J.: Converting quantitative expressions with measurement unit into an orthographic form, and convenient monitoring methods for belarusian. In: Monti, J., Silberztein, M., Monteleone, M., Di Buono, M.P. (eds.) Formalising Natural Languages with Nooj 2014, pp. 175–186. Cambridge Scholars Publishing, UK, Newcastle (2015)

Named Entity Recognition from Arabic-French Herbalism Parallel Corpora

Mohamed Aly Fall Seideh[1(✉)], Hela Fehri[1], and Kais Haddar[2]

[1] MIRACL Laboratory, Higher Management Institute of Gabes,
University of Gabes, Gabes, Tunisia
almedyfall@gmail.com, hela.fehri@yahoo.fr
[2] MIRACL Laboratory, Faculty of Science of Sfax, MIRACL,
University of Sfax, Sfax, Tunisia
kais.haddar@yahoo.fr

Abstract. With the adverse health effects of chemical drugs and antibiotics, herbal medicine has been a resurgence of interest in recent years. Thus, the use of medicinal plants is being largely considered as an effective and lucrative treatment, especially in Asia and Africa. The objective of this work is to achieve an identification system of medicinal plants names from French-Arabic parallel corpora. Corpora are formed by several texts composed from the multilingual encyclopedia Wikipedia. The identification of Named Entities is realized by several types of patterns. These patterns are represented by a set of transducers. The prototype is implemented in NooJ linguistic platform using a set of morphological and syntactic grammars. This prototype is experimented on a French-Arabic parallel corpora collected from Wikipedia. The obtained results are promising given the measures values.

Keywords: Named entity recognition · Herbalism · Morpho-syntactic analysis · NooJ platform

1 Introduction

The Named Entities (NEs) has been a very active field of research for many years. The concept of NEs covers not only proper names but also more complex entities such as multi-word expressions. The NEs are usually typed by taxonomies more or less vast and strongly dependent on the scope or considered needs. They typically cover names designating persons, places or organizations but can also refer to more technical concepts such as diseases. The ability to determine the NEs in a text has been established as an important task for several natural language processing areas, including information retrieval, machine translation, information extraction and language understanding [4].

At one time, herbalism was a honorable profession that laid the foundations of modern medicine, botany, pharmacy, perfumery, and chemistry [10]. Medical herbalism, or simply, herbalism or herbology or phytotherapy, is defined by [2] as "the study of herbs and their medicinal uses". In recent years, interest in herbal medicine has skyrocketed, leading to a greater scientific interest in the medicinal use of plants.

© Springer International Publishing Switzerland 2016
T. Okrut et al. (Eds.): NooJ 2015, CCIS 607, pp. 191–201, 2016.
DOI: 10.1007/978-3-319-42471-2_17

Many international studies have shown that plants are capable of treating disease and improving health, often without any significant side effects. In 2009, the World Health Organization (WHO) estimated that 80 % of the world population use herbal medicines as part of their primary health care [14]. Herbalism terminologies are a necessary resource for phytotherapists and free users of medicinal plants. This renewed interest in the natural treatment make the herbalism NE recognition as an interesting field of study. In herbalism, plants and diseases names are the most relevant NEs. The scarcity of corpora and the variability of plants names in both languages French and Arabic are the main encountered problems.

Today, a powerful resource of collecting a corpus is the web. Besides providing access to an unlimited number of documents, it also hosts a large quantity of multilingual texts [6]. Wikipedia is available in several languages including French and Arabic. These documents are semi-structured and updated continuously. Wikipedia is used by many computer linguist's applications as varied as construction of ontologies and taxonomies, semantic disambiguation, lexicology and translation [9, 12]. The scarcity of resources especially in Arabic means that Wikipedia is an opportunity for creating a French-Arabic corpora.

The linguistic platform NooJ allows the developer to construct, test, and maintain large coverage lexical resources, as well as apply morpho-syntactic tools for Arabic processing [7, 18]. It can recognize all Unicode encodings, which is a very important feature for processing Arabic Script languages. NooJ can recognize rules written in finite-state form or context-free grammar form, facilitating the development of rule-based NER systems [18]. NooJ provides a disambiguation technique based on grammars to resolve duplicate annotations. Arabic is one of the languages that are supported by NooJ [17].

As far as we know, there is no work on NEs in herbalism, much less on the parallel corpara French-Arabic in this field. The growing interest of medicinal plants justifies the need for an automated system of bilingual French-Arabic dictionary. This paper is a first step to achieve this goal. Thus this work aims to extract the NEs of medicinal plants from French-Arabic parallel corpora using the linguistic NooJ platform.

The next section presents a state of the art describing some works on NE recognition and French-Arabic parallel corpora. The third section is devoted to the study of the characteristics and typologies of plant names. The methodological approach for the extraction of NEs will be the subject of the fourth section. The fifth section will be dedicated to the implementation on the linguistic NooJ platform. Finally, in the last two sections, we will present the results and research perspectives.

2   State of the Art

Several actual works focus on the recognition, the extraction or/and the classification of NEs from a corpus or a parallel corpora. [15] describe three approaches for extracting NEs from parallel corpora.

Statistical approach based on IBM models, including using GIZA ++ [15]. The main shortcoming of supervised learning described by [11] is the requirement of a large annotated corpus. Interesting results are obtained by using semi-supervised or unsupervised learning methods. [12] proposed a semi-supervised learning for multi-lingual NE recognition from Wikipedia. [1] proposed two alignment discriminating models. The first model formalizes the alignment task as a multi-class classification task and processes it with a maximum entropy classifier. The second model is based on conditional random fields (CRF).

Linguistic approaches are based on bilingual dictionaries already available, and also on the results of the morpho-syntactic analysis of the source and target sentences [5]. [7] proposed an approach of recognition and translation based on a representation model of Arabic NEs and a set of transducers resolving morphological and syntactical phenomena.

A combination of both approaches where systems that use linguistic and statistical techniques in structured hybrid approaches. Linguistic analysis is carried out before the application of statistical measures, to be helpful in selecting all linguistic admissible candidates over which will be applied numerical tests [4, 13, 16].

[15] used a French-Arabic parallel corpora for the study of the impact of proper names transliteration on the quality of the words alignment. [6] proposed a word alignment for translating medical terminologies in a parallel text corpora. [3] identify proper names in Parallel Medical Terminologies.

We have not met work on herbalism NEs, but several newspapers and organisms and associations exist which include Journal of Medicinal Plant Research[1], Journal of Applied Research on Medicinal and Aromatic Plants[2], European Scientific Cooperative On phytotherapy[3], European Herbs Growers Association[4], International Journal of Phytotherapy[5], International Journal of Phytomedicines and Related Industries[6].

3   Analysis of Plants Names Characteristics

The names of medicinal plants can be in modern language or in botanical one [8], the modern language appellation is the most used: [French-Arabic-(Botanical): thym commun, زعتر شائع za'tar shaai' (Thymus vulgaris), absinthe, شيح ابن سينا shih ibnu siinaa (Artemisia Absinthium), chardon à petits capitules, لسان رفيع الزهرة lisaan rafii alzahrah (Carduus tenuiflorus)]; The scientific name of a plant, or Latin binomial, can be a great source of information. Botanical names are exact and internationally recognized, and each Latin binomial refers to one plant and only one plant. However common names, vary from place to another, and much confusion can result when several plants are called by the same common name. We underline here some problems that have to be treated.

---

[1] http://www.academicjournals.org/journal/JMPR.

[2] http://www.sciencedirect.com/science/journal/22147861.

[3] http://escop.com/.

[4] http://www.europam.net/.

[5] http://www.phytotherapyjournal.com/.

[6] http://www.iospress.nl/journal/medicinal-plants/.

3.1   Synonymy

As well as in Arabic or in French, a plant could have different common names; for example كَمّون الجَبَل *kammun aljabal* or المُو *almuw* in Modern Standard Arabic and Cerfeuil des Alpes, Fenouil de montagne ou Fenouil des Alpes in French indicate the same botanical name Meum athamanticum. The plant name Pois rouge also called haricot paternoster means the plant (Abrus precatorius) while cascavelle, liane réglisse, réglisse marron, graine d'église, graine diable, herbe de diable, soldat, pater noster are other common names. The synonymy represents richness of language, but is also a problem that must be managed to have robust results.

3.2   Polysemy and Inherent Ambiguity

As well as in French or in Arabic, like other languages, we face the problem of ambiguity between two or more NEs. For example consider the following plant name angélique (Angelica archangelica) which could refer to angélique (adjective) or angélique (person name). In Arabic, the plant name ريحان *rayHaan* (Ocimumbasilicum) could refer to a person name also.

3.3   Composed Terms

A lot of plant names are multi-words name as Acanthe à feuilles molles, Arnica des montagnes, Amélanchier à feuilles d'aulne, Centaurée chausse-trappe. And in Arabic also عين العفريت *'aynal'afriit*, أقنثا ناعمة *aaqnithaa naa'imah*, لحاء الغول *liHaa alghuwl*, زهرة العطاس *zahratal'aTTaas*, جكراندة ميموزية الأوراق *jikraandah maymuwziyyat alawraaq*. The recognition of plant names composed by multiple words requires effort to build the proper identification paradigm.

3.4   Some Other Problems of Arabic Language

Problems specific to Arabic language were identified. The resolution or the consideration of these problems can make the task of NEs recognition more easier and more accurate.

Lack of Capitalization. Unlike latin languages, capitalization is not a distinguishing orthographic feature of Arabic script for recognizing NEs such as proper names, acronyms and abbreviations [17]. The ambiguity caused by the absence of this feature is further increased by the fact that most Arabic NEs are indistinguishable from forms that are common nouns and adjectives (non-NEs).

Agglutination. The agglutinative nature of Arabic results in many different patterns that create many lexical variations. Each word may consist of one or more prefixes, a stem or root, and one or more suffixes in different combinations, resulting in a very systematic but complicated morphology [17]. Arabic has a set of clitics that are attached to a NE, including conjunctions such as (Waw, and) and prepositions such as

(Laam, for/to), (k, as), and (baa, by/with), or a combination of both, as in (Waw-Laam, and-for). It is determinant to use a grammar for controlling the agglutination.

Lack of Uniformity in Writing Styles. The ambiguity generated by Arabic tran-scription makes that a NE can be transliterated in a multitude of ways. The lack of standardization is significant and leads to many variants of the same word that are written with different syntax but corresponding to the same meaning. For example the plant name eucalyptus produces اليوكالبتس *alyuwkaalibtis*, اليوكالبتوس alyuwkaalibtuws, الأوكاليبتوس aluwkaalibtuws اليوكليبتوس alyuwkalibtuws; This difference is more difficult to resolve due to the morphology variation. It requires a special treatment.

4 Proposed Method and Implementation Using NooJ Platform

Our proposed method is based on three steps for the recognition of the NEs. Figure 1 shows the building a French-Arabic corpora from Wikipedia as a first step. The second step consists of elaborating dictionaries, morphological and syntactic grammars from identified patterns.

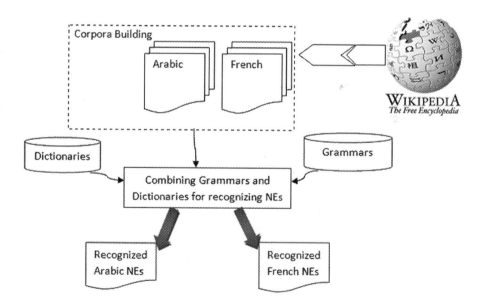

Fig. 1. Proposed method

The third, and the last step consists of implementing the dictionaries, the grammars, and the corpora in the linguistic NooJ Platform and, finally processing linguistic analysis for generating identified NEs.

4.1   Corpora Building

We generate pairs of parallel documents (i.e., documents that are French-Arabic translations of each other) using information contained in the document structure, and links to corresponding documents in the other language. Indeed, after a study of the documents, we noticed that each document provided access to its translation page in the corresponding language. This gives us 65 pairs of parallel documents and a total of 275788 words.

4.2   Dictionaries

In the following, we present plants dictionaries that we have elaborated (Fig. 2).

```
Érable,N+Plante+FLX=abricot
erigéron,N+Plante+FLX=abricot
eucalyptus,N+Plante
anis,N+Plante
grenade,N+Plante+FLX=abricot+DRV=grenade
geranium,N+Plante
abricot,N+Plante+FLX=abricot+DRV=abricot
eupatoire,N+Plante+FLX=abricot
euphorbe,N+Plante+FLX=abricot
euphraise,N+Plante+FLX=abricot
fenouil,N+Plante+FLX=abricot
fenugrec,N+Plante+FLX=abricot
flouve,N+Plante+FLX=abricot
fougère,N+Plante+FLX=abricot
fraise,N+Plante+FLX=abricot+DRV=grenade
fucus,N+Plante+FLX=abricot
fusain,N+Plante+FLX=abricot
gaillet,N+Plante+FLX=abricot
marron,N+Plante+FLX=abricot+DRV=marron
```

Fig. 2. An extract of French Plant dictionary

- A dictionary of plants names: The Arabic plants names dictionary is composed of 715 entries, and the French one is about 668 entries. Some plants names without a paradigm definition are modeled as frozen expression such as Centaurée chausse-trappe in the French dictionary or أضراس الكلب *aDraas alkalb* in the Arabic one.
- A dictionary of plants components (i.e. stem, leaf, bud, root, flower, fruit, seed, stalk): the dictionary of Arabic plants components contains 8 entries and the French one 8 entries (Fig. 3).

أَدُونِـيس, N+Plantea
اذَخَرَه, N+Plantea
أَرَاك, N+Plantea
أَزطَة, N+Plantea
أَزطَمَاشِـيا, N+Plantea
أَزقَظِـيُون, N+Plantea
أَزنِـيـكا, N+Plantea
أَرِيـقَـازُون, N+Plantea
آس, N+Plantea
أَسَازُون, N+Plantea
سَبَانَـخ, N+Plantea
أَضزَاس الـكَـلْب, N+Plan
قِـزفَـة, N+Plantea
إكْـلِـيـل, N+Plantea
زَغْثَر, N+Plantea
زَنَـد, N+Plantea

Fig. 3. An extract of Arabic Plant dictionary

- A dictionary of triggers: a set of triggers are detected like زيت *ziit* for the Arabic (5entries), oil for French (7 entries). The trigger helps to identify Olive oil rather than Olive.

- A dictionary of locations: a lot of plant names contain location, for example Erigéron du Canada, Camomille des champs, or طحلب أيسلندا, *TaHlab ayslandaa*, قصب النيل *qaSab alnyl* contains locations in their names. For the Arabic 18 entries and the French 120 entries.

- A dictionary of adjectives: for the French we used the adjective dictionary of NooJ, and for the Arabic we have created a dictionary composed of 110 entries. Guimauve officinale or قويسة مخزنية *qawysah makhziniyah* are examples of such plants names.

4.3   Transducers Implemented on the NooJ Platform

We have implemented a set of transducers. In the following, we present the morphological grammar one dedicated for resolving agglutination, then examples of Arabic and French syntactic grammars.

Morphological Grammar Resolving Agglutination. Arabic is a highly inflected language which entails a requirement of understanding of its morphological nature.

The inflected Arabic word maybe composed of prefixes such as prepositions and suffixes such as pronouns. The agglutination grammar in Fig. 4 is built to fix this problem.

Syntactic Grammars. A set of patterns are modeled and translated into syntactic grammars using defined dictionaries and inflectional and derivational morphology features. The grammars perform recognition and extraction of plant entities from the input corpus.

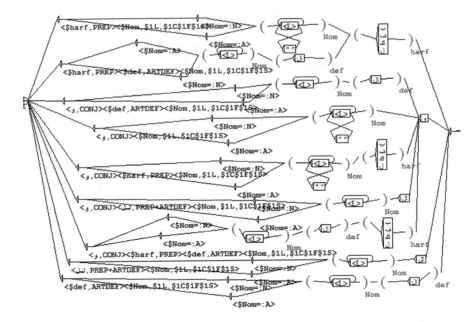

Fig. 4. Extract of the agglutination grammar

The main transducer in Fig. 5 allows recognition of NEs belonging to the Arabic corpus. Each path of each sub-graph represents a set of rules extracted from the studied corpus. The transducer of the sub-graph in Fig. 6 allows the recognition of NEs composed by multiple words like: قنطريون صغير *qanTaryuwn saghiir*, زهرة العطّاس *zahratal'aTTaas*, أوراق الشاي الاخضر *aawraaq alshaay alakhdhar*.

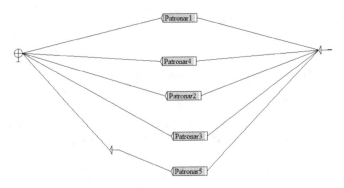

Fig. 5. Arabic main transducer

Patronar1

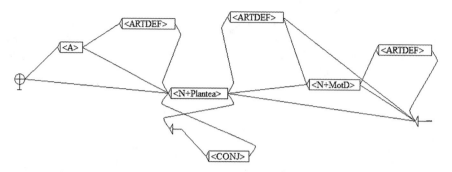

Fig. 6 Extract of the Arabic transducer definition

The main transducer for processing the French corpus in Fig. 7 consists of four patterns representing different identification rules. For example, the transducer in Fig. 8 identifies the plants names such as: plante du sapin, petites poires, feuilles de coca, myrtille, etc.

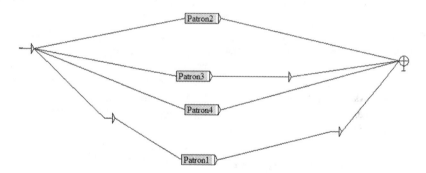

Fig. 7 French main transducer

Patron1

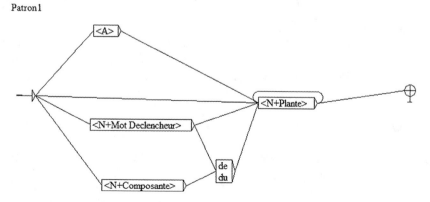

Fig. 8 Extract of the French transducer definition

5   Evaluation Method and Results

[19] present a systematic analysis of different performance measures. We use the following measures for evaluating and comparing the results: Precision, Recall and the F-measure. Precision indicates how many of the extracted entities are correct. Recall indicates how many entities among those to be found, are effectively extracted.

	Arabic corpus	French corpus
Number of text	56	56
Number of words	91930	183858
Precision	0,88	0,84
Recall	0,81	0,89
F-measure	0,84	0,86

The noise for the French NEs recognition mainly comes from the verb-adjective conflict. Indeed, the rules for detecting basilic commun, basilic romain or grand basilic combine the noun and the adjective. When the text contains basilic flétri or basilic fané, the rules return them as NEs and causing a noise.

The noise in Arabic is caused by the confusion between plant name and person name, in the sentence رحب علي كمون بعثمان بطيخ *raHHaba 'aly kammoun bi'uthmaan baTTykh* returns بطيخ *baTTykh* and كمون *kammoun* as plants NEs although they refer family names in this example.

The Arab silence problem is mainly caused by the lack of uniformity in the writing styles, the lack of some entries in the dictionary and the presence of decorative characters. The French silence problem is mainly due to the particular structure of some plants name, such as grande mauve, faux indigo which are not returned. The peculiarity of two successive adjectives can be solved by adding a semantic feature like color.

6   Conclusion and Perspectives

In this paper, we have presented an approach for recognition of medicinal plants NEs from French-Arabic parallel corpora. We have elaborated a set of transducers that have been applied to extract NEs. We have underlined the main problems encountered for the Arabic language. These problems have been largely resolved but some of them require further solutions for improving the F-measure, especially differences in the writing styles and decorative characters. The obtained results are satisfactory and as perspectives, we intend to integrate a learning-based approach.

References

1. Allauzen, A., Wisniewski, G.: Modèles discriminants pour l'alignement mot à mot. TAL **50** (3), 173–203 (2009)
2. Ameh, S.J., Obodozie, O.O., Babalola, P.C., Gamaniel, K.S.: Medical herbalism and herbal clinical research: a global perspective. Br. J. Pharm. Res. **1**(4), 99–123 (2011)

3. Bodenreider, O., Zweigenbaum, P.: Identifying proper names in parallel medical terminologies. Stud. Health Technol. Inform. **77**, 443–447 (2000)
4. Daille, B., Gaussier, E., Lange, J.-M.: Towards automatic extraction of monolingual and bilingual terminology. In: Proceedings of the 15th International Conference on Computational Linguistics (COLING 1994), pp. 515–521 (1994)
5. Debili, F., Zibi, A.: Les dépendances syntaxiques au service de l'appariement des mots. In: Actes du 10ème Congrès Reconnaissance des Formes et Intelligence Artificielle (RFIA 1996) (1996)
6. Deléger, L., Merkel, M., Zweigenbaum, P.: Translating medical terminologies through word alignement in parralel text corpora. J. Biomed. Inform. **42**, 692–701 (2009)
7. Fehri, H.: Reconnaissance automatique des entités nommées arabes et leur traduction vers le français. Ph.D. thesis, Sfax University (2012)
8. Gledhill, D.: The Names of Plants, 4th edn. Cambridge University Press, Cambridge (2008)
9. Goldman, J.-P., Scherrer, Y.: Création automatique de dictionnaires bilingues d'entités nommés grace à Wikipédia. Nouveaux Cahiers de Linguistique Française **30**, 213–227 (2012)
10. Hoffmann, D.: Medical Herbalism: The Science And Practice of Herbal Medicine. Haling Arts Press, Rochester (2003)
11. Nadeau, N., Sekine, S.: A survey of named entity recognition and classification. In: Sekine, S., Ranchhod, E. (eds.) Named Entities: Recognition, Classification and Use. John Benjamins publishing company, pp. 3–28 (2009)
12. Nothan, J., Ringland, N., Radford, W., Murphy, T., Curran, J.R.: Learning multilingual named entity recognition from Wikipedia. Artif. Intell. **194**, 151–175 (2013)
13. Ozdowska, S., Claveau, V.: Inférence de règles de propagation syntaxique pour l'alignement de mots. TAL **47**(1), 167–186 (2006). ATALA
14. Rose Lim-Cheng, N., Co, J.R.C., Gaudiel, C.H.S., Umadac, D.F., Victor, N.L.: Semi-automatic population of ontology of philippine medicinal plants from on-line text. Presented at the DLSU Research Congress, De La Salle University, Manila, Philippines, 6–8 March 2014
15. Semmar, N., Saadane, H.: Etude de l'impact de la translittération de noms propres sur la qualité de l'alignement de mots à partir de corpus paralléles français-arabe. In: 21iéme Traitement Automatique des Langues Naturelles, Marseille, pp. 268–279 (2014)
16. Semmar, N., Servan, C., De Chalendar, G., Le Ny, B.: A hybrid word alignment approach to improve translation lexicons with compound words and idiomatic expressions. In: Proceedings of the 32nd Translating and the Computer Conference, England (2010)
17. Shaalan, K.: A survey of Arabic named entity recognition and classification. Comput. Linguist. **40**(2), 469–510 (2014)
18. Silberztein, M.: NooJ: a Linguistic annotation system for corpus processing. In: Proceedings of the Conference on Human Language Technology Conference and Conference on Empirical Methods in Natural Language Processing, Vancouver, British Columbia, Canada, 6–8 October 2005
19. Sokolova, M., Lapalme, G.: A systematic analysis of performance measures for classification tasks. Inf. Process. Manage. **45**, 427–437 (2009)

Automatic Translation from Belarusian into Spanish Based on Using Nooj's Linguistic Resources

Alena Veka[1]([⊠]) and Yauheniya Yakubovich[2]

[1] Belarusian State University, Minsk, Belarus
helena1993huk@mail.ru
[2] flexSem, Universitat Autònoma de Barcelona, Bellaterra (Barcelona), Spain
Yauheniya.Yakubovich@uab.cat

Abstract. This work is the first step on the elaboration of the Belarusian-Spanish dictionary, which would contain Spanish equivalents for Belarusian words and expressions. The global goal is to create a Belarusian-Spanish dictionary of simple words supplied with different kinds of grammatical information, e.g. category, inflectional and derivational paradigms, and also the semantic information concerning the lemmata. One more point is that the dictionary must comprise a number of set word combinations typical for both languages that would make the translation of idioms possible. Finally, it is important to create some local grammars indispensable to resolve translation problems and to make contextual desambiguation both in Belarusian and Spanish. This article describes a provisional dictionary for a fragment of the Belarusian NooJ module text and some simple local grammars reflecting particular translation problems.

Keywords: Automatic translation · Belarusian · Spanish

1 Introduction

Interaction of nations with one another in the current world has become so developed and widespread that knowing foreign languages today is of high importance.

Of course, it is very advisable to have a good command of foreign languages you need in your everyday communication or for work, but it is not really possible to learn all of them and have an opportunity to make a translation from one language to another by yourself. Very often we need a vocabulary to render words, phrases or complete sentences.

Our work is aimed at helping in translating words and phrases from Belarusian into Spanish. The whole process deals with using an indrawn Belarusian-Spanish dictionary, which contains pairs of Spanish equivalents for Belarusian words and expressions, to make rendering of Belarusian text into Spanish.

The first step was to create a glossary itself. Belarusian-Spanish dictionary represents a set of words and expressions supplied with different kinds of grammatical information, e.g. category, inflectional and derivational paradigms (conjugated forms of verbs), data about the number and gender of nouns and adjectives. Furthermore, this

© Springer International Publishing Switzerland 2016
T. Okrut et al. (Eds.): NooJ 2015, CCIS 607, pp. 202–207, 2016.
DOI: 10.1007/978-3-319-42471-2_18

dictionary was completed with a number of idiomatic expressions typical for both languages. That made the translation of idioms possible.

The fact that both Belarusian and Spanish do not have a strict fixed word order facilitates a lot the translation process. Thus, it is not necessary for the machine to make complex transformations of phases or sentences. More often it is enough just to translate them word by word in order to get an adequate translation of a text under consideration.

The process of translation consists of linguistic analyzing the text, which results in finding concrete text elements, i.e. isolated words, set expressions or special names of places or notions (proper names). Then NooJ finds equivalents for the text elements found in the dictionary. After the shifting of all the items for their analogues in the other language, we can operate with a ready-made translated sentence.

The purpose of this finding is to apply it in practice. Namely, for translating texts from Belarusian into Spanish. First of all, it is innovative because there are no many electronic resources dealing with automatic Belarusian-Spanish translation of the whole text. Then it is typical as this country has tight relationships with some Spanish-speaking countries, e.g. Venezuela.

2   Aims

At the beginning of the work several aims were set by the researchers: to create a NooJ-based dictionary of simple words with grammatical and some semantic annotations both for the Belarusian and Spanish; a dictionary of set words combinations for both languages; all kinds of local grammars that would help resolve translation problems and disambiguate words both in the source and target languages.

By the end of the considered work the resulting dictionary contained simple words with the necessary annotations together with set word expressions for both the Belarusian and Spanish languages. During the working process different kinds of local grammars were worked out.

3   Creating the Dictionary for Automatic Translation

As it was mentioned above the current work deals with bilingual machine translation from Belarusian into Spanish. For the purpose of the research a fragment of the Belarusian module text was chosen. The given text consisted of 924 lexical units.

Doing the research the authors faced the problem of the fact that it was quite challenging to create completely automatic machine Belarusian-Spanish translator. The challenge was that there were no enough resources for creating an independent mechanism of identification of word forms from one language and then transforming them into the appropriate forms of another language units. Thus, it was decided to create a dictionary which would consist of the unchanged forms of the text vocabulary. As a result, the dictionary contains over 940 word forms.

A dictionary in the NooJ software represents a list of word forms with the appropriate characteristics in one language connected with the list of their equivalents in another language. Each Belarusian lexical unit was described with its grammatical peculiarities as well as provided with its direct translation into Spanish. Let us consider an example: *агню, NOUN + FLX = АГОНЬ + TranslationSP="fuego"*. In this line of the dictionary there is particular information on the analyzed word *агню* (fire in English). The line illustrates the data about the grammatical category of the lexeme. Moreover it has the reference to the certain paradigm of the word with the initial form *агню*. With the continuation of the work on the project such paradigms should be used to simplify the dictionary itself, thus making it is possible for the software to find the correct form for translation within the paradigm of the equivalent word in the other language.

The last piece of necessary information in the considered line is the most appropriate variant for translation into Spanish.

Consider the view of the described dictionary on the Fig. 1 below.

Fig. 1. Worked-out Belarusian-Spanish dictionary.

4   Creating Local Grammars

After all the word forms were set with their equivalents, it was another challenge to face. To make the translation highly qualitative it was important to create a set of special grammars for the NooJ software to render certain expressions in the correct way.

To begin with, the whole abstract under consideration was carefully analyzed in order to find the most problematic places for the future translation. While analyzing the abstract, a list of the most challenging phrases for rendering from Belarusian into Spanish was composed.

Considering all the difficult for machine translation word combinations corresponding grammars were introduced.

The first local grammar created by the authors was that allowing to preserve the structure typical for the target language that differs it from Belarusian. This grammar is aimed at transforming each adjective-noun combination into noun-adjective unit. Thus each time the software finds two subsequent words the first of which is an adjective followed by a noun, it swaps their locations as it is illustrated on the Fig. 2.

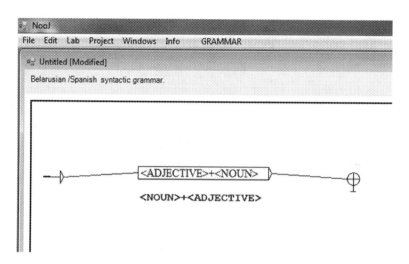

Fig. 2. Local grammar for dealing with adjective-noun lexical units

Let us consider the examples of some other local grammars:

As it is seen on the Fig. 3, there were three positions with the word *рука* in the analyzed discourse. In all these occasions the given lexical unit was to be translated from Belarusian into Spanish using different methods. In the first line it is shown that when the word under consideration is succeeded by the preposition *на* and followed by a noun, it should be rendered into Spanish as *en brazos*. At the same time if it is only followed by a verb, it is translated just as *brazos*. But in case the word is in final position and succeeded by a combination of different parts of speech with a preposition, the equivalent for translation will be the following: *mano*.

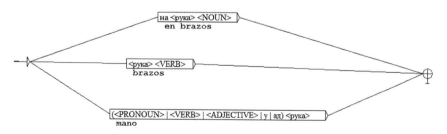

Fig. 3. The example of NooJ grammar for translation of the lexical unit *рука* (*hand* in English).

Consider the example of the analyzed grammar in use below (Fig. 4).

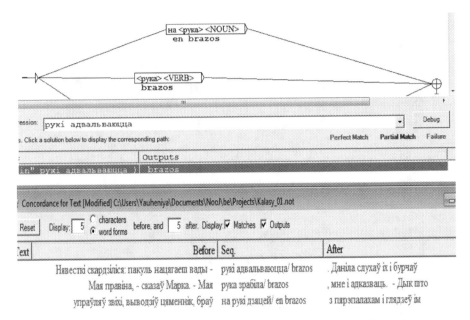

Fig. 4. The example of the grammar on the combinations with the word *рука* in action.

Along with local grammars created to accomplish the rendering of word combinations with the certain nouns, there were produced several grammars for translating lexical units with prepositions. The reason for this arose because of the fact that not all the prepositions of Belarusian coincide in their meaning with those of the target language.

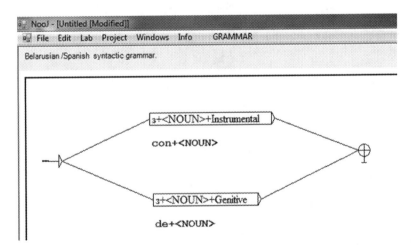

Fig. 5. The example of the local grammar on word combinations with the preposition *з*

Thus it was important to make sure that while the process of transforming the selected discourse from one language into another all the occasions of word combinations with the prepositions would be translated correctly. On the Fig. 5 there introduced the variants for translation the lexical units with the Belarusian preposition *з*. There were come across only two of them through the whole analyzed text. As it is clearly seen on the print screen in the figure below provided the preposition in the Belarusian context is followed by a noun in the Instrumental Case the given preposition would be rendered into Spanish as *con*. As far as the noun after the analyzed preposition is characterized by the Genitive Case, the chosen equivalent for the Belarusian preposition *з* would be *de*.

5 Conclusion

The points covered during the work on the research are not as numerous as it seemed possible at the beginning. However, it is necessary to admit that here the scale of the work done is not as valuable as the quality of the gained results.

First of all the current piece of work proved the possibility of automatic Belarusian-Spanish translation in terms of the NooJ programme. Secondly, as the initial steps were taken on the way to Belarusian-Spanish translation, it is highly important to outline potential directions of development for this issue: to translate all the lemmas (12 184 units) of the Belarusian discourse; to elaborate a dictionary with all the necessary grammatical and even semantic annotations both for the Belarusian and Spanish languages; to make local grammars that would be less dependent on the context.

References

1. Hetsevich, Y., Hetsevich, S.: Overview of Belarusian and Russian electronic dictionaries and their adaptation for NooJ. In: Vučković, K., Bekavac, B., Silberztein, M. (eds.) Formalising Natural Languages with NooJ: Selected Papers from the NooJ 2011 International Conference, Dubrovnik, Croatia, pp. 29–40. Cambridge Scholars Publishing, Newcastle (2012)
2. Hetsevich, Y., Hetsevich, S., Skopinava, A., Lobanov, B., Yakubovich, Y., Kim, Y.: Describing set and free word combinations in Belarusian and Russian with NooJ. In: Koeva, S., Mesfar, S., Silberztein, M. (eds.) Formalising Natural Languages with NooJ 2013: Selected Papers from the NooJ 2013 International Conference, Saarbrucken, Germany, pp. 101–114. Cambridge Scholars Publishing, Newcastle (2014)
3. Silberztein, M.: NooJ manual (2003). www.nooj4nlp.net

A French-Tamazight MT System
for Computer Science

Farida Yamouni[(⊠)]

Mouloud Mammeri University, Tizi Ouzou, Algeria
fariyamo@yahoo.fr

Abstract. Today, industrial and large-audience Machine Translation software are still producing poor quality results. For example when we use Babelfish to translate the compound term: Entrées sorties physiques, we obtain: Entries physical outputs, instead physical input output. Automatic translating software needs increasingly significant and varied terminological resources. Our aim is to develop a French-Tamazight MT system for computer science compound words. NooJ is the linguistic environment of development.

Keywords: Machine translation · Terminology · Compound words · NooJ · Computer science

1 Introduction

Like Systran in other times, Google hastens to explain that this new service can help the user to understand the general meaning of a text in a foreign language, but does not provide accurate translations. User's expectations are great, but they do not understand very well why the machine translation does not make progress faster [1].

For the technical languages or of specialty, work remains to be made by building electronic dictionaries. The construction of a terminology depends on the application in which one wants to use it. The selected terms and their degree of description are different according to what one wants to build [2].

Most of translations are not 'word to word' translation for example "mémoire tampon" has four different translations:

- Buffer;
- Buffer memory;
- Cache storage;
- Read buffer storage.

To obtain a right translation of the compound words, we need to describe them as entries in a specialized dictionary. The first step is building electronic dictionaries and morphological grammars. For building dictionaries, one has to extract terms from texts. The extraction is done manually or automatically. In [3] one can find works on automatic extraction of terminology.

© Springer International Publishing Switzerland 2016
T. Okrut et al. (Eds.): NooJ 2015, CCIS 607, pp. 208–217, 2016.
DOI: 10.1007/978-3-319-42471-2_19

2 Terminology, Specialized Language and Compound Words

2.1 Terminology, Specialized Language [2]

The computer science texts are technical texts and the language is specialized. A specialized language [4, 5] is the use of a language that makes it possible to give an account technically of specialized knowledge. This specialized knowledge is linguistically called by terms that are words, word groups. In a general language, the lexemes constituting the inputs of the dictionary are words; in the case of a specialized language, the lexemes are terms. In the linguistic dictionary "Larousse" [6], we find that any discipline, and with stronger reason any science needs a set of terms, rigorously defined, by which it indicates the concepts which are useful for it: this set of terms constitutes its terminology. The characteristic of the term, compared to the other lexemes of a language, is to have a specialized meaning, i.e. a meaning put in keeping with a field of specialty [7].

2.2 Compound Words

There is not a single definition of a compound word but a certain number of common properties. Most of compound words are compound nouns. We will quote work, [8] on the lexicon of the compound nouns.

A term can be simple if it contains one word or compound if it contains more than one. A compound word is built starting from simple words. A compound noun is a consecutive sequence of at least two simple forms and blocks of separators. A simple form is a nonempty consecutive sequence of characters of the alphabet appearing between two separators. A simple word is a simple form that constitutes an input of dictionary. Related works on compound words can be found in [9–11].

A terminological bank is essentially composed of compound words. Each linguist uses his own terminology to define the compound words and proposes his own criteria to define it.

2.3 Compound Classes

Most of the compound words are compound nouns. In [3] we defined 5 Compounds classes (related to syntax), one for each length:

- Compounds[1] with lenght 2
  - NA – Adressage absolu, absolute addressing;
  - NN – Mémoire tampon, buffer memory;
  - NPN – Adressage par octets, byte addressing;
  - NDN – Formatage de données, data formatting;
  - AN – Arrière-plan, background;
  - PN – Sous programme, subroutine;

---

[1] N: noun, P: preposition or empty, A: adjective, V: verb, C: conjunction, X: adverb, etc.

- NAN – Décalage à droite, right shift;
- NA – Adressage absolu, absolute addressing;
- NN – Mémoire tampon, buffer memory;
- NPN – Adressage, par octets byte addressing;
- NDN – Formatage de données, data formatting;
- AN – Arrière-plan, background;
- PN – Sous programme, subroutine
- NAN – Décalage à droite, right shift;
- NPV – Demande pour émettre, request to send;
- NCN – Sauvegarde et restauration, save and restore;
- VPN – Désactiver par commentaries, disable by comments;
- APN – Lié au calcul, linked to computation;
- XN – Pseudo langage, pseudo language;
- XA – Non valide, not valid.
- Compounds with lenght 3
  - NAPN – Allocation dynamique de mémoire, dynamic allocation memory;
  - NPNPN – Allocation de ressources en batch, batch resources allocation;
  - NPAA – Algorithme du premier, adapté first adapted algorithm;
  - NPXA – Algorithme du mieux adapté, best adapted algorithm;
  - NPXN – Appel de sous programme, subroutine call;
  - NPNA – Architecture à mémoire partagée, shared memory architecture;
  - NPAN – Bit de demi retenue, half carry bit;
  - NXA – Interruption non masquable, not hidden interrupt;
  - NAA – Circuit intégré decimal, decimal intregrated circuit;
  - XNPN – Non retour à zero, nonreturn to zero
  - NACA – Unité arithmétique et logique, arithmetic and logic unit;
- Compounds with lenght 4
  - NX4 – Algorithme préemptif à priorités dynamiques, dynamic priority pre-empted algorithm.
- Compounds with lenght 5
  - NX5 – Traitement différé à flot de travail unique, single job stream batch processing.
- Compounds with lenght 6
  - NX6 – accès multiple par détection de porteuse et détection des collisions, carrier sense multiple access and collision detection;

3   The French-English-Tamazight Computer Science Lexicon

3.1   Building the Tamazight Computer Science Terminology

After having listed the French and English computer science vocabulary, various Tamazight dictionaries on paper (kabyle, touareg, chleuh, mozabite, chaoui), Amawal, mathematical and electricity lexicons were used by the author [12] to extract tamazight single terms and produce compound terms for the translation.

Neology was considered at last resort. Neologisms creation processus are those attested in Tamazight.

3.2   The Rules [12]

The rules are composition and derivation, for example:
Composition (from two lexemes):

- Noun + noun: amaḍan, byte (from "tam": eight and "amḍan": nombre);
- Verb + noun: tasenkelmit, computer science (from "issin": knowledge and "aselkim": computer),
- Noun + verb: tahlaskit, program measurement: (from "ahil": program and "sket": to measure.

Derivation: It is the procedure that allows to derive from a verb, a verbal action noun, an agentive noun, an instrument noun or an adjective. There are two kinds of derivations, nominal and verbal:

- Verbal derivation:
  - Factitive form: sedfu, to amplify (from "dfu": être fortifié);
  - Reciprocal form: amyuqqen, interconnection (from "my", prefix of reciprocity and "qqen": attacher, lier).
- Nominal derivation:
  - Verbal action noun: aseket, converter (from "selket": to transform);
  - Agentive noun: assemlellay, assembler (from "semlil": to assemble);
  - Instrument noun: asunaɣ, plotter(from "suneɣ: "to plott).
  - Nominal derivations based on prefix are also used, agrudem, interface (from "ager": inter and "udem": face).

The translation of a term leads to treat a family.of words, as for translating code, we also translate to encode, encoder, encoding, decoder, to codify.

Many words have been translated directly from English. The basic element was the verb, it allows to build up the family of terms.

Compound words are generally described by one term, one can put a dash between the different parts to highlight them.

One can write: afelmẓiselkim (super mini computer) or afel-mẓi-selkim.

4   Linguistic Resources for Machine Translation

The NooJ platform [13] is used to implement the linguistic resources for Machine translation. We need to build dictionaries containing compound words of computer science terminology, syntactic grammars for translation.

For extracting compounds terms in French and in Tamazight, we used the French-English-Berber lexicon and the French electronic compound dictionary.

4.1 The Electronic Dictionaries

The computer science electronic dictionary for Tamazight terms (about 1500 entries) is built with NooJ, using Saad-Bouzefrane [12] lexicon. An extract is given in the Fig. 1.

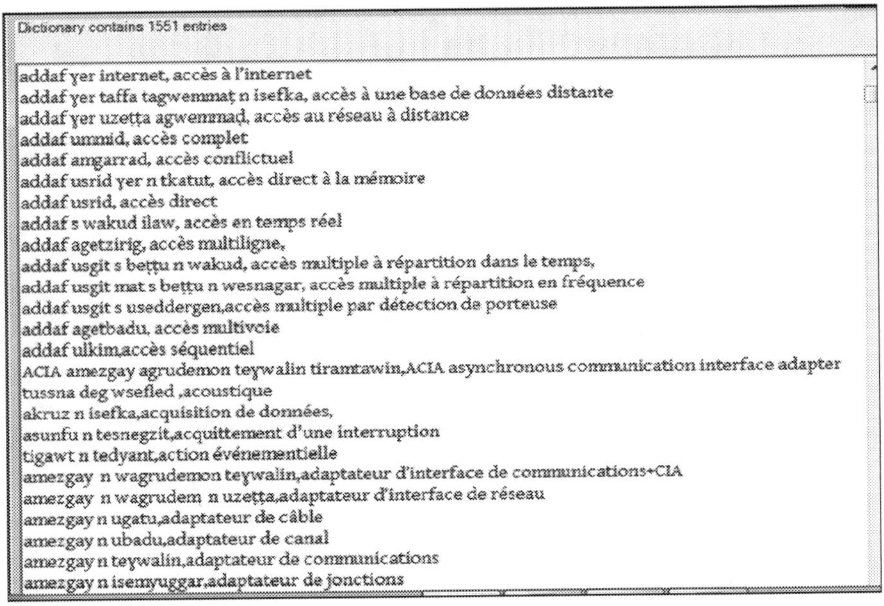

```
Dictionary contains 1551 entries

addaf yer internet, accès à l'internet
addaf yer taffa tagwemmaṭ n isefka, accès à une base de données distante
addaf yer uzeṭṭa agwemmaḍ, accès au réseau à distance
addaf ummid, accès complet
addaf amgarrad, accès conflictuel
addaf usrid yer n tkatut, accès direct à la mémoire
addaf usrid, accès direct
addaf s wakud ilaw, accès en temps réel
addaf agetzirig, accès multiligne,
addaf usgit s beṭṭu n wakud, accès multiple à répartition dans le temps,
addaf usgit mat s beṭṭu n wesnagar, accès multiple à répartition en fréquence
addaf usgit s useddergen,accès multiple par détection de porteuse
addaf agetbadu, accès multivoie
addaf ulkim,accès séquentiel
ACIA amezgay agrudemon teywalin tiramtawin,ACIA asynchronous communication interface adapter
tussna deg wsefled ,acoustique
akruz n isefka,acquisition de données,
asunfu n tesnegzit,acquittement d'une interruption
tigawt n tedyant,action événementielle
amezgay n wagrudemon teywalin,adaptateur d'interface de communications+CIA
amezgay n wagrudem n uzeṭṭa,adaptateur d'interface de réseau
amezgay n ugatu,adaptateur de câble
amezgay n ubadu,adaptateur de canal
amezgay n teywalin,adaptateur de communications
amezgay n isemyuggar,adaptateur de jonctions
```

Fig. 1. Compound words Tamazight dictionary.

4.2 The French Computer Science Dictionary

The electronic computer science dictionary for French compounds with about 10200 entries was developed with NooJ using various sources [2, 3, 14] (Fig. 2).

In the dictionary, for the entry "mémoire paginée":

Mémoire paginée, N + NA + info + FLX = TableRonde

We have:

- "mémoire paginée": the term,
- +N + NA: the categories are Noun, Noun Adjective,
- +info: sémantic class,
- TableRonde: flexional model.

```
Dictionary contains 10251 entries

accès aléatoire,N+NA+info+FLX=AccesAccordé
accès aléatoire à la mémoire,N+NAPN+info+FLX=AccesAléatMem
accès anonyme,N+NA+info+FLX=AccesAccordé
accès arbitraire,N+NA+info+FLX=AccesAccordé
accès arborescent,N+NA+info+FLX=AccesAccordé
algorithme de gestion mémoire,N+NPNPN+info+FLX=algogemem+OS
programme de test machine,N+NPNPN+info+FLX=algogemem+Hild98
programme de gestion canal,N+NPNPN+info+FLX=algogemem+Hild98
mémoire auxiliaire,N+NA+info+FLX=TableRonde
mémoire cryptée,N+FLX=TableRonde
mémoire de masse et auxiliaire,N+NPNPN+info+FLX=NmassAux
mémoire de masse,N+NDN+info+FLX=PommeDeTerre
mémoire paginée,N+NA+info+FLX=TableRonde
abaissement de niveau,N+NDN+info+FLX=AccorDeBase+HILD98
abaissement de niveau d'un titre,N+NPNPN+info+FLX=AccorDeBase+HILD98
abaisser la sélection d'un niveau,V+VPNPN+info+HILD98
abaisser le corps de texte,V+VPNPN+info+HILD98
abaisseur de fréquence,N+NDN+info+FLX=AccorDeBase+HILD98
abandon d'activité,N+NDN+info+FLX=AccorDeBase+HILD98
abandon de déclencheur SQL,N+NPNPN+info+FLX=AccorDeBase+HILD98
abandon de procédure,N+NDN+info+FLX=AccorDeBase+HILD98
abandon prématuré,N+NA+info+FLX=AdrAbsolu+HILD98
abandon système,N+NN+info+FLX=AccordPrecis+HILD98
aberration chromatique,N+NA+info+FLX=TableRonde+HILD98
```

Fig. 2. An extract of the French computer science dictionary

4.3   Construction of the French Tamazight Dictionary for Translation

The NooJ dictionary French-Tamazight for translation is built from the Tamazight dictionary and a part of the French dictionary. We added the translation in Tamazight for the entries. Fig. 3 gives an extract of the FR-TM dictionary.

Each entry in French contains information about source language (Kabyle: kbl, tachelhit: clh, Touareg: mcɛ, Mozabyte: mzb, Chaoui: cw) or lexicon (mathematical: mat, Amawal: mc), used to build the compound words translation.

For example, in Fig. 3, the dictionary entry:

langage de haut niveau, N + Compo + TM = tameslayt m 'swir ɛlayan + mw + kbl contains:

- the entry "langage de haut niveau" in French,
- N: for noun,
- +Compo: compound word
- " + TM" gives the Tamazight compound word translation "tameslayt m 'swir ɛlayan",
- +mw, reference: Amawal lexicon of modern Berber;
- +kbl: reference: Kabyle dictionary.

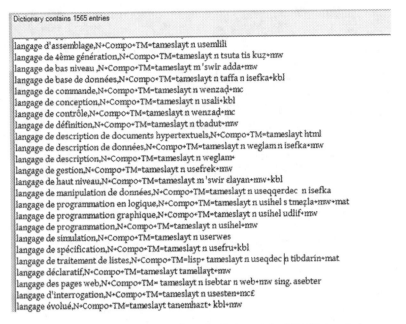

Fig. 3. An extract of compound words dictionary for FR-TM translation.

4.4   Construction of Syntactic Grammar for Translation

To implement compound words translation, we built a syntactic translation grammar with for input Fr and output TM (Fig. 4).

The grammar allows the translation of each compound word in French. It takes as input the compound word in French and gives as output the translation and its annotation in the source language.

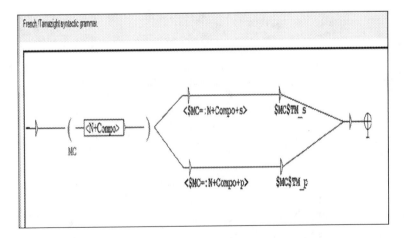

Fig. 4. Syntactic grammar for FR-TM translation.

5   Machine Translation

One can find works on MT using NooJ in [15] with an auxiliary verbs French-Chinese MT and in [16] with a French-Arabic MT for named entities.

Our works concern compound words. Linguistic resources are developed for a French-Tamazight MT system for computer science. NooJ is the environment of development.

5.1   The Linguistic Resources

We developed linguistic resources for the translation of computer science compound words:

- the compound words dictionary for FR-TM translation,
- the French Tamazight syntactic grammar for translation.

In the Tamazight compound words dictionary works remains to do. For each compound word entry, we have just to give the flexional form for the parts of the compound; NooJ will produce automatically, the different flexional forms.

5.2   The Text

The text given in Fig. 5 contains computer science compound words in the source language French. We have terms like "mémoire à bulles magnétiques", "mémoire à condensateur", mémoire à feuillets magnétiques".

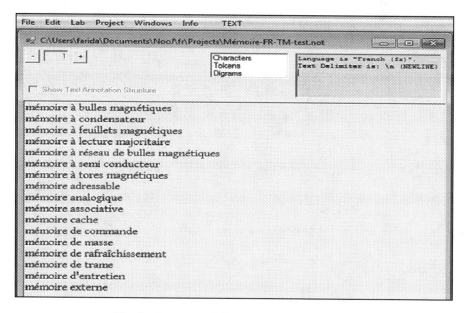

Fig. 5. An extract of the text used for translation.

5.3   The Translation

After the linguistic analysis of the text, we apply the NooJ syntactic grammar defined in Sect. 4.4, the result is the text translated.

The concordance of the text gives the translation from the French source language to the Tamazight output language. For example, in Fig. 6, we have:

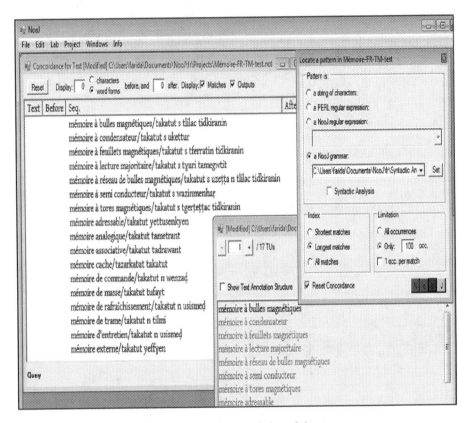

Fig. 6. The results: translation of the text

- mémoire à bulles magnétiques/takatut s tlilac tidikarin.
- "mémoire à bulles magnétiques" is the compound word found in the text. NooJ used the compound noun FR-TM dictionary of Tamazight and the syntactic grammar for the translation.
- "takatut s tlilac tidikarin" is the translation in Tamazight of the compound word in French, "mémoire à bulles magnétiques".

6   Conclusion

We have built a dictionary of computer science words FR-TM. It contains 1500 terms. Most of the entries are compound nouns.

This terminology is used for the translation from computer science compounds, in French, to computer science compounds, in Tamazight. The exact translation is obtained with success for all the terms described in the FR-TM dictionary.

Future works will focus on the enrichment of the FR-TM dictionary, a study of computer science verbs (syntax, semantics), adding inflexional descriptions for entries in the dictionaries FR-TM and Tamazight, and the translation of texts.

References

1. Lebert, M.: La traduction automatique de babel fish à google (2013). https://www.actualitte.com/societe/la-traduction-automatique-de-babel-fish-a-google-traduction-46891.htm
2. Aoughlis, F.: A computer science electronic dictionary for NooJ. In: Kedad, Z., Lammari, N., Métais, E., Meziane, F., Rezgui, Y. (eds.) NLDB 2007. LNCS, vol. 4592, pp. 341–351. Springer, Heidelberg (2007)
3. Aoughlis, F: Construction d'un dictionnaire électronique de terminologie informatique et analyse automatique de textes par grammaires locales. Thèse, Université Mouloud Mammeri, Tizi Ouzou (2010)
4. Fotopoulou, A.: Analyse automatique des textes: Dictionnaires et thésaurus électroniques des termes des télécommunications, Actes de la 5 ème journée ERLA-GLAT Brest, université de Bretagne occidentale (1994)
5. Fotopoulou, A.: Elaboration d'un thésaurus des termes des télécommunications. Technical report, Institut National des télécommunications, Program Human Capital & Mobility (1995)
6. Dubois, J., et al.: Dictionnaire de linguistique, édition Larousse (1973)
7. L'Homme, M.C.: La Terminologie: principes et techniques, PUM, presses Universitaires de Montreal (2003)
8. Jung, R.: Remarques sur la constitution du lexique des noms composés. Langue française **87**, 91–97 (1990)
9. Silberztein, M.: Le dictionnaire électronique des mots composés. Langue Française **87**, 71–83 (1990)
10. Silberztein, M.: Dictionnaires électroniques et analyse automatique de textes: le système INTEX. Edition Masson, Paris (1993)
11. Silberztein, M.: Les groupes nominaux productifs et les noms composés lexicalisés. Lingvisticae Investigationes **17**(2). John Benjamins B.V., Amsterdam (1993)
12. Saad-Bouzefrane, S.: Lexique d'informatique Français - Anglais – Berbère, (amawal n tsenselkimt Tafṛansist - Taglizit – Tamaziɣt), l'Harmattan, Paris (1996)
13. Silberztein, M.: NooJ manual (2006). http://www.nooj4nlp.net
14. Hildebert, J.: Dictionnaire des technologies de l'informatique. vol. 2, Français/Anglais, La maison du dictionnaire (Paris), Hippocrene Books Inc., New York (1998)
15. Ferhi, H.: Reconnaissance automatique des entités nommées arabes et leur traduction vers le français. Thèse, Université de Sfax, Faculté des Sciences Economiques et de Gestion (2012)
16. Wu, M.: The auxiliary verbs in NooJ's French-Chinese MT system. In: Donabédian, A., Khurshudian, V., Silberztein, M. (eds.) Formalising Natural Languages with NooJ, pp. 211–221. Cambridge Scholars Publishing, Cambridge (2013)

Mixed Prolog and NooJ Approach in Japanese Benefactive

Valérie Collec-Clerc[(⊠)]

Laboratoire d'Informatique Fondamentale de Marseille, Marseille, France
valerie.clerccollec@yahoo.fr
http://www.lif.univ-mrs.fr

Abstract. This paper presents our research on analysis and generation of valid Japanese sentences in the context of polite donatory situations of communication. We have used NooJ to extract the relevant constructions and resorted to the logic programming language Prolog to generate these constructions. This paper points out the links between NooJ and Prolog.

Keywords: Japanese · Donatory verbs · NooJ · Prolog

1 Introduction

Our article aims at examining the possibilities of turning linguistic elements of the Japanese language described by the means of the NooJ platform into Prolog items and vice-versa. It is part of our context of study, the purpose of which is the analysis of interpersonal relationships of different social groups to generate sentences according to a given context. These sentences belong to the politeness system of the Japanese language which is composed of utterances in which the speakers position themselves as superior, equal or inferior to the addressees or a third person, according to psychological or social criteria.

Our article also shows the links between NooJ to extract and analyse sentences from a corpus and Prolog to generate them. There is no direct bridge between the two tools.

We will first give a brief explanation of benefactive situations in the Japanese language. Then we will compare NooJ and Prolog for morphosyntactic rules, universe of discourse and interpersonal pragmatic rules.

2 Benefactive Situations

2.1 Donatory Situations

They are mainly featured by the use of donatory verbs or auxiliaries to describe donatory situations.

These situations consist in a communication exchange that describes the action of giving or receiving from the communication partners or people involved in the utterance. The speakers clearly distinguish giving actions from those of receiving and will use a communication strategy depending on their self-positioning in the social scale.

© Springer International Publishing Switzerland 2016
T. Okrut et al. (Eds.): NooJ 2015, CCIS 607, pp. 218–225, 2016.
DOI: 10.1007/978-3-319-42471-2_20

Norio Ota (3) symbolised the use of the donatory verbs with a circle which bears the speaker as a centre and is divided into two equal parts: the giving and receiving actions marking by the use of giving and receiving verbs. The two parts are themselves subdivided according to the social role of the speaker in the speech act: superiority, equality or inferiority.

2.2   The Axis of Giving

The speaker, commonly regarded as inferior to the exchange partner, is the subject of the utterance: the action of giving from the speaker to the partner is described by the use of the humble verb 差しあげる (*sashiageru*).

The speaker commonly, regarded as equal to the exchange partner is the subject of the utterance: the action of giving from the speaker to this partner is described by the use of the verb あげる (*ageru*). The speaker commonly regarded as superior to the exchange partner is the subject of the utterance: the action of giving from the speaker to this partner may be described by the use of both あげる (*ageru*) and やる (*yaru*). The latter is however less and less employed then it is now regarded as derogatory.

2.3   The Axis of Receiving

The speaker is commonly regarded as inferior to the exchange partner:

When the speaker is the subject of the utterance, the action of receiving from this partner is described by the use of the humble verb いただく(*itadaku* to receive).
When the subject of the utterance is not the speaker: the action of receiving from this subject is described by the use of the honorific verb くださる (*kudasaru* to give).

The speaker commonly, regarded as equal or superior to the exchange partner:

When the speaker is the subject of the utterance, the action of receiving from this partner is described by the use of the humble verb もらう(*morau* to receive).
When the partner is the subject of the utterance, the action of receiving is described by the use of the honorific verb くれる (*kureru* to give).

2.4   Verbs and Extraction

The verbs of giving and receiving can be either employed as verbs or as auxiliaries when they are combined with the *te*-form of a verb involving an exchange (doing something for someone, explain, lend....)

森さんが日本の歌を歌ってくれました。

Mori-san ga nihonnouta wo utatte kuremashita
(*utau* (to sing) in the *te* form + *kureru* (affirmative, past))

(Mrs/Mr Morau sang a song for us/me)

鉛筆を貸してくださいませんか。

Empitsu wo kashite kudasaimasen ka?

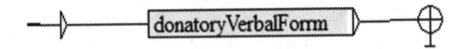

Fig. 1. Nooj graph: donatory forms

Fig. 2. Nooj graph: donatory verbal forms

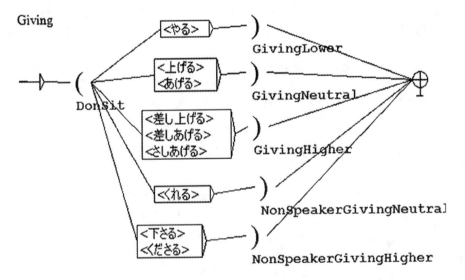

Fig. 3. Nooj graph: giving donatory forms

Receiving

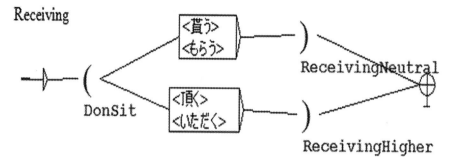

Fig. 4. Nooj graph: receiving donatory forms

(*kasu* (to lend) in the *te* form + *kudasaru* (interrogative and negative, present))
(Couldn't you lend me your pen?)

These following Nooj-graphs extract the donatory forms (Figs. 1, 2, 3 and 4):

3 Prolog for Sentence Generation

We have chosen Prolog for sentence generation. Prolog is a non-procedural programming language which relies on a restriction of the first order logic, called Horn clauses. A Prolog program consists of a set of facts and rules. For examples, a fact like "human(yumiko)." indicates that the argument "yumiko" makes the predicate "human" true. Another one like "student(yumiko,todai)." asserts that the term "(yumiko,todai)" makes the two-argument predicate "student" true.

A rule connects a deductible predicate to a set of facts. To give an example: "mortal (X):- human(X)" means that if an "X" for which "human(X)" is true can be found, it implies that the predicate "mortal" is also true for "X".

In a similar way "sameUniversity(X,Y):- student(X,U), student(Y,U)" is proved to be true if the free variable "U" owns a value which makes both "student(X,U)" and "student(Y,U)" true.

The Prolog rules do not allow negation apart from the negation as failure, that is to say failing to deduce a searched term from the rules and facts. For instance, if there are no facts or rules leading to "human (taro)" "not (mortal (taro))" will be considered as true. In logic, this assertion involves a closed world. In our example, "taro" is not human because the clauses cannot assert it.

Prolog was created to analyse natural language. It also possesses its specific way of expressing grammars, which is called Define Clause Grammar (DCG):

np_acc(W) –> [W], acc_part. A noun W in the accusative can be replaced with the noun W followed by acc_part.
acc_part –> [を]. acc_part can be replaced with the terminal symbol を. The grapheme を (wo) is the particle which is used for the direct object.

In our application facts will be used to create the basic information of universe of discourse, such as "Yumiko is a student of Tokyo University". The DCG is employed to specify the grammatical rules of the Japanese language. Other rules defined the pragmatic aspect in the choice of the words and the grammatical constructions. Communicative contexts are provided through graphic user interfaces.

4   Morphological Rules

The first similarity concerns morphological rules such as the large number of verb inflections that must be defined exhaustively so that NooJ could recognise verbal lemma and Prolog could generate correct sentences. Modal and tense inflections depend on the categories of the Japanese verbs. In the NooJ dictionary this appears as a link between a verb typical of a given category for each lemma, for example FLEX=AU. In Prolog we mix up facts and rules to limit the number of fact clauses that are to be generated by the interpreter.

Hiragana endings of the lemmatized verbal forms mostly enable verbal types to be determined. However, some exceptions like the ending in る(*ru*) that *ichidan* and *godan* verbs have in common must be taken into consideration.

We were driven to build up a NooJ dictionary that contains all the types of lemmatized verbs from standard lexical resources.

The following Prolog rules identify *godan* verbs:

A verb is of *godan* type if it is not irregular, ends in る(*ru*) and does not belong to the *ichidan* type:

godan(V):-

not(irregul(V)),
ending(V,る),
not(ichidan(V)).

A verb is of *godan* type if not irregular, ends in く (*ku*) or ぐ (*gu*) or す(*su*) or つ (*tsu*) or う(u) or む (*mu*) or ぬ (*nu*) or ふ (*fu*):

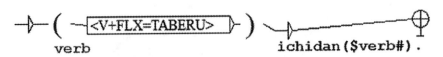

verb   ichidan($verb#).

Fig. 5. Nooj graph: extraction of ichidan verbs

godan(V):-

not(irregul(V)),
ending(V,T),
member(T, [く,ぐ,す,つ,う,む,ぬ,ふ]).

A verb is of *godan* type if it is part of a list of verbs that are *godan* exceptions

godan(V):-

godanException(V).

To these rules must be added a set of Prolog facts that declares irregular verbs, *godan* exceptions and all the *ichidan* verbs ending in る(*ru*). The list of *ichidan* verbs can be extracted from the NooJ dictionary by using a Nooj graph. The graph that extracts the searched inflections is applied to the NooJ dictionary or to a corpus (Fig. 5).

name   studentIn($name#,$name$UNIVERSITY#).

Fig. 6. Nooj graph: extraction of student and university

This graph generates Prolog facts from the verbs that are conjugated like *taberu* (V +FLX=TABERU). They are *ichidan* verbs ending in る(*ru*).

5 Semantic Features

Our second approach deals with semantic features. In standard lexicons it is usual to add information about the term categories (scientific terms, legal terms, etc.). Most of the entries from our resources are categorised this way. The addition of features like "human" is required in Nooj to disambiguate some words in Japanese. As a result, we have purposely used "+human" as a feature.

The context of utterance must be known for correct parsing or generation. It is called universe of discourse. Interpersonal language requires knowing the relationships between communication partners.

We must devise a NooJ dictionary for named entities which meets the context (university, company, etc.).

由美子,ENAM+human+SEX=f+student+UNIVERSITY=東京大学
+ROMAJI=yumiko

This example has its equivalent in Prolog facts

human(由美子, f).
university(東京大学).
studentIn(由美子, 東京大学).

They can also be generated (Fig. 6):

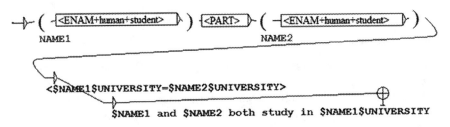

Fig. 7. Nooj graph: same university as a constraint

6   Pragmatic Rules

Pragmatic rules are written in Prolog. They express the choice of words, modals, constructions according to the relative role of the components of the utterance. For instance, from a basic sentence like 作文を見る (*sakubun/wo/miru* essay/case particle/see) which involves a situation in which a student makes a request to the teacher, some modifications lead gradually to the final sentence 作文をご覧になってくだ さいませんか (*sakubun wo goran ni natte kudasaimasen ka*? Couldn't you please have a

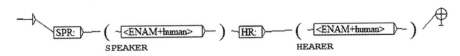

Fig. 8. Nooj graph: extraction of speaker and hearer tags

look at my essay?). This first modification takes the donatory situation into account by turning the verb *miru* into a *te*-form and by adding the benefactive auxiliary *kureru* to it: (*sakubun wo mittekureru*). The second modification applies the following hierarchical link: When a student addresses to a teacher, the former must use honorific verbs. In this example, *miru* and *kureru* are replaced with their honorific suppletive forms, respectively *goran ni naru* and *kudasaru*: *sakubun wo goran ni natte kudasaru*. The third modification considers the relationship between the speaker and the listener by adding the polite suffix *masu* to the verb *kudasaru*: *sakubun wo goran ni natte kudasaru*.

This kind of rules may have its counterpart in NooJ. Therefore, we have inserted the required data to recognise standard social roles like student and professor in our NooJ dictionary for named entities. We have also designed an additional dictionary to identify the donatory verbs, their valences and the associated auxiliaries. NooJ grammars may use the constraints on those data, for instance the subject and the object of the utterance belong to the same university (Fig. 7).

For pragmatic rules, it is also necessary to tell the speaker from the other communication partners. In Prolog, communication partners are direct parameters of Prolog clauses:

situationGenerator (Sentence, Spr, Hr, Verb, Subject, IndirectObject, Object, ...):-
utteranceSituation(Spr, Hr), ...

In NooJ, it is necessary to artificially tag utterance roles in the text. only subject/object can be deduced with syntactic rules and it is not enough with Japanese (Fig. 8).

7 Conclusion and Prospects

In our work we use NooJ for linguistic extraction by the means of grammars and Prolog for sentence pattern reproduction by the means of rules. We try to maintain an equivalence between Nooj and Prolog morphosyntactic rules. A common pragmatic description of the utterance needs closed world and a NooJ dictionary of names and functions of the speech partners. In the real world of text corpora like interviews from newspaper, we need to determine the status of the speech partners such as genders and occupations.

In the future we contemplate turning NooJ descriptions into Prolog clauses or turning parts of Prolog rules into NooJ grammars to enhance the link between the two points of view.

References

1. Kozai, S.: Exceptionally exceptional expressions in Japanese. Japanese Linguistics 101 Kansai Gaidai University, Osaka, Japan (2011)
2. Nariyama, S., Nakaiwa, H., Siegel, M.: Denotating social ranking of referents. In: Proceedings of the 6th International Workshop on Linguistically Interpreted Corpora (2005)
3. Ota, N.: Donatory verbs giving and receiving, Japanese section, York University (2001)
4. Sugimura, R.: Japanese honorifics and Situation Semantics. In: International Conference on Computational Linguistics, pp. 507–510 (1986)
5. Tanaka, S., et al.: Keigo wo totonoeru (Treatment of the honorific form). Asakura Nihongo Shin-Kôza, vol. 5. Asakura Shoten, Tokyo (1983)
6. Terrya, K.: Interpersonal grammar of Japanese. In: A Systemic Functional Grammar of Japanese, vol. 2, pp. 135–205 (2007)
7. Tsujimura, N.: Japanese Linguistics vol II syntax and Semantics vol. III Pragmatics, Sociolinguistics and Language Contact. Routlege, London (2005)

Author Index